# Intergenerational Programs: Understanding What We Have Created

*Intergenerational Programs: Understanding What We Have Created* has been co-published simultaneously as *Child & Youth Services*, Volume 20, Numbers 1/2 1999.

# The *Child & Youth Services*™ Monographic "Separates"

Below is a list of "separates," which in serials librarianship means a special issue simultaneously published as a special journal issue or double-issue and as a "separate" hardbound monograph. (This is a format which we also call a "DocuSerial")

"Separates" are published because specialized libraries or professionals may wish to purchase a specific thematic issue by itself in a format which can be separately cataloged and shelved, as opposed to purchasing the journal on an on-going basis. Faculty members may also more easily consider a "separate" for classroom adoption.

"Separates" are carefully classified separately with the major book jobbers so that the journal tie-in can be noted on new book order slips to avoid duplicate purchasing.

You may wish to visit Haworth's website at . . .

## http://www.haworthpressinc.com

. . . to search our online catalog for complete tables of contents of these separates and related publications.

You may also call 1-800-HAWORTH (outside US/Canada: 607-722-5857), or Fax 1-800-895-0582 (outside US/Canada: 607-771-0012), or e-mail at:

## getinfo@haworthpressinc.com

---

*Intergenerational Programs: Understanding What We Have Created,* Valerie S. Kuehne, PhD (Vol. 19, No. 2, 1999).

*Caring on the Streets: A Study of Detached Youthworkers,* Jacquelyn Kay Thompson (Vol. 19, No. 2, 1999).

*Boarding Schools at the Crossroads of Change: The Influence of Residential Education Institutions on National and Societal Development,* Yitzhak Kashti (Vol. 19, No. 1, 1998). *"This book is an essential, applicable historical reference for those interested in positively molding the social future of the world's troubled youth." (Juvenile and Family Court Journal)*

*The Occupational Experience of Residential Child and Youth Care Workers: Caring and Its Discontents,* Edited by Mordecai Arieli, PhD (Vol. 18, No. 2, 1997). *"Introduces the social reality of residential child and youth care as viewed by care workers, examining the problem of tension between workers and residents and how workers cope with stress." (Book News, Inc.)*

*The Anthropology of Child and Youth Care Work,* Edited by Rivka A. Eisikovits, PhD (Vol. 18, No. 1, 1996). *"A fascinating combination of rich ethnographies from the occupational field of residential child and youth care and the challenging social paradigm of cultural perspective." (Mordecai Arieli, PhD, Senior Teacher, Educational Policy and Organization Department, Tel-Aviv University, Israel)*

*Travels in the Trench Between Child Welfare Theory and Practice: A Case Study of Failed Promises and Prospects for Renewal,* George Thomas, PhD, MSW (Vol. 17, No. 1/2, 1994). *"Thomas musters enough research and common sense to blow any proponent out of the water. . . . Here is a person of real integrity, speaking the sort of truth that makes self-serving administrators and governments quail." (Australian New Zealand Journal of Family Therapy)*

*Negotiating Positive Identity in a Group Care Community: Reclaiming Uprooted Youth,* Zvi Levy (Vol. 16, No. 2, 1993). *"This book will interest theoreticians, practitioners, and policymakers in child and youth care, teachers, and rehabilitation counselors. Recommended for academic and health science center library collections." (Academic Library Book Review)*

*Information Systems in Child, Youth, and Family Agencies: Planning, Implementation, and Service Enhancement,* Edited by Anthony J. Grasso, DSW, and Irwin Epstein, PhD (Vol. 16, No. 1, 1993). *"Valuable to anyone interested in the design and the implementation of a Management Information System (MIS) in a social service agency. . . ." (John G. Orme, PhD, Associate Professor, College of Social Work, University of Tennessee)*

**Assessing Child Maltreatment Reports: The Problem of False Allegations,** Edited by Michael Robin, MPH, ACSW (Vol. 15, No. 2, 1991). *"A thoughtful contribution to the public debate about how to fix the beleaguered system . . . . It should also be required reading in courses in child welfare." (Science Books & Films)*

**People Care in Institutions: A Conceptual Schema and Its Application,** Edited by Yochanan Wozner, DSW (Vol. 14, No. 2, 1990). *"Provides ample information by which the effectiveness of internats and the life of staff and internees can be improved." (Residential Treatment for Children & Youth)*

**Being in Child Care: A Journey Into Self,** Edited by Gerry Fewster, PhD (Vol. 14, No. 2, 1990). *"Evocative and provocative. Reading this absolutely compelling work provides a transformational experience in which one finds oneself alternately joyful, angry, puzzled, illuminated, warmed, chilled." (Karen Van-derVen, PhD, Professor, Program in Child Development and Child Care, School of Social Work, University of Pittsburgh)*

**Homeless Children: The Watchers and the Waiters,** Edited by Nancy Boxill, PhD (Vol. 14, No. 1, 1990). *"Fill[s] a gap in the popular and professional literature on homelessness . . . . Policymakers, program developers, and social welfare practitioners will find it particulary useful." (Science Books & Films)*

**Perspectives in Professional Child and Youth Care,** Edited by James P. Anglin, MSW, Carey J. Denholm, PhD, Roy V. Ferguson, PhD, and Alan R. Pence, PhD (Vol. 13, No. 1/2, 1990). *"Reinforced by empirical research and clear conceptual thinking, as well as the recognition of the relevance of personal transformation in understanding quality care." (Virginia Child Protection Newsletter)*

**Specialist Foster Family Care: A Normalizing Experience,** Edited by Burt Galaway, PhD, MS, and Joe Hudson, PhD, MSW (Vol. 12, No. 1/2, 1989). *"A useful and practical book for policymakers and professionals interested in learning about the benefits of treatment foster care." (Ira M. Schwartz, MSW, Professor and Director, Center for the Study of Youth Policy, The University of Michigan School of Social Work)*

**Helping the Youthful Offender: Individual and Group Therapies That Work,** William B. Lewis, PhD (Vol. 11, No. 2, 1991). *"In a reader-friendly and often humorous style, Lewis explains the multilevel approach that he deems necessary for effective treatment of delinquents within an institutional context." (Criminal Justice Review)*

**Family Perspectives in Child and Youth Services,** Edited by David H. Olson, PhD (Vol. 11, No. 1, 1989). *"An excellent diagnostic tool to use with families and an excellent training tool for our family therapy students. . . . It also offers an excellent model for parent training." (Peter Maynard, PhD, Department of Human Development, University of Rhode Island)*

**Transitioning Exceptional Children and Youth Into the Community: Research and Practice,** Edited by Ennio Cipani, PhD (Vol. 10, No. 2, 1989). *"Excellent set of chapters. A very fine contribution to the literature. Excellent text." (T. F. McLaughlin, PhD, Department of Special Education, Gonzaga University)*

**Assaultive Youth: Responding to Physical Assaultiveness in Residential, Community, and Health Care Settings,** Edited by Joel Kupfersmid, PhD, and Roberta Monkman, PhD (Vol. 10, No. 1, 1988). *"At last here is a book written by professionals who do direct care with assaultive youth and can give practical advice." (Vicki L. Agee, PhD, Director of Correctional Services, New Life Youth Services, Lantana, Florida )*

**Developmental Group Care of Children and Youth: Concepts and Practice,** Henry W. Maier, PhD (Vol. 9, No. 2, 1988). *"An excellent guide for those who plan to devote their professional careers to the group care of children and adolescents." (Journal of Developmental and Behavioral Pediatrics)*

**The Black Adolescent Parent,** Edited by Stanley F. Battle, PhD, MPH (Vol. 9, No. 1, 1987). *"A sound and insightful perspective on black adolescent sexuality and parenting." (Child Welfare)*

**Qualitative Research and Evaluation in Group Care,** Edited by Rivka A. Eisikovits, PhD, and Yitzhak Kashti, PhD (Vol. 8, No. 3/4, 1987). *"Well worth reading. . . . should be read by any nurse involved in formally evaluating her care setting." (Nursing Times)*

**Helping Delinquents Change: A Treatment Manual of Social Learning Approaches,** Jerome S. Stumphauzer, PhD (Vol. 8, No. 1/2, 1986). *"The best I have seen in the juvenile and criminal justice field in the past 46 years. It is pragmatic and creative in its recommended treatment approaches, on target* *concerning the many aspects of juvenile handling that have failed, and quite honest in assessing and advocating which practices seem to be working reasonably well." (Corrections Today)*

**Residential Group Care in Community Context: Insights from the Israeli Experience,** Edited by Zvi Eisikovits, PhD, and Jerome Beker, EdD (Vol. 7, No. 3/4, 1986). *"A variety of highly effective group care settings in Israel are examined, with suggestions for improving care in the United States.*

**Adolescents, Literature, and Work with Youth,** Edited by J. Pamela Weiner, MPH, and Ruth M. Stein, PhD (Vol. 7, No. 1/2, 1985). *"A variety of thought-provoking ways of looking at adolescent literature." (Harvard Educational Review)*

**Young Girls: A Portrait of Adolescence Reprint Edition,** Gisela Konopka, DSW (Vol. 6, No. 3/4, 1985). *"A sensitive affirmation of today's young women and a clear recognition of the complex adjustments they face in contemporary society." (School Counselor)*

**Adolescent Substance Abuse: A Guide to Prevention and Treatment,** Edited by Richard E. Isralowitz and Mark Singer (Vol. 6, No. 1/2, 1983). *"A valuable tool for those working with adolescent substance misusers." (Journal of Studies on Alcohol)*

**Social Skills Training for Children and Youth,** Edited by Craig LeCroy, MSW (Vol. 5, No. 3/4, 1983). *"Easy to read and pertinent to occupational therapists." (New Zealand Journal of Occupational Therapy)*

**Legal Reforms Affecting Child and Youth Services,** Edited by Gary B. Melton, PhD (Vol. 5, No. 1/2, 1983). *"A consistently impressive book. The authors bring a wealth of empirical data and creative legal analyses to bear on one of the most important topics in psychology and law." (John Monahan, School of Law, University of Virginia)*

**Youth Participation and Experiential Education,** Edited by Daniel Conrad and Diane Hedin (Vol. 4, No. 3/4, 1982). *"A useful introduction and overview of the current and possible future impact of experiential education on adolescents.*

**Institutional Abuse of Children and Youth,** Edited by Ranae Hanson (Vol. 4, No. 1/2, 1982). *"Well researched . . . should be required reading for every school administrator, school board member, teacher, and parent." (American Psychological Association Division 37 Newsletter)*

# Intergenerational Programs: Understanding What We Have Created

Valerie S. Kuehne

Editor

*Intergenerational Programs: Understanding What We Have Created* has been co-published simultaneously as *Child & Youth Services*, Volume 20, Numbers 1/2 1999.

The Haworth Press, Inc.
New York • London • Oxford

*Intergenerational Programs: Understanding What We Have Created* has been co-published simultaneously as *Child & Youth Services*TM, Volume 20, Numbers 1/2 1999.

Cover design by Thomas J. Mayshock Jr.

The Haworth Press, Inc., 10 Alice Street, Binghamton, NY 13904-1580 USA

**Library of Congress Cataloging-in-Publication Data**

Intergenerational programs: understanding what we have created / Valerie S. Kuehne, editor.
      p. cm.
      "Has been co-published simultaneously as Child & youth services, volume 20, numbers 1/2, 1999"
      Includes bibliographical references and index.
      ISBN 0-7890-0782-7 (alk. paper)–ISBN 0-7890-0817-3 (alk. paper)
      1. Aged–Family relationships. 2. Aging–Social aspects. 3. Intergenerational relations.
      4. Children and adults. I. Kuehne, Valerie. II. Title.
HQ1061 .I5275 1999
305.2–dc21
                                                 99-051409

# INDEXING & ABSTRACTING

Contributions to this publication are selectively indexed or abstracted in print, electronic, online, or CD-ROM version(s) of the reference tools and information services listed below. This list is current as of the copyright date of this publication. See the end of this section for additional notes.

- *BUBL Information Service. An Internet-based Information Service for the UK higher education community*

- *Cambridge Scientific Abstracts*

- *Child Development Abstracts & Bibliography*

- *CNPIEC Reference Guide: Chinese National Directory of Foreign Periodicals*

- *Criminal Justice Abstracts*

- *ERIC Clearinghouse on Counseling and Student Services (ERIC/CASS)*

- *ERIC Clearinghouse on Elementary & Early Childhood Education*

- *Exceptional Child Education Resources (ECER), (CD/ROM from SilverPlatter and hard copy)*

- *Family Studies Database (online and CD/ROM)*

- *IBZ International Bibliography of Periodical Literature*

- *Index to Periodical Articles Related to Law*

- *International Bulletin of Bibliography on Education*

- *Mental Health Abstracts (online through DIALOG)*

- *National CCenter for Chronic Disease Prevention & Health Promotion (NCCDPHP)*

- *National Criminal Justice Reference Services*

- *OT BibSys, American Occupational Therapy Foundation*

- *PASCAL, c/o Institute de L'information Scientifique et Technique. Cross-Disciplinary electronic database covering the fields of science, technology % medicine, Also available on CD-ROM, and can generate customized retrospective searches. For more information: INIST, Customer Desk, 2, allec du Parc de Brabois, F-154514 Vandoeuvere Cedex, France; http//www.inst.fr*

(continued)

- *Psychological Abstracts (PsycINFO)*
- *Referativnyi Zhurnal (Abstracts Journal of the All-Russian Institute of Scientific and Technical Information*
- *Sage Family Studies Abstracts (SFSA)*
- *Social Planning/Policy & Development Abstracts (SOPODA)*
- *Social Sciences Index (from Volume 1 & continuing)*
- *Social Work Abstracts*
- *Sociological Abstracts (SA)*
- *Sociology of Education Abstracts*
- *Studies on Women Abstracts*
- *Violence and Abuse Abstracts: A Review of Current Literature on Interpersonal Violence (VAA)*

## Special Bibliographic Notes related to special journal issues (separates) and indexing/abstracting:

- indexing/abstracting services in this list will also cover material in any "separate" that is co-published simultaneously with Haworth's special thematic journal issue or DocuSerial. Indexing/abstracting usually covers material at the article/chapter level.
- monographic co-editions are intended for either non-subscribers or libraries which intend to purchase a second copy for their circulating collections.
- monographic co-editions are reported to all jobbers/wholesalers/approval plans. The source journal is listed as the "series" to assist the prevention of duplicate purchasing in the same manner utilized for books-in-series.
- to facilitate user/access services all indexing/abstracting services are encouraged to utilize the co-indexing entry note indicated at the bottom of the first page of each article/chapter/contribution.
- this is intended to assist a library user of any reference tool (whether print, electronic, online, or CD-ROM) to locate the monographic version if the library has purchased this version but not a subscription to the source journal.
- individual articles/chapters in any Haworth publication are also available through the Haworth Document Delivery Service (HDDS).

To my mother,
Agnes Dyck Shahariw
(1919-1991)
and
to my son,
Nathan William Kuehne
who did not have the opportunity to share an intergenerational relationship.

# ABOUT THE EDITOR

**Valerie S. Kuehne, PhD,** is Associate Professor in the School of Child and Youth Care at the University of Victoria in British Columbia. She has been investigating relationships between older adults and youth for 15 years, in both the United States and Canada. With a background in pediatric nursing and professional experience working with all age groups, Dr. Kuehne has researched intergenerational relationships as they occur in families and in various community contexts, such as schools, child day care centers, and adult day care centers. She has written more than 20 publications that have appeared in such journals as *Developmental Psychology, Intergenerational Journal of Aging and Human Development, Journal of Applied Gerontology, Child and Youth Care Forum,* and *Child & Youth Services* (The Haworth Press, Inc.). Dr. Kuehne is a member of numerous professional societies, including the Society for Research in Child Development, Canadian Association on Gerontology, American Society on Aging, Generations United, and the Canadian Psychological Association. She is frequently sought out for her expertise in intergenerational program research and serves as a speaker and consultant to community and university groups around North America.

# Intergenerational Programs: Understanding What We Have Created

## CONTENTS

## EPILOGUE

# Foreword

Over the past two decades, intergenerational programming has come to play an increasingly prominent role in communities around North America. Bringing people of different ages to work together in meeting community needs is a strategy that makes sense because of the growth in the proportion of healthy, knowledgeable, and experienced older adults in our population, and because of violent crime, drug abuse, academic difficulties, and other problems that seem to plague young people especially. These trends have raised new questions, challenges and opportunities regarding the roles and responsibilities of elders, youth, and families in today's world. How can we meet the needs of both young and old in innovative ways? What can we do to foster a sense of interdependence across generations and provide opportunities for people of all ages to engage in meaningful activities throughout the life course?

By tapping into previously underutilized human resources and challenging assumptions about older and younger people, intergenerational programmers have been finding creative and cost-effective answers to these questions. During the 1970s and 1980s, a number of isolated, small-scale, yet highly innovative intergenerational programs were created, usually with the explicit goals of breaking down age-related stereotypes and negative attitudes while fostering understanding across ages. Since then the scale and number of intergenerational programs have grown dramatically and intergenerational coalitions have formed locally, regionally, nationally, and internationally. Moreover, as the notion that elders and youth should be seen more as community assets than as liabilities has gained momentum, a gradual shift toward providing more specific intergenerational services seems

---

[Haworth co-indexing entry note]: "Foreword." Henkin, Nancy Z. Co-published simultaneously in *Child & Youth Services* (The Haworth Press, Inc.) Vol. 20, No. 1/2, 1999, pp. xix-xxi; and: *Intergenerational Programs: Understanding What We Have Created* (ed: Valerie S. Kuehne) The Haworth Press, Inc., 1999, pp. xvii-xix. Single or multiple copies of this article are available for a fee from The Haworth Document Delivery Service [1-800-342-9678, 9:00 a.m. - 5:00 p.m. (EST). E-mail address: getinfo@haworthpressinc.com].

to be taking place in communities across North America. In the last decade, we have witnessed the emergence of intergenerational approaches to literacy development, the prevention of drug abuse and adolescent pregnancy, educational reform, and long-term care. Professionals from different disciplines are collaborating to provide holistic, community-based, intergenerational solutions to problems in each of these areas.

As we approach the millennium, we appear to be at a critical juncture in the development of intergenerational programming–one in which careful research and evaluation stand to play a significant role. There is a widespread view among those in the field that the intergenerational approach to meeting various community needs is on the verge of "going to scale": Becoming integrated into the overall missions of large-scale organizations and service delivery systems, especially in the United States. Success in this next level of growth depends on a concerted effort to disseminate what we know about the work we have done. We have learned much over the last twenty years and providing the best program models for large scale replication depends on documenting our successes and challenges effectively and understanding them fully.

Yet while research and evaluation provide the necessary tools for such tasks, they have been too infrequently used; much more scholarly research is needed. Too many intergenerational programs are designed and implemented without any effort to document their process or impact, and they generate only subjective, anecdotal evidence of their effectiveness. Programmers are sometimes discouraged that generalizable research and evaluation studies can require more resources than their program budgets have available, or that new strategies and sociometric tools must be developed to fully understand their program processes or effects on young children and frail elders, for example.

This volume provides an important, first opportunity for those conducting intergenerational program research and evaluation to contribute their knowledge to the field in a single volume. This compilation of research and evaluation papers provides all those working in the field with access to the best contemporary knowledge and critical thinking regarding the concepts that underlie intergenerational programs, the interactions that constitute them, and their outcomes. Sample research designs and measures appropriate for intergenerational program settings and participants provide evaluation and research direction to both beginning and experienced programmers. Questions and challenges guide both intergenerational program developers and researchers to some of the most important issues in the field at this time. Finally, this volume communicates to community leaders and policy makers that intergenerational programs can be demonstrably effective in meeting many of the human and social needs found in our communities. For all of us–young, old, and in-between–the timing of this message couldn't be better.

*Nancy Z. Henkin*

# Introduction

As a researcher interested in intergenerational relationships for almost fifteen years, it is my pleasure to introduce you to this collection of research and evaluation papers dedicated to intergenerational programs. Programs bringing children, youth, and older adults together have proliferated in communities around North America over the past three decades. They are the "creations" of community members, often human service and education professionals, who attempt to meet community needs and make good use of existing community resources for a stronger, more caring society. Goals such as improving school attendance, school-based learning, self-esteem, attitudes toward aging and older persons, and reducing substance use, social isolation, and troublesome behaviors are all among those suggested by intergenerational programs described in this volume and in volumes before (e.g., Brabazon & Disch, 1997; Newman & Brummel, 1989).

The importance of a collection of papers such as this one has increased over the years. With the millennium fast approaching and substantial momentum now behind intergenerational approaches to human services, education and policy making, this volume is well timed to contribute to the creation of national and international strategies for building and maintaining caring communities that foster generational interdependence and mutual responsibility.

My goals for this volume are twofold: To provide assistance to those interested in understanding how intergenerational programs work and to provide a collection of papers that demonstrate the breadth and depth of knowledge that research and evaluation studies have revealed about intergenerational programs in communities around North America. It is my hope that both beginning and sophisti-

[Haworth co-indexing entry note]: "Introduction." Kuehne, Valerie S. Co-published simultaneously in *Child & Youth Services* (The Haworth Press, Inc.) Vol. 20, No. 1/2, 1999, pp. 1-3; and: *Intergenerational Programs: Understanding What We Have Created* (ed: Valerie S. Kuehne) The Haworth Press, Inc., 1999, pp. 1-3. Single or multiple copies of this article are available for a fee from The Haworth Document Delivery Service [1-800-342-9678, 9:00 a.m. - 5:00 p.m. (EST). E-mail address: getinfo@haworthpressinc.com].

cated intergenerational practitioners and researchers will learn something new about how to study the intergenerational programs created in their communities, that research and evaluation in various forms can contribute toward advancing knowledge in this field, that intergenerational programs can and do contribute toward building strong communities, and that by studying intergenerational programs we increase the depth of our understanding of these "social creations," specifically their processes and effects on those who participate as well as society at large.

The volume begins with papers examining and critiquing the conceptual bases for intergenerational programming and related research. Ward, VanderVen, and Smith and Yeager argue for a closer link between theory and intergenerational program development and research. The second group of papers provide data supporting intergenerational program effects on participating children, youth, families and human service administrators. The effects of program participation described by Brabazon, Griff, Taylor et al., and Travis and Stremmel are wide ranging, providing directives for future work to both programmers and researchers. The third group of papers presents systematic and detailed examinations of intergenerational interactions. Using primarily observational data collection methods, Angersbach and Jones-Forster and Newman et al. focus our attention on the ways in which intergenerational program participants communicate with one another in two diverse community settings. In the final group of papers, Kocarnik-Ponzetti and Ponzetti, Vernon, Strom and Strom, and Cook question and challenge both intergenerational programmers and researchers. These papers argue for community participation in intergenerational research initiatives and provide examples of how such participation can work both theoretically and in real communities–locally, nationally and internationally. They also highlight some of the challenges associated with designing and researching intergenerational programs and make recommendations to address these challenges. In the Epilogue, Abrams and Giles describe the book's contributions to the intergenerational field and they identify gaps in the theoretical and empirical work, along with suggested theoretical approaches.

In sum, it is my sincere hope that this first collection of research papers contributes to the growing body of knowledge in the intergenerational field. It is just a beginning–there is much work to do to bring the volume of research and evaluation knowledge to the level of program development. Yet good work must be done, and quickly, if we are to provide evidence of the effects of intergenerational programs on our communities and begin to answer important questions regarding the nature of these created relationships. It is exciting work that benefits us all.

*Valerie S. Kuehne*

# SECTION ONE:
# CONCEPTUAL FOUNDATIONS FOR INTERGENERATIONAL PROGRAM RESEARCH

# The Intergenerational Field Needs More Ethnographic Research

## Christopher R. Ward

**SUMMARY.** Dominant approaches to intergenerational research may be inadequate to meet new challenges to the intergenerational field, such as increasing complexity of program settings, interdisciplinary collaboration, and a mandate to address social problems. An ethnographic approach to intergenerational work may be an effective strategy for meeting these challenges. An ethnographic approach involves a holistic perspective using field-based methods of data collection and a cross-cultural research base. As ethnographic methods have been used successfully in related areas such as education, gerontology, and child development, researchers are encouraged to integrate this perspective into studies of intergenerational programming. Various resource materials are described for practitioners and researchers interested in learning more about the ethnographic approach. *[Article copies available for a fee from The Haworth Document Delivery Service: 1-800-342-9678. E-mail address: getinfo@haworthpressinc.com <Website: http://www.haworthpressinc.com>]*

**KEYWORDS.** Ethnography, research, field, holistic, intergenerational

Intergenerational programs involve ongoing, organized interactions between members of younger and older age-groups for the benefit of

---

Christopher R. Ward is affiliated with the Intergenerational Studies Program, Community College of Denver, Campus Box 850, P.O. Box 173363, Denver, CO 80217-3363.

[Haworth co-indexing entry note]: "The Intergenerational Field Needs More Ethnographic Research." Ward, Christopher R. Co-published simultaneously in *Child & Youth Services* (The Haworth Press, Inc.) Vol. 20, No. 1/2, 1999, pp. 7-23; and: *Intergenerational Programs: Understanding What We Have Created* (ed: Valerie S. Kuehne) The Haworth Press, Inc., 1999, pp. 7-23. Single or multiple copies of this article are available for a fee from The Haworth Document Delivery Service [1-800-342-9678, 9:00 a.m. - 5:00 p.m. (EST). E-mail address: getinfo@haworthpressinc.com].

all participants. Over the past twenty to thirty years, these programs have grown in number and complexity, and they are increasingly valued for their application to a wide range of social problems (Newman, Ward, Smith, Wilson, & McCrea, 1997). The need to understand the contributions of intergenerational programs to address various social problems has created new challenges for intergenerational researchers. This paper will discuss how an increased use of ethnographic research approaches may not only broaden the scope of intergenerational research but also may help practitioners and policy makers better comprehend and address the complexities of professional settings and communities in which intergenerational approaches are used to meet social needs.

## INTERGENERATIONAL RESEARCH: A SURVEY

Theories and methods drawn from psychology dominated the intergenerational field through its first three decades. As noted in several reviews of the literature, many researchers have examined children's and youths' attitudes about aging and about the elderly (Green, 1981; Kite & Johnson, 1988; Lutsky, 1981). Only a few studies have looked at older persons' attitudes toward the young (e.g., Seefeldt, Jantz, Serock, & Bredekamp, 1982). Applied researchers and evaluators have investigated how intergenerational programs may change the attitudes of members of the younger or older generation toward each other (e.g., Chapman & Neal, 1990). Other studies have examined how specific individual characteristics such as life-satisfaction or self-esteem may be enhanced by program participation for both service providers (Newman, Karip, & Faux, 1995; Saltz, 1971) and for service recipients (Reinke, Holmes, & Denney, 1981). Most of these studies used standardized instruments and formal observational tools as primary methods of data collection.

Apart from the psychological approach, the amount and variety of intergenerational research have been limited. A few studies have examined the effects of intergenerational programs on student learning (Cooledge & Wurster, 1985; Powell, Wisenbaker, & Conner, 1987). Others have focused on participant behaviors. For example, Kuehne (1989) categorized the interactions between children and older adults in an intergenerational program in an adult day center as falling into positive or negative categories and found that most observed interactions were positive.

Recently, new perspectives on research and theory-building have appeared from outside the network of scholar-practitioners who have largely shaped the intergenerational field. For example, Fox and Giles (1993) suggested the need for a refined theory of intergenerational contact and for better understanding of the communication that occurs between younger and older individuals. Ryan, Hamilton, and See (1994) examined the use of "baby talk" by younger persons when talking with frail elderly individuals. Compared with persons in more neutral speech situations, the older persons who received such talk were less satisfied with the intergenerational interaction.

Seeming to reflect the field's general orientation toward psychology, most intergenerational researchers have tended to use quantitative research methods more frequently than qualitative methods. It would appear that qualitative methods have gained only limited acceptance over the last decade. In one of the few studies using this methodology, McGowan (1994) found positive outcomes for elderly persons who participated in a reminiscence project with college students. McGowan used intensive, qualitative interviews to examine the effects of project participation.

Research approaches that are based in psychology and which involve the use of quantitative methods were used widely in the intergenerational field during its formation and initial growth. Studies using this approach contributed to a greater understanding of youths' attitudes toward aging and the elderly. As a result, practitioners also understood the changes that might occur in intergenerational program participants across a significant, if narrow, range of individual measures, for example, life satisfaction.

More research is needed in many areas of the intergenerational field. For example, more studies are needed to examine the shared perspectives of younger and older participants in intergenerational programs and of those who interact in other multigenerational settings. A continued focus on concepts measured by standardized scales may miss the richness of what older and younger persons think and feel about each other. For example, researchers have not generally asked, "What shared values and understandings do participants (young and old) need to work successfully together?"

Most studies of intergenerational programs have not been designed to explore in depth what these programs "look like from the inside." Nor have they examined how the perspectives of younger and older participants may differ or coincide. No studies discuss ways in which detailed observations of a specific intergenerational program may be related to the larger programmatic context, such as the surrounding community or school district. Moreover, there is little in the literature that describes precisely how old and young interact in non-program settings such as churches, work, or school.

Other limitations of previous research include a dependence on a narrow range of individual measures that may have been developed for other purposes, such as measures of life satisfaction. Thus response categories may not be appropriate for use with children, youth, and older adults in intergenerational contexts.

The quantitative approach to research has been useful for describing specific kinds of program impact. However, this approach may be inadequate for achieving a broader, holistic understanding of the way that groups or systems function—a key feature of intergenerational programs.

Researchers must utilize new approaches if intergenerational research is to serve practitioners' needs and enhance the field's scholarly credibility. An increased use of ethnographic approaches to research and the integration of insights from anthropology may help to achieve these goals, since both permit researchers to examine closely and with rigor the experiences and perspectives of intergenerational participants in context.

Ethnographic research is not without its drawbacks. Ethnographers must spend generous amounts of time in the field, time that administrators or funders may not be willing to support. Critics of ethnographic approaches question the generalizability of findings from ethnographic studies with a limited number of cases—sometimes only one. In response, ethnographers have argued that culture is shared and that people do not hold beliefs, values, ideas, and ways of doing things in isolation. Saying that culture is shared means that what is learned by individuals in one setting is likely to be linked to the cultural rules shared by people in another, similar setting.

## THE NATURE OF ETHNOGRAPHY

Ethnographers use the concept of culture to organize the many ideas and behaviors found in any complex group (Spindler & Spindler, 1997). That concept has several variations. For some, the concept of culture is materialistic, with an emphasis on behavior and customs. For others, the concept is more ideational, with the focus being on people's ideas, beliefs, and knowledge (Fetterman, 1989). The latter interpretation is appropriate for exploring group members' shared beliefs about who is old, who is young, and about what constitutes generational differences or similarities. When culture is defined primarily as being shared knowledge, the ethnographer's task is to describe the cultural rules that members of a group share and which they may use to guide their behavior. In the intergenerational field, this concept of culture might be used in applied research, such as in studies of the knowledge shared by intergenerational professionals about younger and older people, about the institutions that serve both age-groups, and about how to create and run successful programs.

Using a concept of shared cultural knowledge may also be helpful to intergenerational programmers for understanding the barriers to working across systems. For example, when child care providers and long-term care practitioners work together, they are, in effect, bringing together two different sets of cultural rules. To work together successfully, members of each service-group must learn the cultural rules of the other's system. Ethnographic studies are designed to elicit such shared systems knowledge in rich detail. On a practical level, those responsible for promoting collaboration among systems can utilize the insights and knowledge from research to teach practitioners from each system about the other system: Its values, ways of doing things, and shared understandings.

Several other characteristics of the ethnographic approach seem to make it especially suitable for the intergenerational field: (a) the locations include naturalistic settings and their contexts, (b) the focus is on the perspective of the insider, (c) researchers are personally involved in the research, and (d) both the informal, often implicit, agenda and the open and clearly stated agenda are of interest.

## A Holistic Approach

To use an ethnographic approach is to seek a complete "picture" of a specific group of people. History, politics, religion, and other aspects of daily life become part of what the researcher attempts to bring into the picture (Fetterman, 1989). Ethnographic researchers spend long periods of time among those from whom they are learning. This intense, long-term engagement contrasts with traditional methods of intergenerational research in which a pre-defined set of information is gathered using paper-and-pencil questionnaires or short interviews. This holistic perspective seems well-suited to the intergenerational field in which practitioners are often called upon to appreciate and integrate the cultural perspectives, systems, and needs of several groups of people simultaneously.

*Naturalistic settings and their contexts.* Research undertaken within the everyday settings of human activity is the hallmark of ethnographic studies. It seems likely that this perspective could be easily applied to studies of a wide range of intergenerational programs and activities. Moreover, ethnographers do not study people in isolation (Atkinson & Hammersley, 1994). For example, in an intergenerational program, the attendance rate of one group of participants may be low. Yet if the program's context is understood–why members of that group do and do not attend or what is keeping many from attending–attendance may be interpreted differently.

Ethnographers are especially interested in how the values and ways of doing things in a specific setting may reflect those of the society of which that setting is a part. Frequently, there appear to be close links between a local setting and the larger culture, suggesting that the behaviors of youths and older adults in a specific intergenerational program are not idiosyncratic. It seems reasonable that cultural rules exert a strong influence on the attitudes, language, and behaviors directed by one age-group toward another in an intergenerational setting. Ethnographers studying intergenerational programs would take these factors into account as they gathered and analysed their data.

*Focus on the perspective of the insider.* Researchers who use an ethnographic approach examine what members of a given group think about certain things, how they view themselves, and how they interpret specific events. The researcher is a learner of culture, with the members of the group instructing him or her–often at length and in their own words–regarding their "insider's" knowledge of their culture. This approach seems to contrast with the traditional perspective in which younger and older individuals may be viewed as "subjects" who teach researchers via answers to specific questions often on standardized measures (Spradley & McCurdy, 1972). A focus on the insider's perspective seems important because intergenerational programs serve mainly younger and older people whose ideas and perspectives are often overlooked and discounted by society overall (McCrea & Smith, 1997). Ethnographers often use insiders' perspectives directly (e.g., to create analytic categories) and by so doing may help enhance the social status of both the young and the old.

*Researcher is personally involved.* Ethnographic researchers conduct their fieldwork within the group and the activities under investigation (Wolcott, 1995). This emphasis on extensive work with participants would necessitate a major change in the way that most intergenerational research has been conducted to date. A variety of formal and informal data-gathering techniques would be employed. Intergenerational researchers using this method would spend much more time interacting with people in the natural setting than typically has been done in the past.

It could be argued that the intense personal involvement of ethnographic researchers in their studies may compromise objectivity in terms of data collection and interpretation. However, for those utilizing an ethnographic approach, personal involvement in the research situation is a major contribution–not a hindrance–to a good analysis. Moreover, most ethnographers seem to view the concept of objectivity as impossible whereas researchers who typically use quantitative methods view objectivity as a necessary goal of their work.

*Interest in the informal or hidden curriculum or agenda.* Some ethnographers are interested in the informal cultural rules that may guide group activities as opposed to more formal, institutional (and often written) kinds of rules. For example, some have studied the "hidden" curriculum of educational institutions to see what schools are teaching in addition to or in place of their formal curriculum (Gearing & Epstein, 1982). An increasing number of researchers are interested in the potential effects of intergenerational programs on problematic youth behaviors such as poor school performance. Detailed ethnographic descriptions of the interactions that take place in an intergenerational program may yield valuable information about the implicit cultural messages that are being communicated between younger and older age-groups within this specific school context.

## ETHNOGRAPHY IN RELATED FIELDS

Although little ethnographic research has been carried out to date in the intergenerational field, the young and the old have been the subject of ethnographic studies completed by researchers in related fields. For example, Moffat (1992) found that among 160 ethnographies written about the United States between 1980 and 1992, 21 focussed on the young and 11 on the old. All 32 of these were written by persons of a different cohort or generation than the subjects under study. Through these studies, ethnographic researchers have contributed to fields such as gerontology, child development, and education. In some cases these researchers have examined the relationships between generations or conducted their fieldwork in settings common to intergenerational programs. In other cases they have developed methods that can be utilized in intergenerational research or have described the intergenerational activities encountered in their fieldwork.

The study of aging comprises a growing subfield in anthropology (Cohen, 1994; Schweitzer, 1991); anthropologists have long been interested in the relationships among persons of different age groups and the ways that age inequalities shape the lives of older people and their relations with the young (Foner, 1984). Some anthropologists provide insights particularly useful to intergenerational practitioners. Drawing on ethnographic fieldwork in the former Yugoslavia and California, Simic (1991) compared the value systems and behavior related to aging in mainstream Anglo-American culture and in southern Yugoslav culture. He found that white, middle-class Americans value self-realization and independence; southern Yugoslavs hold an ideal that stresses kinship ties and interdependence. From these differing sets of core values come contrasting views of intergenerational relationships, findings that would be very useful for intergenerational program designers.

Within the field of gerontology, researchers have conducted their ethnographic studies in the types of settings where intergenerational programs frequently occur, such as long term care facilities (e.g., Myerhoff, 1978). In one recent study, Foner (1994) described the work of nursing home aides and their experiences as employees and caregivers. Such description could provide useful information for intergenerational program designers on the work life perspectives of this group of potential program participants and could help to ensure that the intergenerational program created is compatible with or enhances their experience.

Ethnographic approaches have also been used extensively in studies of children and youth. One of these studies (Tobin, Wu, & Davidson, 1989) is based on a research model well suited for the intergenerational field. Through comparisons of daily practice in preschools, Tobin and his colleagues demonstrated the links between respective cultural values of Japan, the United States, and the People's Republic of China, and the values transmitted in these countries' preschools. Preschool activities were videotaped daily; footage then was reviewed by persons from each preschool's culture, followed by persons from the other two cultures. A similar methodology using tapes of intergenerational program activities and discussions across generations and cultures could generate useful cultural findings for the intergenerational field.

Ethnographic methods have been useful in studies of education, including schooling (Spindler, 1997). School-based ethnographies often investigate topics relevant to intergenerational programs, such as how various groups relate within the school context (Fordham, 1996) or how community values are transmitted to the next generation (Foley, 1990). Researchers who use ethnographic methods to study schools have sometimes described intergenerational programs they encounter in their fieldwork. For example, Ernst (1994) investigated how an elementary English-As-a-Second-Language program helped language-minority students succeed in school. One of the program components was an intergenerational school volunteer program through which older adults worked with the students as they learned English. The intergenerational program gave the immigrant children individual instruction and attention while also providing persons to fill the roles of "grandparents," since their biological grandparents had remained in their home countries.

## ETHNOGRAPHY AND MEETING NEW CHALLENGES

The intergenerational field is facing many new challenges for both researchers and practitioners. Some of these challenges are discussed below, along with some suggestions for meeting these challenges through an increased use of ethnographic approaches.

### Program Complexity

Intergenerational programs can be viewed as complex structures. They include participants from at least two age-groups, of course, as well as the staff and agencies that serve the participants. Personnel from each agency or institutional system bring to the program a specific combination of training, viewpoints, and procedures, all of which must be integrated with those of other systems. Intergenerational programs also may have several sources of funding, two or more sets of regulations under which to operate, and participants with different expectations about activities. Despite all of this complexity, the intergenerational experience is shared by all, providing a common "culture" for participants.

Thus it is not surprising that practitioners often indicate that "more is going on" in intergenerational programs than can be measured with standardized instruments. Typically, this view is voiced by a researcher or evaluator who used standardized measures and who found few effects from a program that both practitioners and participants perceived as having been a rich, dynamic intergenerational experience.

Such "more is going on" observations may reflect the multiplicity of perspectives among the various professional groups involved in intergenerational programming and evaluation. This phenomenon also may be observed in encounters between younger and older persons in non-program settings such as the workplace. These encounters may be even more complicated than those in structured programs, because direct, real-world exchanges between younger and older individuals are related to all sorts of issues, often beyond the scope of typical program activities. Most psychological studies have used predetermined categories of behavior that may not be adequate to describe all of what individuals are experiencing. As a result, practitioners may lack rich, descriptive data about program activities and intergenerational encounters.

Ethnographic research can yield in-depth, detailed descriptions of a wide range of activities as well as the nuances of intergenerational interactions and exchanges. An ethnographic approach also may provide a framework for examining what participants see themselves doing in intergenerational programs and interactions by clarifying the categories and labels that participants use to make sense of intergenerational encounters (Spradley, 1980; Spradley & McCurdy, 1972).

## Mandate to Solve Social Problems

In the last decade, many practitioners, policy makers, and funders have advocated a broader, more demanding mission for the intergenerational field. Intergenerational programs may now be expected to help solve the social ills facing the young, the old, and society at large. These programs have been described as vehicles to diminish drug abuse, raise school grades, reduce crime, improve the economic well-being of the poor, pass on knowledge about the workplace, and transmit community values (Newman, Ward, Smith, Wilson, & McCrea, 1997). However, it is difficult to study the relationship between an intergenerational program and specific outcomes. Little is known about the mechanisms by which intergenerational programs may relieve social problems. We lack good descriptions of how intergenerational efforts differ from other human service programs serving the same populations.

Studies using an ethnographic approach may provide more complex, detailed information about how programs work and about their potential effects. Ethnographic researchers might attempt to describe how intergenerational programs evolve and how participants' subjective experiences may change over time. In addition, the intergenerational field is becoming more deeply involved in the partnering of systems. The ways in which the members of these systems work together can make or break an intergenerational program. An ethnographic approach seems well-suited for capturing the complexities of collaboration across systems and for describing how a collaboration succeeds or fails.

## Beyond Intergenerational Programs: Intergroup Relations

The intergenerational field is focused on inter-group relations–how younger and older individuals interact socially, culturally, politically, and economically. Yet we have few detailed studies of public or private interactions between the youngest and the oldest generations. How do members of younger and older age-groups interrelate in shared spaces such as parks or in multi-generational organizations such as churches or workplaces? In contemporary North American society, which values, symbols, activities and policies contribute to intergenerational exchange and which to intergenerational conflict?

An increased use of ethnographic approaches in intergenerational research may help answer those questions. For example, an ethnographic approach seems well-suited to examine the long-term, community-wide effects that school volunteer programs may have on communities and on the support that older adults give to public education. There is a substantial body of literature on how to carry out school-related ethnographic studies (e.g., Wilcox, 1982) and how to tie findings to broader issues of inter-group relations (e.g., La Belle & Ward, 1994).

## A COMPARATIVE PERSPECTIVE

Research in the intergenerational field is largely a North American enterprise. Much of the rationale for the field's development and the specific nature of that development are based on the conditions and values of a highly industrialized Western society. There is little evidence of an international perspective, particularly in research. This is unfortunate considering important world-wide demographic changes such as the growing proportion of older adults in the population (Kristof, 1996) and the potential for growth of an international movement for intergenerational research. An intergenerational movement might include the perspectives of societies in which care for the young and for the old remain family responsibilities and where there is not a large social welfare apparatus as there is in North America and Western Europe. In these societies, issues related to changes in intergenerational relations within the family might be considered of great importance, whereas public policy issues related to generational equity and allocation of public funds may be seen as being less important.

Most comparative intergenerational studies to date have examined if and how attitudes toward aging, as measured on standardized scales, may differ across cultures (Jantz, 1981; McCracken, Fitzwater, Lockwood, & Bjork, 1995; Seefeldt, 1984; Zandi, Mirle, & Jarvis, 1990). Typically, the question of interest has been, "Is ageism universal?" However, there are many other basic questions about intergenerational relations that might be addressed in comparative ethnographic studies. For example: What is the nature of cross-generational encounters in other societies? How do other cultures "divide" up the human life-span–are there always categories for young people, old people, and people "in the middle?" Do people in various societies think it necessary to have older adults as role models for children and youth? Do people in various societies see inequalities between the generations? Finding the answers to these and other related questions would contribute to our knowledge of intergenerational relations in other societies. The use of ethnographic methods may also contribute to new approaches for intergenerational research and programming in North America and around the world.

## PRACTICAL CONSIDERATIONS

Practitioners interested in becoming involved in ethnographic intergenerational research can refer to a variety of introductory works for guidance and direction. Fetterman (1989) and Spradley and McCurdy (1972) include step-by-step descriptions for ethnographic research. Spradley (1980) is a useful supplement to either volume.

Bernard (1994) argued for an ethnographic approach that is both quantitative and qualitative, and provided detailed information on various techniques. Wolcott (1995) discussed specific aspects of a qualitative approach to research. Together, these two volumes provide a useful overview of the concepts and methods typically used in ethnographic research. Those seeking a particularly detailed overview are referred to the handbook by Denzin and Lincoln (1994).

Ethnographic studies themselves are another important source of information for those considering the use of ethnographic approaches to research. For example, Foner (1994) studied how nursing home workers seem to relate to other individuals in their work setting, including the older residents. The nursing home setting is one likely to be familiar and of interest to many in the intergenerational field.

Zinsser (1991) used an ethnographic approach to examine how parents in a working-class neighborhood seem to value local family- and friendship-based child care settings as opposed to more formal, professional settings. Researchers in the intergenerational field may find this study a useful model for exploring how communities perceive the interactions between and respective roles of their older and younger members.

Examples of creative research methodology can be found in other works. Tobin, Wu, and Davidson (1989) discussed the use of videotape to record daily activities in a preschool setting. The videotapes can be used to promote discussion among various groups of their beliefs about preschool education. The videotaping of intergenerational encounters may yield rich data, that may lead to important insights about the nature of these interactions and about the subjective interpretations of them by younger and older participants.

## CONCLUSIONS

Practitioners and scholars in the intergenerational field are facing new challenges and should consider approaches to research that can help them to address the challenges. Methods and insights from ethnography and anthropology can provide the foundation for one such approach. Ethnographic methods emphasize the concept of culture, a holistic perspective, the importance of context, and the value of insider perspectives. These methods also may bring to the intergenerational field a much-needed cross-cultural perspective, which can contribute to its internationalization.

The potential benefits of an ethnographic approach to intergenerational programming and research are extensive. It may be especially beneficial to build upon the ethnographic methods and concepts being used in the areas of education, child development, and gerontology. Intergenerational practitioners can benefit from more in-depth descriptions and analyses of intergenerational programs than are typically gained from traditional approaches. Researchers will be able to study programs and program participants in more complex ways.

However, it may be that the full extent of ethnography's contribution to the intergenerational field will become apparent only as researchers move beyond studying what programs "do" to examining a wide range of daily intergenerational encounters in the workplace, in organizations, and in shared public spaces.

## REFERENCES

Atkinson, P., & Hammersley, M. (1994). Ethnography and participant observation. In N. Denzin & Y. Lincoln (Eds.), *Handbook of qualitative research* (pp. 248-261). Thousand Oaks, CA: Sage Publications.

Bernard, H. R. (1994). *Research methods in anthropology: Qualitative and quantitative approaches* (2nd ed.). Thousand Oaks, CA: Sage Publications.

Chapman, N., & Neal, M. (1990). The effects of intergenerational experiences on adolescents and older adults. *The Gerontologist, 30*, 825-832.

Cohen, L. (1994). Old age: Cultural and critical perspectives. *Annual Review of Anthropology, 23*, 137-158.

Cooledge, N., & Wurster, S. (1985). Intergenerational tutoring and student achievement. *The Reading Teacher, 39*, 343-346.

Denzin, N., & Lincoln, Y. (Eds.). (1994). *Handbook of qualitative research.* Thousand Oaks, CA: Sage Publications.

Ernst, G. (1994). Beyond language: The many dimensions of an ESL program. *Anthropology and Education Quarterly, 25*(3), 317-335.

Fetterman, D. (1989). *Ethnography: Step by step.* Newbury Park, CA: Sage Publications.

Foley, D. (1990). *Learning capitalist culture: Deep in the heart of Tejas.* Philadelphia: University of Pennsylvania Press.

Foner, N. (1984). *Ages in conflict: A Cross-cultural perspective on inequality between old and young.* New York: Columbia University Press.

Foner, N. (1994). *The caregiving dilemma: Work in an American nursing home.* Berkeley, CA: University of California Press.

Fordham, S. (1996). *Blacked out: Dilemmas of race, identity, and success at Capital High School.* Chicago: University of Chicago Press.

Fox, S. & Giles, H. (1993). Accommodating intergenerational contact: A critique and theoretical model. *Journal of Aging Studies, 7*(4), 423-451.

Fujita, M., & Sano, T. (1988). Children in Japanese and American day care centers: Ethnography and reflective cross-cultural interviewing. In H. Trueba & C. Delgado-Gaitan (Eds.), *School and society: Learning content through culture* (pp. 73-97). New York: Praeger.

Gearing, F., & Epstein, P. (1982). Learning to wait: An ethnographic probe into the operations of an item of hidden curriculum. In G. Spindler (Ed.), *Doing the ethnography of schooling: Educational anthropology in action* (pp. 240-247). New York: Holt, Rinehart, and Winston.

Green, S.K. (1981). Attitudes and perceptions about the elderly: Current and future perspectives. *International Journal of Aging and Human Development, 13*(2), 99-119.

Henderson, J., & Vesperi, M., (Eds.). (1995). *The culture of long term care: Nursing home ethnography.* Westport, CT: Bergin & Garvey.

Jantz, R. (1981). Children's attitudes towards the elderly: A look at Greek and American children. *Theory and Research in Social Education, 9*(2), 1-22.

Kite, M., & Johnson, B. (1988). Attitudes toward older and younger adults: A meta-analysis. *Psychology and Aging, 3*(3), 233-244.

Kristof, N. D. (1996, September 22). Aging world, new wrinkles. *The New York Times,* Section 4, p. 1, 5.

Kuehne, V. (1989). "Younger friends/older friends": A study of intergenerational interactions. *Journal of Classroom Interaction, 24*(1), 14-21.

La Belle, T., & Ward, C. (1994). *Multiculturalism and education: Diversity and its impact on schools and society.* Albany, NY: State University of New York Press.

Lutsky, N. (1981). Attitudes toward old age and elderly persons. In C. Eisdorfer (Ed.), *Annual review of gerontology and geriatrics.* (Vol. 1, pp. 287-336). New York: Springer.

McCracken, A., Fitzwater, E., Lockwood, M., & Bjork, F. (1995). Comparison of nursing students' attitudes toward the elderly in Norway and the United States. *Educational Gerontology, 21,* 167-180.

McCrea, J., & Smith, T. (1997). Social issues addressed by intergenerational programs. In S. Newman, C. Ward, T. Wilson & J. McCrea (Eds.), *Intergenerational Programs: Past, Present, and Future* (pp. 37-51). Washington, DC: Taylor & Francis.

McGowan, T. (1994). Mentoring-reminiscence. A conceptual and empirical analysis. *International Journal of Aging and Human Development, 39*(4), 321-336.

Moffatt, M. (1992). Ethnographic writing about American culture. *Annual Review of Anthropology, 21,* 205-229.

Myerhoff, B. (1978). *Number our days.* New York: Dutton Press.

Newman, S., Karip, E., & Faux, R. (1995). Everyday memory function of older adults: The impact of intergenerational school volunteer programs. *Educational Gerontology, 21*(6), 569-580.

Newman, S., Ward, C., Smith, T., Wilson, J. & McCrea, J. (1997). *Intergenerational programs: Past, present, and future.* Washington, DC: Taylor & Francis.

Powell, J., Wisenbaker, J., & Connor, R. (1987). Effects of intergenerational tutoring and related variables on reading and mathematics achievement of low socioeconomic children. *Journal of Experimental Education, 55*(4), 206-211.

Reinke, B., Holmes, D., & Denney, N. (1981). Influence of a "friendly visitor" program on the cognitive functioning and morale of elderly persons. *American Journal of Cognitive Psychology, 9*(4), 491-506.

Ryan, E., Hamilton, J., & See, S. (1994). Patronizing the old: How do younger and older adults respond to baby talk in the nursing home? *International Journal of Aging and Human Development, 39*(1), 21-32.

Saltz, R. (1971). Aging persons as child-care workers in a foster grandparent program: Psycho-social effects and work performance. *Aging and Human Development, 2,* 314-340.

Schweitzer, M. (1991). *Anthropology of aging: A partially annotated bibliography.* New York: Greenwood Press.

Seefeldt, C. (1984). Children's attitudes toward the elderly: A cross-cultural comparison. *International Journal of Aging and Human Development, 19*(4), 319-328.

Seefeldt, C., Jantz, R., Serock, K., & Bredekamp, S. (1982). Elderly persons' attitudes toward children. *Educational Gerontology, 8,* 493-506.

Simic, A. (1991). Aging, world view, and intergenerational relations in America and Yugoslavia. In J. Sokolovsky (Ed.), *The Cultural Context of Aging* (pp. 89-107). New York: Bergin & Garvey.

Spindler, G. (Ed.) (1982). *Doing the ethnography of schooling: Educational anthropology in action.* New York: Holt, Rinehart and Winston.

Spindler, G., & Spindler, L. (1997). Ethnography: An anthropological view. In G. Spindler (Ed.), *Education and the cultural process: Anthropological approaches* (pp. 50-55). Prospect Heights, IL: Waveland Press.

Spradley, J. (1980). *Participant observation.* New York: Holt, Rinehart and Winston.

Spradley, J., & McCurdy, D. (1972, reprinted 1988). *The cultural experience: Ethnography in complex society.* Prospect Heights, IL: Waveland Press.

Tobin, J., Wu, D., & Davidson, D. (1989). *Preschool in three cultures.* New Haven: Yale University Press.

Wilcox, K. (1982). Ethnography as a methodology and its application to the study of schooling: A review. In G. Spindler (Ed.), *Doing the ethnography of schooling: Educational anthropology in action* (pp. 457-488). New York: Holt, Rinehart and Winston.

Wolcott, H. (1995). *The art of fieldwork.* Walnut Creek, CA: Alta Mira Press.

Zandi, T., Mirle, J., & Jarvis, P. (1990). Children's attitudes toward elderly individuals: A comparison of two ethnic groups. *International Journal of Aging and Human Development, 30*(3), 161-174.

Zinsser, C. (1991). *Raised in East Urban: Child care changes in a working class community.* New York: Teachers College Press.

# Intergenerational Communities:
# Where Learning and Interaction
# Go Hand-in-Hand

Barbara J. Smith
Annette Yeager

**SUMMARY.** The authors argue for intergenerational programs based on two contemporary orientations to teaching and learning: constructivist and sociocultural. They provide examples of school-based intra- and inter-generational activities that challenge conventional notions about the capabilities of young children and speak to the learning benefits of collaborative decision-making. The authors offer several specific guidelines for intergenerational program developers and researchers that focus on assessing the learning potential of intergenerational initiatives. They also recommend case studies and participatory research approaches as particularly useful for gaining insight into intergenerational learning processes. *[Article copies available for a fee from The Haworth Document Delivery Service: 1-800-342-9678. E-mail address: getinfo@haworthpressinc.com <Website: http://www.haworthpressinc.com>]*

**KEYWORDS.** Constructivist, sociocultural, teaching, learning, research, intergenerational

Community centers and other sites, such as museums and schools, provide a range of programs that span the learning needs and interests

---

Barbara J. Smith may be reached at 9 Blvd du Chateau, 92200, Neuilly-Sur-Seine, France. Annette Yeager is a retired teacher educator and may be reached at R.R. #4, Simcoe, Ontario VN3Y 4K3, Canada.

[Haworth co-indexing entry note]: "Intergenerational Communities: Where Learning and Interaction Go Hand-in-Hand." Smith, Barbara J. and Annette Yeager. Co-published simultaneously in *Child & Youth Services* (The Haworth Press, Inc.) Vol. 20, No. 1/2, 1999, pp. 25-32; and: *Intergenerational Programs: Understanding What We Have Created* (ed: Valerie S. Kuehne) The Haworth Press, Inc., 1999, pp. 25-32. Single or multiple copies of this article are available for a fee from The Haworth Document Delivery Service [1-800-342-9678, 9:00 a.m. - 5:00 p.m. (EST). E-mail address: getinfo@haworthpressinc.com].

of many people. Most of these programs are geared to particular age-groups. Bridge, for instance, is an activity that usually draws adults, whereas driver education courses tend to be more popular with teenagers.

Programs do exist, however, that transcend age-based boundaries and promote more interaction among persons of varying ages. Parent-tot swimming lessons are a popular physical activity in many communities. In a computer workshop at the Disney Institute in Florida, 7-year-olds write stories with 80-year-olds. The young authors of *Foxfire*, a publication originating at Raban Gap-Nacoochee School in the Appalachian mountains, based their articles about local history and folklore on interviews conducted with their elders (Wigginton, 1972). At a high school in Ontario, Canada, in a day-care center staffed by volunteers from a local women's shelter, many young mothers were guest speakers in sex education classes. One school administrator attributed a reduction in the rate of teenage pregnancy to the open and honest exchange between these mothers and the adolescents.

Intergenerational programs often have an informal, natural quality. However, we have also noticed in these settings a sophisticated, interactional learning process. It is to this latter dimension that we address our attention. We will provide a brief overview of two contemporary orientations to learning along with pertinent illustrations from both intra- and inter-generational programs. We will pose several questions that can guide intergenerational communities in assessing the learning potential of their programs. We will conclude with some recommendations for future research.

## *LEARNING AS A TOOL FOR GROWTH AND CHANGE*

Traditional notions of learning are deeply embedded in our personal histories of education. Many of us believe, for example, that information is transferred from the teacher to the learner, that the learner passively consumes what is presented. Much of the thinking in contemporary education, however, reflects a very different orientation.

According to the constructivist orientation, learners are the generators of knowledge. It is the educator's responsibility to create the kind of conditions that will enable the learner to "construct" understanding

(Kelly, 1955). Bannister and Fransella (1980) wrote that, "Education-al growth is not the accumulation of more and more pieces of informa-tion, but the development of an increasingly complex structure for organizing and interrelating ideas" (p. 95).

One activity that seemed to foster learning, from a constructivist orientation, occurred in an urban public school west of Toronto. Fif-teen students, ages 8 and 9 years old, assumed the role of teacher with respect to students in kindergarten, and grades 1, 2, and 3. As these young "teachers" developed their lesson plans and put them into operation, they were constructing, simultaneously, both a deeper un-derstanding of the subject matter (health and physical education) and a more sophisticated understanding of teaching and learning (Smith, 1996).

A year after this peer-teaching project had ended, the classroom teacher and a school librarian discussed their perceptions of its lasting and influential impact. Their comments seemed to illustrate the types of outcomes that are often associated with constructivist approaches to education.

Teacher:

> We (grade 5 class) were having physical education one day and the gym was being used by the kindergartens. I decided that the kids would be able to go in and help. It was interesting to watch them go in–even though they wouldn't want to play with them. The peer teachers especially seemed to get them organized quick-ly into groups, playing different ball games . . . And as well, the rest of my class followed along because they had those examples [the peer-teachers] to follow. (Smith, 1996, p. 132)

School librarian:

> To see them [peer teachers] taking a leading role I think we'll really . . . see them come out as school 'leaders' in the next couple of years, where [otherwise] they might not have been. Laura was a child who would always be led where now she's taking the lead. I see that when she comes down to do work . . . she's not sitting back in her group. When she's doing research, she's talking and speaking up and having a position on things

which she never would have done before . . . Lyle–the same thing
. . . It's interesting. The children that chose to do it [peer teach-
ing]–the bulk of them were not your outgoing "natural leader"
type children. (Smith, 1996, p. 131)

These teachers' perceptions of their pupils seem to challenge conventional wisdom about the capabilities of young children. Might
community-based intergenerational programs consider giving younger
children similar responsibilities? If 8- and 9-year-olds are capable of
instructing younger children, might not they be capable of playing
other, significant community roles than those typically afforded them?
These children might, for example, teach younger children at the local
library. Older children could be active participants in teaching seniors.
Many young children have sufficient levels of cognitive and decision-
making capabilities to help support school/community breakfast and
lunch programs. Regardless of setting, all participants in programs
such as these stand to gain a great deal in terms of skills and knowledge, personal competence, and satisfying community-based interactions.

The potential for children to assume responsible community roles
seemed apparent in a program at a public school in southwestern
Ontario. Students in a grade 7 classroom were given the responsibilities for setting up, presenting, and assessing the school's salute to
Canada's Fitweek. Working in one of the five teams (program, public-
ity, sponsor, registration, and evaluation teams), students organized
the event. Community members were invited to the school on four
consecutive evenings to take part in various physical activities. The
Fitweek events were an outstanding success. Students were awarded
"points" for bringing family and community members to the school,
and the students who had accumulated the highest scores at the end of
the week were given prizes.

It seems reasonable that the Fitweek activities would be viewed as
an intergenerational program. From a sociocultural perspective on
learning, however, programs such as this have the potential for even
more intergenerational involvement. If community members had participated along with the children in the design, organization, and follow-up of the program, the experience could have been more collaborative and, perhaps as a consequence, more learning-intense.

According to the sociocultural perspective, interaction with others is central to learning. The founder of the socioculturalism movement, Vygotsky (1978), coined the phrase, the *zone of proximal development* (ZPD). The ZPD is where the novice learns "under adult guidance or in collaboration with more capable peers" (p. 86). Here, learning is indicated by specific changes in language used by the novice. As the novice becomes more of an expert, he or she appropriates the language of the expert.

The notion of a zone of proximal development seemed reflected in the activities at a public school west of Toronto. In this school, fifth-grade students were asked to evaluate a playground leadership program in which seventh-grade students provided structured activity for students in grade 2 over a period of 2 months. The fifth graders were assisted in designing a plan for gathering assessment data prior to and during this program.

Six teams of student researchers participated in conducting taped interviews with teachers, students, and administrators. One student team used videotapes of playground activity obtained before, during, and after the project to compare the quality and quantity of the activities. An adult researcher and the student researchers spent many hours together designing the research instruments, analyzing the data, and interpreting the results.

The findings were presented to the school staff, who, from all appearances, took the students' ideas and recommendations seriously. This investigation of playground activity was perceived as being a rewarding experience for all involved.

How can such sociocultural learning be facilitated within the context of contemporary intergenerational programs? Perhaps communities could utilize their intergenerational resources for planning and coordinating local celebrations. Young people could work with seniors to organize Halloween safety blitzes, nutrition awareness activities, literacy programs, Heart-Health Month events, blood-donor clinics, organ-donation promotions, fire-safety challenges, baby-sitting courses, and so on. Although collaborative projects take time to implement, it is necessary to ensure that all community voices are heard and that the activities are relevant to a wide range of community members. Successful outcomes may be facilitated when participant interaction involves the exchange of ideas, the development of common goals, and collaborative decision-making.

## LEARNING-ORIENTED CHALLENGES
## FOR INTERGENERATIONAL COMMUNITIES

The constructivist and sociocultural approaches to learning seem to suggest the following questions, which might be used for assessing intergenerational programming and for charting future directions. The responses to these questions may be used also to develop new program features that may maximize learning for all participants.

1. To what extent are participants working in collaboration with others of dissimilar ages?
2. Do participants share equally in the decision-making process regarding program goals?
3. To what extent are participants making reciprocal contributions to others' growth and development?
4. Are there benefits for all community members?

## A CALL FOR RESEARCH

Everyone connected to an intergenerational program has a vested interest in ensuring that the program is well-designed and implemented. To achieve this common goal, appropriate research techniques and program evaluation methods must be used. Recommended approaches include the use of case studies (Glaser, 1978; Glesne & Peshkin, 1992; Lincoln & Guba, 1985) and participatory research (Hall & Kassam, 1985; Park, Brydon-Miller, Hall, & Jackson, 1993; Selener, 1997).

The case-study format is useful for examining the process through which individuals in communities learn together. Although this kind of documentation of the learning process is rarely done, it can provide important information that can be used for interim program changes and outcome evaluations. It also may lead to specific research questions about the nature of intergenerational interactions in learning contexts. Reports concerning intergenerational programs routinely describe activities and accomplishments: Very seldom do such accounts detail the twisting and turning pathways and the stops and starts encountered when participants are learning and growing together.

Participatory research is action-oriented. Those involved in this kind of research are all stakeholders who work together to solve practical problems and to bring about change in their community. When discussing the roots of participatory research in the struggles of marginalized "communities," Selener (1997) described it as " . . . a process through which members of an oppressed group or community identify a problem, collect and analyze information, and act upon the problem in order to find solutions and to promote social and political transformation" (p. 17). Some of the issues that intergenerational communities might address through the use of participatory research include: (a) changing patterns of community participation, (b) upgrading equipment and facilities, (c) maintaining programs in the face of funding cutbacks, and (d) resource-sharing among programs. The solutions and changes that emerge from such participatory research may benefit persons of all ages in these communities, and may have potential for an impact beyond the immediate community.

## *A FINAL COMMENT*

Successful intergenerational programs may take a variety of forms and they are found in a diversity of community settings. Constructivist and sociocultural orientations, which traditionally have been applied to "classroom learning," offer new ways to view and to assess the learning that takes place in community-based intergenerational programs. Achieving a greater understanding of what happens in community-based intergenerational programs, including those in schools, also may help us to better understand learning in its more "traditional" sense. This includes the potential benefits for very young children who are engaged in learning relationships with much older children. Our discussion of these learning paradigms provides some direction and guidelines for intergenerational-program developers, researchers and evaluators as they strive to enhance community-based learning between members of all age-groups.

## REFERENCES

Glaser, B. (1978). *Theoretical sensitivity.* Mill Valley, CA: Sociology Press.
Glesne, C., & Peshkin, A. (1992). *Becoming qualitative researchers: An introduction.* White Plains, NY: Longman.
Hall, B., & Kassam, Y. (1985). Participatory research. In T. Husen, (Ed.), *International Encyclopedia of Education* (p. 85). Oxford: Pergamon Press.

Kelly, G. (1955). *The psychology of personal constructs.* NY: Norton.

Lincoln, Y. S., & Guba, E. G. (1985). *Naturalistic inquiry.* Beverly Hills, CA: Sage.

Park, P., Brydon-Miller, M., Hall, B., & Jackson, T. (1993). *Voices of change: Participatory research in the United States and Canada.* Toronto: OISE Press.

Selener, D. (1997). *Participatory action research and social change.* Ithaca, NY: The Cornell Participatory Action Research Network.

Smith, B. J. (1996). *Constructing understandings of teaching and learning: An inquiry into peer teaching.* Unpublished doctoral dissertation, University of Toronto.

Vygotsky, L. (1978). *Mind in society.* Cambridge, MA: Harvard University.

Wigginton, E. (1972). *The foxfire book.* NY: Anchor Press.

# Intergenerational Theory:
# The Missing Element
# in Today's Intergenerational Programs

## Karen VanderVen

**SUMMARY.** Various modifications to current theories of human development are suggested along with potential applications to intergenerational programming. It is argued that a new intergenerational theory of human development should be developed that accounts for an increase in life span, contemporary societal values, and the role of environmental variables in shaping behavior. Such an intergenerational theoretical approach should be used to examine the potential developmental outcomes for specific age-group dyads engaged in programmatic activities. Implications of such an approach for research and program evaluation are also suggested. *[Article copies available for a fee from The Haworth Document Delivery Service: 1-800-342-9678. E-mail address: getinfo@haworthpressinc.com <Website: http://www.haworthpressinc.com>]*

**KEYWORDS.** Intergenerational theory, research development

Intergenerational programs are proliferating. "Common sense," as well as the bulk of empirical evidence, seems to indicate that pairing older and younger people in various activities and contexts such as schools, child and older adult care centers, residential and group homes, may yield positive developmental benefits (Calhoun, Kingson &

Karen VanderVen is affiliated with the Program in Child Development and Child Care, School of Social Work, University of Pittsburgh, Pittsburgh, PA 15260.

[Haworth co-indexing entry note]: "Intergenerational Theory: The Missing Element in Today's Intergenerational Programs." VanderVen, Karen. Co-published simultaneously in *Child & Youth Services* (The Haworth Press, Inc.) Vol. 20, No. 1/2, 1999, pp. 33-47; and: *Intergenerational Programs: Understanding What We Have Created* (ed: Valerie S. Kuehne) The Haworth Press, Inc., 1999, pp. 33-47. Single or multiple copies of this article are available for a fee from The Haworth Document Delivery Service [1-800-342-9678, 9:00 a.m. - 5:00 p.m. (EST). E-mail address: getinfo@haworthpressinc.com].

Newman, 1997; Newman & Brummel, 1989). That such programs or interventions serve two vulnerable populations simultaneously–thereby being cost-effective–seems a powerful rationale for community support. Intervention is defined here as activity or activities designed to influence the course of human development in a positive way; thus intergenerational programs are considered as being primarily developmental in nature and purpose.

Two demographic trends seem to suggest a need to utilize whatever potential that intergenerational programs may have for enhancing human well-being. First, there is the general domain of social problems that can affect people of all ages. These include poverty, violence, family dysfunction, alcohol and drug abuse (Children's Defense Fund, 1996), boredom, and lack of engagement in meaningful activity (Barnes, 1991; Czikszentmihalyi, 1990). Second, not only is the North American population aging, but people are living longer; there has been a documented increase in the proportion of people living into their eighties and nineties (Dychtwald, 1989; Seelye, 1997).

It is important to ensure that intergenerational programs are designed from a strong knowledge base (Kettner, Moroney, & Martin, 1990). Traditionally, the social sciences have advanced by an interactive process among theory, research, and practice in which each of the elements is influenced by the others. In the intergenerational field, however, there has been no strong theoretical base to complete this knowledge-generating triangle.

Most of our theoretical ideas about the rationale, design, and implementation of intervention strategies for both children and older adults come from the human development literature. However, the relationship of intergenerational programs to a developmental theory base is weak. The theoretical rationale for intergenerational activities is usually based on developmental themes associated with a specific age group (e.g., early childhood, post-retirement) and how contact with members of another age-group might enhance that development. Perceived benefits often are described in emotional, social, or cognitive terms such as increased self-esteem, sense of purpose (older adults), being important, competence, and (children's) development of a more positive attitude towards the elderly (Kuehne & Sears, 1993; Seefeldt, 1989).

Although the developmental literature provides valuable insights, I contend that it is itself inadequate as a basis for effective intergenera-

tional program design. Theorists and researchers in the intergenerational field must extend existing concepts to create an *intergenerational-developmental* theory.

Toward that end, the present discussion will focus on two topics:
(a) critique of current human developmental theories, specifically Eriksonian theory, highlighting lags and gaps, and (b) some suggestions
for creating an intergenerational developmental theory which can be
used to inform intergenerational program design and to study the
nature of intergenerational interactions.

## CURRENT DEVELOPMENTAL THEORY: A CRITIQUE

### Narrow Theoretical Focus

There are several shortcomings in current developmental theories
that are typically applied to intergenerational issues. One problem
pertains to their narrow theoretical focus. For example, although there
are numerous theories of lifespan development, Erik Erikson seems
clearly the predominant theorist used when considering intergenerational programs (Newman, Ward, Smith, Wilson & McCrea, 1997).
More recent and also highly relevant lifespan theorists such as Kegan
(1982) or Levinson (1978, 1996), are mentioned rarely in the intergenerational literature.

### Limited Developmental Range

Most contemporary theories of development share a shortcoming:
They fail to account sufficiently for the period of *old-old* age (i.e.,
beyond 75 years of age). Current concepts of aging may need revising
to accommodate the increase in life expectancy. For example, Erikson's stage of *generativity* may last many more years into the life span
now than it did in previous generations. The related question is, might
there be a shift in the age range to which specific developmental
phases pertain? In response, a possible new period, *late-late adulthood*
(after age 80) is being considered as an addition to Levinson's model
of adult development (Perlmutter & Hall, 1992).

### Cultural Limitations

Today's post-modern perspective (Ray, 1996; Rosenau, 1993)
stresses that any theory of personality is highly situated in and deter-

mined by the particular cultural context existing at the time of its creation. While Eriksonian theory considers human development in interaction with social context, some critics have argued that it reflects the prevalent values of its time also and that it fails to accommodate a feminist perspective. For example, in Erikson's model of lifespan development (Erikson, 1950; Levine, 1989), the phase known as *identity vs. role confusion* is followed by *intimacy vs. isolation*. Chodorow (1997) argues that the process of identity formation for young women may be quite different than that described by Erikson. In fact, Levine (1989) suggested that even Erikson believed that male identity formation focused on "establishing independence and autonomy" while female identity formation "is tied to relationships" (p. 131).

It seems important for any theory of human development to acknowledge the potential impact of cultural factors and social values on individual functioning. Potentially relevant issues in contemporary Western society include racial and ethnic diversity and an awareness of gender-related power imbalances. The *post-modern* perspective emphasizes equality, pluralism, and reducing oppression (Rosenau, 1993).

### Linear Thinking

Most developmental theories can be categorized as either stage or phase theories (Levine, 1989) according to their view of development across the lifespan. Phase theories are characterized by their sequential progression related to age, whereas stage theories focus on sequentially ordered stages. With their "alternating periods of stability, instability, and transition," stage theories may be viewed as more *dynamic* in nature than are phase theories; however, "both stage and phase theorists agree that development unfolds sequentially, that one period or balance predictably follows another" (Levine, 1989 p. 85). Thus, all current phase and stage theories could be viewed as essentially *linear*. A linear approach focuses on common trajectories for all individuals within a specific age-range as opposed to considering multiple pathways and contextual factors in the course of development, and less predictability in developmental outcomes.

Both phase and stage theories were developed prior to the paradigmatic shift from a linear perspective to a view that includes the concepts of *dynamic systems* and *chaos* (Goerner, 1995). Much contemporary developmental research seems to reflect this new perspective suggesting that a new intergenerational theory should consider this paradigm as well.

## PROPOSALS FOR AN INTERGENERATIONAL THEORY

### Greater Differentiation

As Eriksonian theory has been the primary source for intergenerational program development (Cohon, 1989; Newman, Ward, Smith, Wilson & McCrea, 1997; ReVille, 1989), it will be used as an example of the differentiation needed in theories that pertain to the upper age ranges in the lifespan. According to Eriksonian theory, the phase conflicts of generativity vs. stagnation and integrity vs. despair may extend across many years in mid- and late-adulthood. The increased numbers of adults living between 75 and 90 years in the Western world may necessitate expanding current notions of old age. Also, it raises the question of whether a single overarching developmental theme can be considered relevant for individuals across such a long period. For purposes of examining intergenerational relationships, it may be necessary to identify the specific developmental tasks and characteristics associated with the full range of older adulthood. As an example, I would suggest adding the following *subdifferentiated* levels to Erikson's phase of generativity.

*Efficacy vs. Passivity.* I would hypothesize that this sub-phase may occur around the age of 50 years, when investment in the next generation, often exemplified by raising children and serving the community, would remain salient developmental tasks, but may be accompanied by a sense of efficaciousness or instrumentality (i.e., feeling able to have an influence in some endeavor). Some studies have suggested that this phase may be an especially vital period in women's development, as energy that was previously expended while caring for young children becomes available for tasks outside of the home (Mitchell & Helson, 1990; Sheehy, 1974). Even for women who do not have their children until well into their 30s and 40s (usually following the establishment of careers), this sub-phase could still be relevant in that these women bring a great deal of personal competence to the act of child rearing and there are many options for identity (re)formation resulting from their multiple life experiences (Helson & McCabe, 1994).

*Investment vs. Detachment.* The proposed sub-phase of efficacy vs. passivity might gradually be supplanted by one focused on investment (vs. detachment). The investment sub-phase involves heightened perceptions of meaning and significance with respect to one's personal belongings and surroundings, as well as to personal relationships. This suggested addition to Erikson's model seems to follow from findings that such feelings are experienced by many individuals as they grow older (Freud, 1988). The focus of this phase is not on the acquisition of material goods per se, but instead on an increased appreciation of one's life with all that it entails. Characteristics associated with this developmental period may intensify gradually, as the older person's friends and family members die. It seems possible that a sense of continuity may be bolstered by one's attachment to cherished objects and relationships.

### Combinatory Approach

Intergenerational programs seem to provide a good example of the process of invention: Pairing differently-aged individuals helps to *invent* new relationships. To understand the potential meaning and significance of these new relationships, it may be useful to apply a *combinatory* approach in which both the pairing and the nature of the interaction between pairs is considered.

*Pairings.* One aspect of the combinatory approach involves examining the number and nature of potential intergenerational dyads. To visualize this task, imagine listing on one side of a sheet of paper all the stages, phases, or periods of development for any given model of human development (e.g., infancy, early childhood, adolescence, adulthood, retirement, old age). Imagine preparing an identical list on a second sheet of paper, and then sliding one list up and down alongside the other. This process would indicate all the possible intergenerational dyads there could be for any given model of development (VanderVen, 1996b). The more differentiated the developmental model being used, the more numerous would be the possible pairings. Several questions arise from this way of thinking. For example, for each dyad member, what might be the developmental implications associated with this specific pairing? How might the personal characteristics of individual members of the dyad influence this dynamic?

*Nature of interactions.* Studying personal relationships as a psychosocial entity in themselves was advocated by Safilios-Rothschild (1981). She recommended that "studies of relationships should start from the individuals, map all the relationships in which they are involved and examine the interrelations between the different types of relationships" (p. 377).

To create the knowledge base for an intergenerational theory, studies are needed to examine the nature of interactions within specific intergenerational dyads. Such studies would be aimed at identifying some of the individual variables that are associated with a given developmental outcome.

There are two other important reasons for studying the psychological dynamics of intergenerational relationships. First, there is a need to identify the relationship factors that may lead to negative outcomes for either member of the dyad. Despite the support for intergenerational programming, the possibility of negative effects is rarely discussed. Second, if intergenerational programs continue to proliferate, it may be necessary to develop a new approach to training human-service practitioners. This is because current approaches to the education of human-service workers tend to focus on individuals instead of on the *relationships* between individuals. The challenges of "relating to a relationship" in such a way as to support the development of both members of the dyad were discussed by Anglin (1984).

*Pair-work,* which occurs when a practitioner works with two children or two youths, each with a different level of social perspective-taking, is an example of how the dyadic relationship may help to enhance the social skills of both members (Karcher, 1996; Selman, Watts & Schultz, 1997). This method may be useful for examining the role of perspective-taking in the dyadic relationship. Within the dyadic context, individuals may share experiences, may feel connected to each other, and may feel understood and cared about (Selman, Watts & Schultz, 1997). To date, pair-work has been used primarily with youths, and thus it is unknown whether this effect may occur in other age-group pairings. However, it seems reasonable to suppose that one benefit of intergenerational programming may be increased social perception and social skills for both the younger and the older participants.

The concepts discussed above may have important implications for training practitioners to facilitate productive intergenerational activities. It seems necessary to define the specific competencies needed in this area and to provide practitioners with special training to do this sensitive work.

## Paradigm Shift from Linear to Dynamic Models

A linear approach to research often involves breaking down phenomena into smaller parts for examination, and focusing on a specific cause or *input* as it leads to a specific effect or *output*. The relationship of a given variable to its social context is rarely considered (Vander-Ven, 1996a). In contrast, "dynamic systems" or "chaos" theory approaches view phenomena as interconnected. According to the dynamic perspective, one input may lead to multiple outputs and context plays a large part in determining the nature of the system, which itself continues to grow and change (Goerner, 1995).

Applications of dynamic systems theory to human development can be found in the work of Fischer and Hogan (1989), van Geert (1995), and Thelen (1996). Salient ideas are that (a) variations in behavior are interpreted according to stage of development, (b) self-organizing patterns of behavior are formed over time, and (c) development may follow multiple pathways and that it is multiply determined by factors both outside and inside the individual in an open and interactive process over time.

To some extent, traditional lifespan and adult-development theories use some dynamic notions, for example, energy focusing on developmental tasks, development interacting with the environment. However, both phase and stage models of human development are essentially linear in approach.

Thus far I have attempted to show the limitations and shortcomings of a linear perspective to research and human development as it is applied to the intergenerational field. I propose that an effective intergenerational theory should comprise the major characteristics of a dynamic perspective. It seems to follow that such an intergenerational perspective would: (a) conceptualize development from a constructivist approach, which includes the notion that people of all ages "construct" their development through the meaning they make from their experiences (Kegan, 1982); (b) view the "purpose" of development as taking multiple and often novel directions rather than achieving the status quo; (c) consider development as a recursive process, that is, continually "feeding back" into itself; (d) derive its knowledge base from the experiential accounts of "developing" individuals as well as from more quantitative studies, and (e) acknowledge that the social and cultural context exerts a strong influence on not only the course of individual development, but also on the perspective of developmental researchers.

The implications of an intergenerational theory based on dynamic systems concepts seem considerable. According to this perspective, examining the relationships between members of different age-group dyads is not a simple case of "clapping" them together, as in the notion of *cold fusion*, and predicting a singular outcome. For example, two individuals, one young and one old, both labeled as having "low self esteem" are placed together, perhaps in an intergenerational program situation; a linear approach would result in the expectation that they both will emerge from the experience with "raised self esteem." Instead, there might be no effect on either's self esteem or lower self esteem for one but not for the other. Similarly, using Eriksonian theory to predict what an adult in the generativity stage might "bring" to an intergenerational dyad is an example of linear thinking. There are great variations in personality characteristics of adults in this stage. Thus, given the potential for complexity in intergenerational relationships, linear thinking seems simplistic and may lead to inaccurate programmatic and research conclusions. Rather, the study of intergenerational pairings should be viewed as integrating two dynamic systems for the purpose of investigating the many possible developmental outcomes for each dyad member.

### Attention to Post-Modernist Perspectives

Post-modern perspectives, which include critical theory and deconstruction, seem not to have affected "mainstream gerontology" (Cole, cited by Ray, 1996), though they do appear to have influenced the social sciences of anthropology and sociology (Rosenau, 1993). It could be argued that any newly-created developmental theory should take into account the central tenets of post-modernism.

One of the central issues in the post-modern perspective is the role of power. According to critical theorists in this area, knowledge is crucial for personal empowerment. This may be particularly true for beleaguered or under-served groups (e.g., children or elderly individuals), who may be subjugated by the elite through their relative lack of knowledge (Soto, 1996). Knowledge that is used for purposes of empowerment has been called *emancipatory* knowledge (Morgaine, 1994). The concept of emancipatory knowledge should be included in an intergenerational theory for two reasons:

1. Emancipatory knowledge may be a useful way of viewing the basic values that shape theory and for examining the needs of younger and older age-groups.
2. The notion of emanicipatory knowledge is relevant to the design of intergenerational programs, in terms of both content and structure. It seems important to facilitate a high level of self-determination for all program participants in which the notion that people who are used to submitting to others are encouraged to realize that they can not only assertively strive to meet their needs but also that the program model allows for input into content and structure, rather than simply being imposed.

Gender issues are another fundamental concern in post-modern perspectives and should be addressed by a new intergenerational theory. The results of recent empirical studies of mid-life development suggest that, for women, this may be a time of self-realization and personal empowerment, while for men, mid-life may be a time of becoming more psychologically "feminine" (e.g., Sheehy, 1974; Levine, 1989). Such findings may have important implications for intergenerational pairings. For example, some older women may provide excellent role models for young girls at risk for premature sexual behavior by showing them how women can be both self-directed and achievement-oriented.

### Integration of Child Development and Life Span Theory

It seems reasonable to suppose that many concepts from currently existing child-development theories (e.g., *resilience*) might be effectively integrated into an intergenerational theory, along with those from a lifespan perspective on aging. Using the personal stories and commentaries of older adults, Erikson, Erikson, and Kivnick (1988) illustrated the energy and vitality that often continues into old age. By giving recognition to the growth potential of older adults, Erikson et al. may have contributed to the eventual integration of developmental theories across the lifespan.

The following examples describe aspects of child- and adult-development theories that can be further integrated to provide an embracing lifespan theory:

*Learning in a social context.* Most developmental theories stress the role of social factors (e.g., cultural context and personal interactions) in shaping and enhancing learning in children (Vygotsky, cited in Wertsch, 1985). However, the importance of social factors is often neglected in theories of adult development. For example, Vygotsky's notion of the *zone of proximal development* refers to an individual's maximum ability to learn when supported by another person who has assumed a coaching role. Continued support may help the recipient to achieve increasingly higher levels of learning, a process known as *scaffolding* (Berk & Winsler, 1995). An intergenerational theory would focus equal attention on the potential development of both members of an intergenerational dyad to learn as a function of a social interaction.

*Constructivism.* Most currently existing theories about learning in children tend to be constructivist in their approach (DeVries & Kohlberg, 1987; Fosnot, 1989). According to this view, the acquisition of knowledge is not simply a passive process of one individual receiving information from another. Rather, knowledge is constructed from both past experience and the meaning of that experience. This newly-constructed knowledge then serves as a lens for taking in and constructing the meaning of future experiences.

Rarely have the tenets of constructivism been applied to the study of older adults. It seems possible that this would be a fruitful area of research, as older persons may have, simply by living longer, more complex cognitive structures. Kegan's lifespan theory (1982) relies heavily on *meaning-making* in development. It suggests that the individual may achieve balance across the lifespan by resolving the tension between self and others (i.e., when there is not undue focus on either the self or on others).

*Risk and resilience.* Several developmental psychologists have examined various developmental factors that may put children and youths at risk for negative outcomes (*risk*) as well as those that may contribute to the ability to withstand negative influences (*resilience*). Some of the factors that have been identified as potentially increasing resilience in youths include: (a) strong interpersonal relationships, at least with one caring person; (b) being held responsible for someone or something (*required helpfulness*), and (c) involvement in interesting and challenging activities (Noam, 1996; Werner, 1990). Intergenerational activities may contain elements that promote resilience in young people. It seems possible that the application of these concepts to the study of adults may also yield important information about resilience in older people.

*Flow.* Czikszentmihalyi's (1990 ) concept of *flow* refers to an optimal emotional state, in which involvement in an activity is so absorbing and compelling that the person "loses" himself or herself. It may be that the concept of flow can be usefully applied to the experiences of intergenerational relationships and in related research.

## IMPLICATIONS FOR INTERGENERATIONAL PROGRAMMING AND RESEARCH

A new intergenerational theory may facilitate the design of more effective intergenerational programming and related research in a number of ways. For example, the post-modern perspective suggests that program participants should participate in all aspects of program design, implementation, and evaluation. Focusing on the importance and various dimensions of relationships formed between program participants may influence how younger and older persons are "matched" in intergenerational programs and may facilitate an emphasis on the evolving nature of the relationships rather than narrowly defined program outcomes typical of many evaluations. Relationship-based research and evaluation may well benefit from the use of qualitative methods of inquiry, including in-depth interviews and oral history, in which participants are able to express their direct experience in intergenerational relationships. Longitudinal studies using these methods could document the evolution of such relationships over time. Both of these research approaches represent an application of dynamic systems theory to research methodology.

In addition to intergenerational programs involving dyads of younger and older persons, trigenerational programs are now appearing that engage three individuals of varying ages (e.g., youth, middle age, old age) in ongoing activities. As a result, the apparent benefits of intergenerational relationships may also accrue to the "generation in the middle," as well as to practitioners who work with a wide range of age-groups.

The future seems exciting for the theorists, researchers, and practitioners who work in the intergenerational area as more is learned about the potential of intergenerational relationships to enhance the quality of many lives. Developing intergenerational-developmental theory will greatly support this effort.

## REFERENCES

Anglin, J. (1984). Counselling a single parent and child: Functional and dysfunctional patterns of communication. *Journal of Child Care, 2*(2), 33-45.

Barnes, F. (1991). From warehouse to greenhouse: Play, work and the routines of daily living in groups as the core of milieu treatment. In J. Beker & Z. Eisikovits (Eds.), *Knowledge utilization in residential child and youth care practice.* (pp. 123-155). Washington, DC: Child Welfare League of America.

Berk, L. & Winsler, A. (1995). *Scaffolding children's learning: Vygotsky and early childhood education.* Washington, DC: National Association for the Education of Young Children.

Calhoun, G., Kingson, E. & Newman, S. (1997). Intergenerational programs and public policy: A context for growth and change. In S. Newman, C. Ward, T. Smith, J. Wilson & J. McCrea (Eds.), *Intergenerational programs: Past, present, and future* (pp. 143-159). Washington, DC: Taylor & Francis.

Children's Defense Fund. (1996). *The state of America's children yearbook.* Washington, DC: Children's Defense Fund.

Cohon, D. (1989). Intergenerational program research to refine theory and practice. In S. Newman & S. Brummel (Eds.), *Intergenerational programs: Imperatives, strategies, impacts, trends* (pp. 217-232). New York: The Haworth Press, Inc.

Czikszentmihalyi, M. (1990). *Flow: The psychology of optimal experience.* New York: Harper & Row.

DeVries, R. & Kohlberg, L. (1987). *Constructivist early education: Overview and comparison with other programs.* Washington, DC: National Association for the Education of Young Children.

Dychtwald, K. (1989). *Age wave.* Los Angeles: Jeremy P. Tarcher.

Erikson, E. (1950). *Childhood and society.* New York: Norton.

Erikson, E., Erikson, J. & Kivnick, H. (1986). *Vital involvement in old age.* New York: W.W. Norton.

Fischer, K. & Hogan, A. (1989). The big picture for infant development: Levels and variations. In J. Lockman & N. Hazen (Eds.), *Action in social context. Perspectives on early development* (pp. 275-305). New York: Plenum.

Fosnot, C. (1989). *Enquiring teachers, enquiring learners. A constructivist approach for teaching.* New York: Teacher's College Press.

Freud, S. (1988). *My three mothers and other passions.* New York: New York University Press.

Goerner, S. (1995). Chaos and deep ecology. In F. Abraham & A. Gilgen, (Eds.), *Chaos theory in psychology* (pp. 3-18). Westport, CT: Praeger.

Helson, R., & McCabe, L. (1994). The social clock project in middle age. In B. Turner & L. Troll (Eds.), *Women growing older: Psychological perspectives* (pp. 64-93). Thousand Oaks, CA: Sage.

Karcher, M. (1996). Pairing for the prevention of prejudice: Pair counselling to promote intergroup understanding. *Journal of Child and Youth Care Work, 11*, 119-143.

Kegan, R. (1982). *The evolving self.* Cambridge: Harvard University Press.

Kettner, R., Moroney, R., & Marin, L. (1990). *Designing and managing programs: An effectiveness-based approach.* Newbury Park, CA: Sage Publications.

Kuehne, V.S. & Sears, H. (1993). Beyond the call of duty: Older volunteers committed to children and families. *Journal of Applied Gerontology, 12*(4), 425-438.

Levine, S. (1989). *Promoting adult growth in schools: The promise of professional development.* Boston: Allyn and Bacon.

Levinson, D. (1978). *The seasons of a man's life.* New York: Knopf.

Levinson, D. & Levinson, J. (1995). *The seasons of a woman's life.*

Mitchell, V., & Helson, R. (1990). Women's prime of life: Is it the 50s? *Psychology of Women Quarterly, 14*, 451-470.

Morgaine, C. (1994). Enlightenment for emancipation. *Family Relations, 43*, 325-335.

Newman, S. & Brummel, S. (Eds.) (1989). *Intergenerational programs: Imperatives, strategies, impacts, trends.* New York: The Haworth Press, Inc.

Newman, S., Ward, C., Smith, T., Wilson, J., & McCrea, J. (Eds.). (1997). *Intergenerational programs: Past, present, and future.* Washington, DC: Taylor & Francis.

Perlmutter, M., & Hall, E. (1992). *Adult development and aging* (2nd ed.). New York: John Wiley & Sons, Inc.

Ray, R. (1996). A post-modern perspective on feminist gerontology. *The Gerontologist, 36*(5), 674-68.

ReVille, S. (1989). Young adult to old age: Looking at intergenerational possibilities from a human development perspective. In S. Newman & S. Brummel (Eds.), *Intergenerational programs: Imperatives, strategies, impacts, trends* (pp. 45-53). New York: The Haworth Press, Inc.

Rosenau, P. (1993). *Post-modernism and the social sciences: Insights, inroads and intrusions.* Princeton, NJ: Princeton University Press.

Safilios-Rothschild, C. (1981). Towards a social psychology of relationships. *Psychology of Women Quarterly, 5*(3), 377-384.

Seelye, K. (1997, March 27). Future U.S.: Grayer and more Hispanic. New York. *New York Times*, p. A 18.

Seefeldt, C. (1989). Intergenerational programs: Impact on attitudes. In S. Newman & S. Brummel (Eds.), *Journal of Contemporary Society, 20*(3/4), 185-194.

Selman, R., Watts, C., & Schultz, L. (Eds.). (1997). *Fostering friendship. Pair therapy for treatment and prevention.* Hawthorne, NY: Aldine De Gruyter.

Sheehy, G. (1978). *Passages.* New York: E.P. Dutton.

Soto, L. (1996). *Constructivist theory in the age of Newt Gingrich: The post-formal concern with power.* Paper presented at the National Association for the Education of Young Children (NAEYC) pre-conference meeting, Dallas, TX.

Thelen, E. (1995). Motor development: A new synthesis. *American Psychologist, 50*(2), 79-95.

van Geert, P. (1995). *Dynamic systems of development.* New York: Harvester/Wheatsheaf.

VanderVen, K. (1996a). *A synergistic approach to transforming early childhood education in a post-modern era: The influential leader and emergence of early childhood care/education as a profession.* Paper presented at the Annual Institute for Professional Development, National Association for the Education of Young Children, Minneapolis.

VanderVen, K. (1996b). *Emergent issues in intergenerational studies and practice.* Presentation to intergenerational studies class. Boston, MA: Wheelock College.

Wertsch, J. (1985). *Vygotsky and the social formation of mind.* Cambridge, MA: Harvard University Press.

# SECTION TWO:
# INTERGENERATIONAL PROGRAM IMPACT

# Student Improvement
# in the Intergenerational
# Work/Study Program

## Kevin Brabazon

**SUMMARY.** This exploratory study of the Intergenerational Work/Study Program examined whether structured intergenerational relationships may be associated with a change in the school attendance and achievement of high school students considered to be at-risk for dropping out of high school. Two separate regression analyses were performed to measure the contribution of 11 independent variables to (a) prediction of attendance levels, and (b) earned course credits. The R for the regression for credits was non-significant. For attendance levels, R for regression was significantly different from zero, $F(11, 219) = 4.24$, $p < .0001$. Whether the school of enrollment was categorized as alternative or mainstream, as well as time spent in group intergenerational activities and time spent in one-on-one intergenerational activities all contributed significantly. Altogether, 18% (13% adjusted) of the variability in attendance levels was predicted by knowing scores on these 11 variables. *[Article copies available for a fee from The Haworth Document Delivery Service: 1-800-342-9678. E-mail address: getinfo@haworthpressinc.com <Website: http://www.haworthpressinc.com>]*

**KEYWORDS.** Intergenerational, research, high school, work study

The Intergenerational Work/Study Program (IWSP) is a dropout prevention program for at-risk high school students operated by New

---

Kevin Brabazon is affiliated with the New York State Intergenerational Network, Brookdale Center on Aging, 425 East 25th Street, 8th Floor, New York, NY 10010.

[Haworth co-indexing entry note]: "Student Improvement in the Intergenerational Work Study Program." Brabazon, Kevin. Co-published simultaneously in *Child & Youth Services* (The Haworth Press, Inc.) Vol. 20, No. 1/2, 1999, pp. 51-61; and: *Intergenerational Programs: Understanding What We Have Created* (ed: Valerie S. Kuehne) The Haworth Press, Inc., 1999, pp. 51-61. Single or multiple copies of this article are available for a fee from The Haworth Document Delivery Service [1-800-342-9678, 9:00 a.m. - 5:00 p.m. (EST). E-mail address: getinfo@haworthpressinc.com].

*51*

York City's Department for the Aging (DFTA) in collaboration with the City's Board of Education (NYC BOE). Students at 16 high schools are typically recruited for the program according to records of their below-average credit accumulation, poor attendance, or both. These two factors are considered to be indicators of students' likelihood of dropping out of school (Banerjee, 1988), and thus, improvements in one or both of these criteria are considered indicators of successful participation in the program.

The best measure of the success of the IWSP would be the graduation status of each student participant. However, because of the difficulty of reliably tracking each student beyond the one year they typically spend in the IWSP, it is generally considered acceptable to use amount of credit accumulation and/or frequency of absenteeism as alternative measures of program success (Anthony & Young, 1995). These are the measures that the NYC BOE typically uses to assess the performance of dropout prevention programs that it funds or operates directly. The primary objective of these programs is to achieve demonstrated improvement in either attendance, credit accumulation, or both, for at least 50% of the participating students.

Although most other programs do not reach these goals (Banerjee, 1988), the IWSP has regularly exceeded them, showing improvement for between 80% and 90% of participating students. The Interface Foundation evaluated the success of the IWSP program in its first year (1987) and found that 95% of participating students graduated high school (Banerjee, 1988). Measures of graduation success rates were not taken for subsequent years. Thus for the present study, I analysed data for the alternative measures of program success (i.e., credit accumulation and attendance).

At the end of the second year in the program, a teacher at each participating high school was required to record: (a) the amount of students' credit accumulation, (b) the recorded number of *days absent* during the semester before entering the IWSP, and (c) the recorded number of *days absent* across each semester spent in the program. Over the 5 years in which these data were gathered, the average credit accumulation rate per semester for students before entering the program was less than 3.0, and the average absenteeism rate was over 22 days. However, New York City's high school students typically need to accumulate 5 credits per semester to graduate on time. This discrepancy forms the basis for selecting students for the IWSP: Gaining only 2.5 credits per semester, it would take a student 8 years to graduate, and it seems unlikely that many of them would stay in school for that long a period. In addition, 22 days absence per semester is an absenteeism rate of almost 25%–not a good basis for learning!

The improved performance of students in the IWSP is now well documented by staff of the IWSP Program who produce regular summary reports of student improvement, and the program is considered an effective intervention model. The Charles Stewart Mott Foundation funded the model for national replication, and it has been established in several other cities. The present study examined the relative contribution of the various factors that seem to promote the positive behavioral changes observed in participating students.

There has been a proliferation of intergenerational programming in the United States since the mid-1980s. A survey by the New York State Intergenerational Network in 1990 identified over 500 programs in New York State alone. These programs deal with a wide range of issues, including, (a) long term care (Hegeman, 1985), (b) education (Friedman, 1990), (c) aging (Family Friends Resource Center, 1991/1994), (d) youth service (Stout, Boyd & Volanty, 1992), (e) child care (Southeast Florida Center on Aging, 1990), (f) medical care (Isabella Geriatric Center, 1995), (g) foster care (Corporation for National Service, 1990), and, (h) home care (Couch, 1992). Although intergenerational programs should not be regarded as a panacea, often they are developed in response to what are perceived as unmet social needs. The IWSP is one such program in New York State that attempts to reduce the drop-out rate of students at selected New York City high schools.

## *METHOD*

### *Program Description*

The IWSP operates by placing students in several different kinds of internship sites[1] where they gain basic work experience and employability skills. Typically, they attend these sites for 10-12 hours a week. Administrators at these sites are required to provide assignments that guarantee students at least 50% of their time interacting with older adults. The goal is to ensure the development of interpersonal relationships between the students and older adults at the work sites, thus ensuring the availability of "grandparent" figures to the students. Relationships with "grandparent" figures are thought to improve the students' self-esteem, life-coping skills, motivation, attitude, and planning skills (New York City Department for the Aging, 1990). The 50% interaction requirement is the primary factor that distinguishes the IWSP from other non-intergenerational work/study programs.

In addition to measuring students' attendance and credit accumulation, managers and evaluators of intergenerational work/study programs consider the following questions:

> *How can the work-mix be optimally developed based around three categories of assignments?* The three categories are: (a) non-intergenerational[2] services, such as office or kitchen work; (b) group intergenerational activities, such as social and recreational activities, and (c) one-on-one intergenerational services such as escort work, home-delivered meals, or case assistance [support for case managers].

> *Which sites contribute to the greatest improvements in students?* Sites are classified into four groups: (a) *Congregate,* which comprises program sites for the well but increasingly frail elderly; (b) *home care*, which refers to agencies that serve the frail homebound population; (c) *nursing home*, which pertains to residential, health-related facilities that service a very frail, medically dependent population, and (d) *other*, which includes all other types of program sites, including housing developments.

> *Which schools contribute to the greatest improvements in students?* Participating schools are classified into three groups by the NYC Board of Education: (a) *Alternative*–these are schools with flexible activities and special programs that cater to students who are not doing well in the regular high school system (i.e., they have shown poor academic performance, are drop-outs, or are returning older students); (b) *Project Achieve*–these are comprehensive high schools that fall into the lowest quartile in student attendance rates, and (c) *Comprehensive*–this category includes most of the Comprehensive High Schools, as well as a few Vocational Schools.

In addition to addressing these questions, there is an interest in improving the program by directing the program coordinator's attention and other resources to where they are most needed. This might be considered a basic management control issue. As students are classified by the NYC BOE according to ethnicity and gender, members of those ethnic or gender groups that perform least well can be identified and receive the time, attention, and special programming that may help them. This can be viewed as a "win-win" situation because it puts the program's discretionary resources where they can do the most to improve the program overall, while helping the students who need it most. This approach seems to promote principles of both equality and achievement.

### *Measures*

Two separate measures of student performance were used as dependent variables: *Credit Improvement* (Credit Impr) and *Absence Decrease* (Abs Decrs). *Credit Impr* represents the difference between the number of credits a specific student is awarded during the first semester spent in the IWSP and during the last semester prior to entering the program. *Abs Decrs* was measured as the difference between the number of absences during the first semester in the IWSP as compared to that of the previous semester.

The following variables were chosen as the independent variables because they may be viewed as being important factors in predicting student performance:

*The number of semesters a student has been in high school (# Sem H S).* Those students who have attended high school for longer periods of time than most others are generally older and may have a more receptive attitude toward the IWSP. Conversely, however, those who have been in high school for relatively shorter periods of time may be less entrenched in negative habits and more susceptible to change. Length of time in school was measured here by the overall number of semesters spent in high school rather than grade, as some students have been held over 1 or 2 years in the same grade.

*Gender.* This variable was included because approximately two-thirds of the total number of participating students were female and differential outcomes by gender could influence recruiting patterns or allocation of resources.

*Ethnicity.* Student ethnicity was defined by three categories: Black, Hispanic, or Other. The latter includes White and a very small number of other groups. Because there were three possible values, two dummy variables were included, African Am (Black or Non-Black) and Latino (Hispanic or Non-Hispanic). The influence of the primarily White "Other" category is captured in the intercept (the constant in the equation).

*School of enrollment.* The student participants were attending schools that were categorized as follows: Project Achieve, Alternative or Comprehensive/Vocational. Two dummy variables were created, *Proj Ach* (Project Achieve School or Non-Project Achieve School) and *Alt HS* (Alternative High School or Non-Alternative High School). The effect of attending a "mainstream" school (i.e., Comprehensive or Vocational) is captured in the intercept/constant.

*Percentage of time spent in intergenerational work assignments.* Two separate measures were used for this variable because of the qualitatively different characteristics of group activities and one-on-one assignments. The first measure, *Interg %*, includes both types of intergenerational assignments. The range of possible values for this variable was from 50% to 100%, as one of the standards of the IWSP is that at least 50% of each student's time must be spent on intergenerational assignments. The second, *1 on 1%*, refers to the percentage of work assignment time spent in one-on-one activities. The possible values for this variable were from 0% to 100%. Therefore, the values for *Interg %* will always be greater than or equal to *1 on 1%* because the former includes time spent in intergenerational groups as well as one-on-one assignments. The difference between the two measures represents the percentage of time spent in group intergenerational activities. The older individuals who participated in the one-on-one activities tend to be generally frail and it was felt that the support that students may receive from a group environment was absent. In addition, one-on-one activities conducted in conjunction with a home care agency are less likely to be monitored by a supervisor and thus require a higher degree of independence and responsibility from students.

*Site type.* There were four categories of worksites participating in the IWSP: (a) nursing homes, (b) congregate sites,[3] (c) homecare agencies, and (d) other sites, which include housing complexes and programs of a hybrid character. Thus, three dummy variables were used, *N H Dum* (nursing home), *Congr Dum* (congregate site), and *H Care Dum* (home care agency). The impact of all other kinds of worksites is captured in the intercept/constant.

There were two reasons for choosing the specific independent variables used here. The first was that IWSP supervisors have some control over these variables and that any meaningful findings from the present study could be followed up by active initiatives. Second, the data for many other variables that might have potential significance (e.g., economic circumstances of students, educational level of parents, family size, family income, local unemployment level) were not available for analysis.

## RESULTS

Two separate, standard multiple regressions were performed. The first was a regression between the amount of credit accumulation as the dependent variable and gender, ethnicity, school type, frequency of intergenerational activities, and type of worksite as independent variables (i.e., a total of 11 independent variables entered into the regression equation). The second regression analysis was between the recorded frequency of absenteeism as the dependent variable and the same set of independent variables used in the first regression.

The regression for credit accumulation was nonsignificant. With respect to the regression for frequency of absenteeism, Table 1 displays the unstandardized regression coefficients ($B$), the standard errors of B, the standardized regression coefficients (ß), the semipartial correlations ($sr^2$) and $R$, $R^2$, and adjusted $R^2$. $R$ was significantly different from zero, $F (11, 230) = 4.24$, $p < .0001$. Only three of the independent variables contributed significantly to prediction of frequency of absenteeism: (a) One of the dummy school variables, *Alt HS* ($sr^2 = .09$), (b) percentage of time spent in intergenerational activities, *Interg %*, ($sr^2 = .03$), and (c) percentage of time spent in one-on-one intergenerational activities, *1 on 1%* ($sr^2 = .06$). Altogether, 18% (13% adjusted) of the variability in absenteeism frequency was predicted by knowing scores on these three independent variables.

The results indicated that students attending Alternative Schools had higher predicted levels of absenteeism than students attending Comprehensive or Vocational High Schools. Findings showed also that greater levels of the mixed category of integenerational activity were associated with predictions of lower levels of absenteeism. However, greater levels of one-on-one intergenerational activity predicted *higher* levels of absenteeism. Relative to the other independent vari-

TABLE 1. Standard Multiple Regression of Demographic, School, Work Activities, and Work Sites on Recorded Absenteeism (N = 231)

| Variable: | B | SE B | $\beta$ | $sr^2$ (unique) |
|---|---|---|---|---|
| INTERCEPT | − 12.900 | | | |
| # Sem H S | .019 | .736 | .002 | |
| Gender | − 1.150 | 2.397 | − .030 | |
| African Am | − .642 | 3.173 | − .018 | |
| Latino | − .744 | 3.176 | − .020 | |
| Proj Ach | 6.262 | 3.877 | .107 | |
| Alt H S | 13.240**** | 2.647 | .345 | .09 |
| Intergen % | − .191** | .078 | − .221 | .03 |
| 1 on 1% | .291*** | .076 | .328 | .06 |
| N H Dum | 4.921 | 3.914 | .121 | |
| Congr Dum | 2.632 | 3.436 | .074 | |
| H Care Dum | − 4.004 | 4.490 | − .069 | |

** $p < .01$
*** $p < .001$
**** $p < .0001$

$R^2 = .18$
Adj. $R^2 = .13$
$R = .42$****

ables in the regression equation, attending an Alternative school versus a mainstream school made the greatest contribution to prediction of absenteeism levels.

## DISCUSSION

The finding that attending Alternative Schools was associated with predictions of lower levels of attendance than was attending Comprehensive or Vocational High Schools was consistent with the results of the Interface evaluation, which was completed after the first three semesters of IWSP's operation. The consistency of this finding across two separate evaluations suggests that it is a reliable one.

The most important finding of the present study was that greater amounts of time spent in intergenerational work assignments were associated with predictions of increased attendance at school, attendance being a measure of effectiveness for most drop-out prevention programs in New York City. That predictions of absenteeism for the *1 on 1%* variable were in the opposite direction from those for the *Interg %* variable suggests further that, for the purpose of increasing school attendance, one-on-one services should not be offered exclusively, but should be combined with group intergenerational activities.

The third work assignment option in the IWSP is performing non-intergenerational activities such as office or kitchen work. As the impact of these activities was reflected in the intercept of the regression equation, the positive impact of intergenerational assignments must be interpreted relative to that of non-intergenerational assignments. The results suggest that intergenerational work assignments in this program may produce better student performance than non-intergenerational assignments.

The gender, ethnicity, and site-type variables were not found to be significant predictors of absenteeism, relative to the set of independent variables included in the equation. Thus, as compared to the impact of school attended and intergenerational work assignments, it seems unlikely that different recruitment or placement patterns for students would produce better outcomes for the IWSP overall.

There were a number of shortcomings with the data used in this project. First, the data used to compute *percentage of time spent in intergenerational work assignments* was taken from the reports of 90 participating sites. This information represents the overall allocation of student work time at each site, as opposed to that for individual students. Hence, all students working at the same site had the same percentage breakdown of work time assigned to them. It was our opinion that there was sufficient variability across the 90 work sites to justify the inclusion of the intergenerational work assignment variables. However, this issue should be addressed more fully in future studies of this type.

Second, there was a considerable amount of missing data (i.e., student records) from schools in two Boroughs (Counties) of New York City. Because of a potential bias effect, *Borough* was not included in the analysis as an independent variable. However, the bias may be reflected in other variables, such as the Project Achieve School variable, because of the uneven distribution of schools by Borough.

Finally, multicollinearity may exist among the variables, *1 on 1%*, *H Care Dum*, and *N H Dum*, because one-on-one assignments are more likely to be given at these two worksites. However, it seemed likely that the high number of alternative work assignments available at both site-types would minimize the potential effects of multi-collinearity on the results of analysis.

The findings of this study may be generalizable only to programs involving activities and populations similar to those in the IWSP. However, there are many commonalities between the IWSP and other drop-out prevention programs. To this extent, other programs using a work-study approach might benefit, as did the IWSP, from including intergenerational assignments in the work mix.

## CONCLUSION

Many critics of intergenerational services have dismissed "soft" justifications for these programs such as improved life satisfaction of participants. The results of our evaluation of the IWSP indicated that intergenerational activities may contribute also to improved attendance at school in at-risk teenagers. More studies of this kind, using empirical data collection methods that are both relatively easy and cost-effective, will undoubtedly help to support and promote intergenerational approaches to social service delivery.

## NOTES

1. The basic types of sites include senior citizen centers with congregate lunch programs, home care agencies and nursing homes.

2. Non-intergenerational services are included in the IWSP at the request of participating sites because of their functional needs. In order to maintain the integrity of the intergenerational program overall, students are not allowed to spend more than 50% of their time in such assignments.

3. Ambulatory older adults typically meet together for congregate meals, recreation, education and social services. They are together for a portion of the day and return home when activities are concluded.

## REFERENCES

Anthony, R. N. & Young, D. W. (1995). *Management control in nonprofit organizations*. Burr Ridge, Illinois: Irwin Publishers.

Banerjee, N. (1988). *Older and wiser: An intergenerational drop-out prevention effort*. New York: Interface Foundation.

Corporation for National Service. (1990). *The foster grandparent program: Bridging the generation of need.* Washington, DC: Author.

Couch, L. (Ed.) (1992). *Let us serve them all their days: Young volunteers serving elderly homebound persons.* Washington, DC: National Council on the Aging.

Family Friends Resource Center. (1991/1994). *Family friends: Heart medicine money can't buy, family friends: A program guide, and family friends replication manual.* Washington, DC: National Council on the Aging.

Friedman, S. (Ed.) (1990). *Closing the gap: An intergenerational discussion model guide for replication.* Kensington, MD: Interages.

Hegeman, C. (1985). *Child care in long-term care settings.* Albany, NY: Foundation for Long Term Care.

Isabella Geriatric Center. (1995). *Health career partnerships.* New York: Author.

New York City Department for the Aging. (1990). *Between friends: Creating intergenerational work/study programs for youth at-risk and older adults: A guide for concerned communities.* New York: Author.

Southeast Florida Center on Aging. (1990). *Intergenerational child care: Program development.* Dade County, FLA: Little Havana Activities and Nutrition Centers of Dade County.

Stout, B., Boyd, S., & Volanty, K. (1992). *Y.E.S. youth service provider guide.* Lubbock, TX: Home Economics Curriculum Center, Texas Tech University.

# Intergenerational Play Therapy: The Influence of Grandparents in Family Systems

## Merle D. Griff

**SUMMARY.** The study examined the effects on parental stress and perceptions of child behavior of an intergenerational family intervention that involved grandparents in the therapeutic process, a family intervention without grandparents, and a control group. It was expected that family therapy with grandparents would (a) reduce the amount of stress reported by parents in their parenting role more than therapy without grandparents, and (b) result in grandparents' perceptions of improvements in their grandchildren's behavior. Eighteen families were randomly assigned to the experimental groups. Subjects included parents and their children, aged 2 to 6 years, and either maternal or paternal grandparents. The results showed that grandparents had a positive influence on their children's treatment of their grandchildren, but they did not change their perceptions of their grandchildren's behavior. It was concluded that grandparents may be an important source of emotional support and may exert a positive influence in changing family systems. *[Article copies available for a fee from The Haworth Document Delivery Service: 1-800-342-9678. E-mail address: getinfo@haworthpressinc.com <Website: http://www.haworthpressinc.com>]*

**KEYWORDS.** Intergenerational play therapy, grandparents

Merle D. Griff is affiliated with the S.A.R.A.H Center Intergenerational Project, 800 Market Avenue North, Canton, OH 44702.

[Haworth co-indexing entry note]: "Intergenerational Play Therapy: The Influence of Grandparents in Family Systems." Griff, Merle D. Co-published simultaneously in *Child & Youth Services* (The Haworth Press, Inc.) Vol. 20, No. 1/2, 1999, pp. 63-76; and: *Intergenerational Programs: Understanding What We Have Created* (ed: Valerie S. Kuehne) The Haworth Press, Inc., 1999, pp. 63-76. Single or multiple copies of this article are available for a fee from The Haworth Document Delivery Service [1-800-342-9678, 9:00 a.m. - 5:00 p.m. (EST). E-mail address: getinfo@haworthpressinc.com].

In recent years, there has been increasing interest in the ecological factors involved in the parenting process and child development (Bronfenbrenner, 1986; Furstenberg, 1985). Particular attention has been focused on how stressful life events may affect an individual's parenting ability. Taken together, the results of many studies indicate that major life stressors such as poverty, emotional and social isolation, and chronic unemployment may have a deleterious effect on parenting (Belsky, 1984; Egeland & Farber, 1984; Nakagawa, Teti, & Lam, 1992; Werner & Smith, 1982). Some researchers believe that stress affects the caregiver's ability to respond sensitively and appropriately to the child (e.g., Pianta & Egeland, 1990). Parents who suffer from significant stressors in their daily lives may be more likely to resist proposed changes in the family system and to use negative and punitive behavioral management techniques (Cox, Owen, Lew, & Henderson, 1989; Pianta & Egeland, 1990; Webster-Stratton & Hammond, 1988).

Family therapy is based on the notion that an individual's problems are best understood when examined in the contexts of the nuclear family and the extended family. There is a growing recognition by child therapists in general that positive behavioral changes may be brought about more effectively by influencing the child's environment rather than by attempting to control the child's behavior directly (Schaefer & Briesmeister, 1989). Many family therapists have recognized that " . . . without engaging the children in a meaningful interchange across the generations, there can be no family therapy" (Ackerman, 1970, p. 407). Proponents of family therapy have developed therapeutic methods that address the needs of the entire family system and build on family strengths.

Recognition of the importance of play for children has led some family therapists, such as Whitaker (1982), to blend play- and family-therapy approaches. The integration of play elements into family-therapy sessions allows children to actively participate in ways that accommodate their chronological age and developmental capabilities. The introduction of play also provides a nonverbal pathway for children through which they may communicate their perceptions and observations.

Some family therapists have adapted both structured and non-directive family-therapy approaches to include grandparents. Although Bowen (1966) did not involve grandparents directly in the treatment process, he did assign to each of the parents one or more tasks to be completed with their own family. Framo (1976) shifted the focus from problems between parents and children to the marital relationship between the parents and their relationships with their family of origin. Ingersoll-Dayton, Arndt, and Stevens (1988) found that family-therapy approaches that involved at least three generations of family members resulted in more positive outcomes for family members than those with two.

There is little research literature regarding the ways in which grandparents may influence parenting behaviors in their adult children or influence specific behaviors in their grandchildren. Although studies have been done of a variety of intergenerational programs, the programs being studied usually include older adults and children who are not related to them. This general approach is based upon the beliefs that contact with extended family members is limited and that intergenerational contact must now be consciously orchestrated (Waters, 1991).

Ingersoll-Dayton, Arndt, and Stevens (1988) examined differences among three separate family-therapy approaches. The first of these was a traditional, two-generational family intervention that included only parents and children. In the second, therapists met with parents and children in family-therapy sessions but encouraged members of the family to maintain contact with grandparents outside of these sessions. The majority of these out-of-session contacts involved conversations between parents and grandparents that focused on prior unresolved issues or on ways in which the grandparents could offer emotional support to the parents. In the third approach, grandparents were invited to participate in family-therapy sessions along with parents and children. The results obtained by Ingersoll-Dayton et al. showed that using a three generational approach that included out-of-session contact with grandparents led to more families accomplishing their treatment goals than did using either the two generational family-therapy approach or the three generational approach that involved grandparents in-session only.

Treatment goals tend to focus on facilitating change in two areas: (a) helping parents to resolve their children's behavior problems, such as aggressive and withdrawn behaviors, and (b) assisting parents to provide environments that facilitate growth and development. Typically, growth and development are measured by the families' perceptions of the overall functioning of the family unit, the "manageability" of their children, and parents' affect toward the children.

Some researchers have examined factors that may enable parents to assimilate newly-acquired parenting skills and information into their daily lives (Pharis & Levin, 1991; Telleen, Herzog, & Kilbane, 1989). The results of these studies point to the need of primary caregivers to have ongoing emotional and social support in their parenting roles. Overall, the findings suggest that it may be the parents' perceptions of receiving social and emotional support that enable them to maintain positive changes with their children and to move beyond dependency on the social-services bureaucracy. When parents perceive having some degree of support, they may feel a greater sense of independence, and may be able to manage their family's daily life with increased feelings of confidence and success.

Notwithstanding the relative effectiveness of specific therapeutic interventions, environmental stressors such as single-parenthood and low income may continue to impact on the family system long after such interventions. Pharis and Levin (1991) found that a significant factor in parents' being able to initiate and maintain positive changes was their perception of some type of ongoing, emotional support. Unfortunately, grandparents are not always perceived as being capable of providing this support. Instead, grandparents may be viewed by their adult children as being old people who are to be "cared for" or "dealt with," rather than as potential sources of strength and energy for family members. This perception seems to differ from the view that most grandparents have of themselves. In my own therapeutic work, I found that many grandparents have expressed the desire to offer ideas and contributions to their families that are based on their life experience. Many have expressed feelings of being cast aside and of being excluded from important family matters and concerns, especially those regarding their grandchildren's behaviors and problems.

## *INTERGENERATIONAL PLAY THERAPY*

The notion that parents might benefit in their parenting role from consistent emotional support led to the development of a therapeutic approach that directly involves grandparents in the therapeutic process along with their children and grandchildren. According to this approach, grandparents are included in the targeted changes in the family system and are provided with the means for expanding their role in the family. Familial change is promoted through active participation in time-limited, structured, family play-therapy sessions. The intergenerational play-therapist helps to reconceptualize the grandparents' role in the family so that they are better able to: (a) offer ongoing emotional support to parents in specific ways, and (b) continue to reinforce any positive changes that occur in the family. As the grandparent role evolves, parents' perceptions toward their children and their parents may change.

In the present study, the effects of intergenerational play therapy were compared to those of family play therapy as well as to no intervention on measures of parental stress, feelings of competence in the parenting role, and of the children's behavior. It was thought that directly involving grandparents in therapeutic intervention would help to alleviate parental feelings of stress and aid in the behavior change process. Thus, the hypotheses were that: (a) parents who participated in intergenerational play therapy would perceive decreased stress in their parenting role when compared to parents who participated in family play therapy or in no therapy, and (b) there would be a significant, positive change in grandparents' perceptions of their grandchildren's specific behaviors over the course of therapy.

## METHOD

### Participants

Participants were selected from the intake list of a community mental-health center in northeast Ohio. The sample included the parents or primary caregiver of male and female children who were between 2 and 6 years of age as well as the children's maternal or paternal grandparent(s). The decision concerning which grandparent would participate in the session was made by the parents. However, the therapist's recommendation to the families was that the best choice probably would be the grandparent who had the most daily contact with the parents and the children. None of the grandparents who participated were living in the same home with their children and grandchildren at the time of the study.

Intake assessors randomly assigned 18 families to one of the three treatment groups: (a) the delayed treatment group (control), consisting of six families who remained on the waiting list for 9 weeks; (b) six families who participated in nine family play-therapy sessions, and (c) six families who participated in nine intergenerational play-therapy sessions.

## *INSTRUMENTS*

*Child Behavior Checklist* (CBCL; Achenbach, 1983). The CBCL follows a standardized format by which parents are asked to describe their children's behavioral problems and competencies. This information may be provided by the child's parent or by any other adult who knows the child well. Test norms are for children ranging in age from 2-16 years. The CBCL generates three scores, the *Internal T*, the *External T*, and the *Total T*. The Internal T score represents internalizing behaviors such as withdrawn or anxious/depressed behaviors. The External T score represents externalizing behaviors such as aggression or attention problems. The Total T score represents behaviors that are positively associated. A content validation analysis of the CBCL showed that all of the social competence items and 116 of the 118 behavior problem items were significantly correlated with clinical status (Achenbach, 1983). Achenbach also reported the strong construct validity of the CBCL, pointing to significant correlations between all of the behavior problems on the CBCL and total scores on other widely-accepted parental ratings of child behavior.

*Parental Stress Inventory* (PSI; Abidin, 1990). The PSI is a screening and diagnostic instrument that is used to identify parent-child systems under stress, as well as patterns of dysfunctional parenting. Its primary focus is on the self-reported behaviors of parents of preschool children. Two uses for this instrument are for the pre-and-post measurement of the effectiveness of a particular intervention, and for researching the effects of stress on parenting behavior (Abidin, 1990). The PSI test manual reports adequate alpha reliability coefficients and varying levels of concurrent and construct validity.

Parents complete the PSI by rating their own behaviors in the parenting role. The PSI consists of two subscales, *Child Domain* and *Parent Domain*. The Child Domain score reflects such things as the child's being continually demanding of the parent, and the child's reinforcing the parent for being "good and loved." High scores in the Child Domain are interpreted as indicating children whose behavior makes it difficult for parents to fulfill their parenting role in a positive and healthy manner (Abidin, 1990).

The Parent Domain score reflects the adults' self-reported sense of competence in the parenting role and their self-reported degree of social isolation from other adults. High scores in the Parent Domain indicate that there are sources of stress and potential dysfunction in the parent-child system that may undermine the parent's ability to function in the parenting role (Abidin & Edelbrock, 1990).

## Procedures

During an initial meeting, parents and grandparents were provided with the rationale of the study, a description of the proposed intervention, and the purpose of having the three experimental groups. Participants were then asked to sign letters of informed consent.

Parents completed the CBCL and the PSI: Grandparents completed the CBCL. Both parents and grandparents completed the measures following the first phase of treatment (third session), following the second phase (sixth session), and following the last session (ninth session). They completed these instruments at the end of the sessions, while still at the mental-health agency. Supervised child-care was available for the time that it took them to complete both instruments.

Parents in the delayed-treatment group completed the same instruments during the initial interview and again after 3 weeks, after 6 weeks, and after 9 weeks. The tests were administered to participants in this group during a home visit.

## Intervention

*Intergenerational Play Therapy* consists of four phases that typically extend across 8-10 sessions. There are similar phases for the *Family Play Therapy*, except that grandparents are not included. Therapy sessions were held once a week for 9 weeks.

*Phase One: Planning.* The first session is with the parent(s) and the child, taking a developmental history and performing a family assessment. Although parents are invited to bring the grandparents to this initial session, most prefer to attend alone. The second session is a planning meeting during which the goals of the intervention are jointly established and specific activities are chosen for the therapy playroom. Grandparents are included in this session.

*Phase Two: Development of therapeutic relationships.* The second phase consists of two sessions, which are used primarily for observation. Here the therapist interacts with the child through play, with the parent and the grandparent observing. This time is used to "teach" the parent and/or grandparent to identify a problem behavior using basic observation techniques. The therapist also may want to focus the family's attention on the positive aspects of the child's behavior. This can be done through the use of direct statements by the therapist at the time of observation and/or at the end of the session. Directing attention to positive behaviors also can be accomplished by the adults' viewing of videotapes recording the child's activities during a given session.

*Phase Three: The beginning of change.* For these sessions, the therapist invites the parent and the grandparent to interact with the child through play. This way the therapist can provide immediate feedback to the adult and give positive reinforcement for specific behaviors. It is during these sessions that the therapist also has an opportunity to influence the parent-child interactions. Suggestions for change that are made to the parent involve specific methods of interaction and communication that seem consistent with the parent's unique interactive style. Suggested behavioral changes are demonstrated by the therapist.

Grandparents are asked to support and to reinforce these changes during the subsequent week at home. This can be done through either the use of verbal reinforcement made immediately after the parenting behavior is observed or through non-verbal means, such as encouraging a smile with direct eye contact. At the beginning of the subsequent session, parents are asked about the changes made, and grandparents are asked to provide a constructive report of the parents' progress in making these changes. Also, both grandparents and parents review the changes made by grandparents in their role.

*Phase Four: Changing roles for parents and grandparents.* In this phase the therapist takes a "back seat" in the play sessions with the child and encourages the parent to take a more active part in the interactions. The therapist remains present to draw attention to and thereby support any positive changes observed in the parent-child interaction. In this way parents are encouraged to use newly-acquired skills within a safe and supportive environment. During these sessions, the therapist also models specific behaviors to the grandparents, showing them how and when to give emotional support to the parent.

This provides an opportunity to reinforce the grandparents in their changing role within the family.

A final session is held with the family to (a) evaluate their progress toward the goals that were established during the first session, (b) to develop a plan for the maintenance of positive changes, (c) to assess the need for additional sessions, and (d) to determine the need for further intervention, such as individual counseling or marital therapy.

## RESULTS

Separate analyses of variance were used to examine the effects of intervention on the CBCL and the PSI. Multiple comparisons were done, where appropriate, using Bonferroni procedures. An alpha level of .05 was used for all other analyses. There were no significant pre-test differences between any of the groups on any of the scales.

The first hypothesis was that parents who participated in intergenerational play-therapy would report an increased sense of competence in their parenting role as compared to parents who participated in family-play therapy. For the CBCL there was a significant overall effect of group for the mean Total T scores, $F(2,52) = 9.2008$, $p < .0003$. Post-hoc multiple comparisons revealed that the intergenerational group had significantly lower scores than the parents-only group ($t(38) = 3.8610$, $p < .0003$) and the control group ($t(42) = 3.8610$, $p < .0008$). None of the group mean Internal T scores were significantly different from each other. The mean External T scores significantly differed by group, $F(2,52) = 13.1320$, $p < .0001$. Post-hoc comparisons showed that the intergenerational group had significantly lower External T scores than the control group ($t(42) = 3.5331$, $p < .0008$) and the parents-only group ($t(38) = 5.0744$, $p < .0001$).

For the PSI, the groups did not differ significantly on the Total Stress score. There was a significant overall effect of group for Child Domain Scores, $F(2,52) = 6.4821$, $p < .0029$. Post-hoc analyses revealed that the intergenerational group had significantly lower mean scores on Child Domain than the parents-only group, $t(38) = 3.3470$, $p < .0015$. The average Parent Domain scores for each group were not significantly different from each other.

The second hypothesis stated that there would be a significant change in the grandparents' perceptions of their grandchildren's behavior over the course of therapy, as measured on the CBCL. Although scores were in the hypothesized direction, none was significantly different from the others.

## DISCUSSION

### *Parental Responses on the Child Behavior Checklist*

The Total T scores for the intergenerational group was nearly 10 points lower than either of the other two groups, a statistically significant difference. This finding indicates that parents who participated in family therapy accompanied by their own parents saw more improvements in their children's behavior than did parents in the other groups.

One possible explanation for the nonsignificant Internal T score is that internalizing behaviors, such as symptoms of anxiety or depression, are not easily observable. Also, they may not be as disruptive to the family on a daily basis as are more externalized behaviors, such as aggressive actions. Thus, changes in internalizing behaviors may not be as readily perceived by parents over a relatively short period of time. It seems likely that these behaviors are not as much the focus of attention in the daily life of a family, as compared to more overtly disruptive behaviors.

As indicated above, the significant overall difference among the groups for the average Total T scores was due primarily to group differences in average scores on the External T subscale. The average score for the intergenerational group was 9 points lower than for the control group and 13 points lower than for the parents-only group. External T scores reflect behaviors that most parents state as wanting to change "immediately" when they are asked to establish treatment goals. Items on this subscale include verbally and physically aggressive behaviors, refusal to follow rules, and impulsive behaviors. These tend to be the kind of behaviors that parents seem most motivated to try to change in their children as compared to other problem areas. The results indicated that parents in the intergenerational group perceived more positive changes in externalizing behaviors following therapy than did parents in the other two groups.

Grandparents were asked to support parents when they initiated positive changes by reinforcing new patterns of communication and interaction, both within and outside of therapy sessions. This was meant to help parents to become aware of the impact they were having on their children. It was intended also to make parents feel supported emotionally by having their behavior reinforced throughout the difficult process of change. Our findings suggest that the significant improvement in External T scores for the intergenerational group was attributable in part to the grandparents' efforts in this area.

### Parental Stress Inventory

Results indicated that neither time of administration nor group membership had a significant effect on either the average Total Stress scores or the average Parent Domain subscale scores. However, the experimental groups did differ on the Child Domain subscale, a not unusual pattern of differences on the PSI, according to Abidin (1990).

The reason for the nonsignificant differences on the Parent Domain subscale is unclear. Perhaps it was because some specific items within this domain were inappropriate for use with the population studied here. For example, *Relationship with Spouse/Significant Other* does not reflect the living situation of most of the parents who were in this study, who were either never-married or divorced single-parents or whose relationships with a significant other tended to be turbulent and transitory. Also, an informal examination of the Parent Domain item scores suggested that some parents in this study may have been in poor health. This speculation seems consistent with Callahan's (1989) suggestion that low-SES mothers who report high levels of parenting stress might be more likely to seek medical care for health-related problems.

On the Child Domain subscale, the intergenerational group obtained a mean score that was 18 points lower than the parents-only group and 11 points lower than the control group. From an informal examination of the six areas covered by this subscale, it appeared that the Distractibility/Hyperactivity and Demandingness items contributed the most to the overall group differences. High ratings on the Demandingness construct reflect parents' views of their children as being too demanding of them. These demands may be expressed in behaviors such as crying, whining, or frequent requests for attention. High ratings on the Distractibility/Hyperactivity dimension reflect such observed behaviors as appearing not to listen, restlessness, and short attention span (Abidin, 1990). Parents in the intergenerational group gave significantly lower ratings in these areas than did either of the other groups. Thus, it seemed that the presence of grandparents made a significant impact on the behaviors described in both these subscales.

### Grandparent Responses on the Child Behavior Checklist

Although there was no significant effect of time of administration for grandparents' scores on the CBCL, there was, as expected, a decremental change in the Internal T scores with each administration of the instrument. Perhaps grandparents are more apt than parents to be concerned with the behaviors evaluated by the Internal T subscale. During the initial intake, many grandparents stated that they observe externalizing behaviors in their grandchildren *only when* their grandchildren are with their parents. Of apparently greater concern to many grandparents are the internalizing behaviors, such as their grandchildren being shy or sad (*Withdrawn*) or feeling unwanted, fearful, or lonely (*Anxious/Depressed*). That this type of behavior tends to be more difficult to change as well as more slow to change may account for the modest, albeit steady decrease in Internal T scores over the 9-week period of the study.

Some therapists assume that a specific family's problems originated with the grandparents. This view, coupled with society's often negative and intolerant views of older adults, may preclude some clinicians from perceiving grandparents as being a vital asset to the family rather than a liability. The findings from this study suggest a need to examine further the specific ways in which grandparents may help their families to deal with stress and how they may help their children to make positive changes in child-rearing practices and family interactions.

When grandparents are involved in the therapeutic process, there may be decreased resistance to change within the family system. My clinical experiences have shown that some grandparents, when they are not included in the change process, try to undermine their children's attempts to adopt new parenting techniques. The use of new methods of discipline or adapting rules and standards to the child's developmental level may be misinterpreted by some grandparents as being implicit criticisms of their own parenting. However, when they are included in the therapeutic process, grandparents are more likely to become an integral part of positive change. Thus it is wise to seek grandparents' advice and guidance and integrate their observations and recommendations into new modes of family interactions. It seemed evident that the grandparents who participated in Intergenerational Play Therapy sessions were proud of their role. It appeared generally that they understood the parameters of their new role with their children and grandchildren. Many of them expressed deep satisfaction in finding ways to offer ongoing emotional support to their children and to provide reinforcement for positive changes in the family system.

Intergenerational Play Therapy requires clinicians to have a broad knowledge base in human development. They should be familiar with a given age-cohort's general attitude toward raising children and with their developmental and behavioral expectations of children. It should be kept in mind that many grandparents in lower-SES families are middle-aged as opposed to elderly, and they may hold different views from older-aged cohorts of grandparents.

One of the limitations of the present study was the limited timeframe for measuring the impact of grandparents on changes in the family system. Another was that most of the grandparents studied here were female. Further research is needed to examine the contributions of grandfathers to the effects of family therapy in terms of providing emotional support and influence in changing family systems.

## REFERENCES

Achenbach, T. M. (1983). *Manual for the Child Behavior Checklist and Revised Child Behavior Profile.* Burlington, VT: Department of Psychiatry, University of Vermont.

Abidin, R. R. (1990). *Parenting stress index manual (3rd ed.).* Charlottesville, VA: Pediatric Psychology Press.

Ackerman, N. W. (1970). Child participation in family therapy. *Family Process, 9*(4), 403-410.

Belsky, J. (1984). The determinants of parenting: A process model. *Child Development, 51,* 437-447.

Bowen, M. (1966). The use of family theory in clinical practice. *Comprehensive Psychiatry, 7,* 345-374.

Bronfenbrenner, U. (1986). Ecology of the family as a context for human development: A research perspective. *Developmental Psychology, 22,* 723-742.

Callahan, J. F. (1989). *Parenting stress and health care utilization.* Unpublished doctoral dissertation, University of Virginia, Charlottesville.

Cox, M. J., Owen, M. T., Lewis, J. M., & Henderson, V. K. (1989). Marriages, adult adjustment, and early parenting. *Child Development, 60,* 1015-1024.

Egeland, S., & Farber, E. (1984). Infant-mother attachment: Factors related to its development and changes over time. *Child Development, 55,* 193-210.

Framo, J. L. (1976). Family of origin as a therapeutic resource for adults in marital and family therapy: You can and should go home again. *Family Process, 15,* 753-771.

Furstenberg, F. F. (1985). Sociological ventures in child development. *Child Development, 56,* 281-288.

Ingersoll-Dayton, B., Arndt, B., & Stevens, D. (1988, May). Involving grandparents in family therapy. *Social Casework: The Journal of Contemporary Social Work,* 280-289.

Nakagawa, M., Teti, D. M., & Lamb, M. E. (1992). An ecological study of child-mother attachments among Japanese sojourners in the United States. *Developmental Psychology, 28*(4), 584-592.

Pharis, M.E., & Levin, V.S. (1991). "A Person to Talk to Who Really Cared": High-risk Mothers' Evaluations of Services in an Intensive Intervention Research Program. *Child Welfare, 70*(3), 307-320.

Pianta, R. C., & Egeland, B. (1990). Life stress and parenting outcomes in a disadvantaged sample: Results of the Mother-Child Interactions Project. *Journal of Clinical Child Psychology, 19,* 329-336.

Schaefer, C. & Briesmeister, J. M. (1989). *Handbook of parent training.* New York: John Wiley & Sons.

Telleen, S., Herzog, A., & Kilbane, T. L. (1989). Impact of family support program on mother's social support and parenting stress. *American Journal of Orthopsychiatry, 59*(3), 410-419.

Waters, R. (1991, October). Young and old alike. *Parenting,* 74-79.

Webster-Stratton, C., & Hammond, M. (1988). Maternal depression and its relationship to life stress, perceptions of child behavior problems, parenting behaviors, and child conduct problems. *Journal of Abnormal Child Psychology, 11,* 123-129.

Werner, E. E., & Smith, R. S. (1982). *Vulnerable but invincible: A longitudinal study of resilient children and youth.* New York: McGraw Hill.

Whitaker, C. A. (1982). A family is a four-dimensional relationship. In J. R. Neil & D. P. Kniskern (Eds.), *From psyche to system* (pp. 185-202). New York: Guilford Press.

# The Mentoring Factor:
# Evaluation of the Across Ages'
# Intergenerational Approach
# to Drug Abuse Prevention

Andrea S. Taylor
Leonard LoSciuto
Margaretta Fox
Susan M. Hilbert
Michael Sonkowsky

**SUMMARY.** Across Ages is a comprehensive, intergenerational mentoring program designed to reduce adolescent drug abuse and to help older adults (55+) maintain active roles in their communities. For an outcome evaluation, students in classrooms from Philadelphia public schools were randomly assigned to one of three conditions: A curriculum and community service condition (Program Group), a curriculum, service, and mentoring condition (Mentoring Group), or a Control Group. Eight modified scales and three original scales were completed by 562 students in a pretest and posttest design. Results suggest that the Program Group participants, as compared to the Control Group participants, showed significant improvement in their sense of well-being,

Andrea S. Taylor is affiliated with the Center for Intergenerational Learning, Temple University, 1601 N. Broad Street, Philadelphia, PA 19122. Leonard LoSciuto and Susan M. Hilbert are affiliated with the Institute for Survey Research at Temple University, 502 University Services Building, 1601 N. Broad Street, Philadelphia, PA 19122. Margaretta Fox may be reached at 1380 1st Avenue, New York, NY 10021. Michael Sonkowsky is affiliated with the School District of Philadelphia, 22nd Street and the Parkway, Philadelphia, PA 19123.

[Haworth co-indexing entry note]: "The Mentoring Factor: Evaluation of the Across Ages' Intergenerational Approach to Drug Abuse Prevention." Taylor, Andrea S. et al. Co-published simultaneously in *Child & Youth Services* (The Haworth Press, Inc.) Vol. 20, No. 1/2, 1999, pp. 77-99; and: *Intergenerational Programs: Understanding What We Have Created* (ed: Valerie S. Kuehne) The Haworth Press, Inc., 1999, pp. 77-99 Single or multiple copies of this article are available for a fee from The Haworth Document Delivery Service [1-800-342-9678, 9:00 a.m. - 5:00 p.m. (EST). E-mail address: getinfo@haworthpressinc.com].

knowledge about elders, reactions to situations involving drug use, and attitudes toward community service. Participants in the Mentoring Group also improved in their attitudes toward school, the future, and elders. Implications for further research and practical considerations for program replication are discussed. *[Article copies available for a fee from The Haworth Document Delivery Service: 1-800-342-9678. E-mail address: getinfo@haworthpressinc.com <Website: http://www.haworthpressinc.com>]*

**KEYWORDS.** Intergenerational, research, drug use, prevention, mentoring

Across Ages is an intergenerational mentoring program designed to reduce drug abuse among "at risk" youth and to improve the lives of older adults (55+) in poor, urban communities. Working as advocates, nurturers, role models, and friends, older mentors help children develop the awareness, self-confidence, and life skills they may need to resist drugs and to meet some of the unique challenges facing today's youth. In return, mentoring allows older adults to retain their roles as productive members of the community and thus to maintain their self-worth at a time of life when many older people feel isolated and under-appreciated.

Across Ages is a school-based project coordinated by the Center for Intergenerational Learning at Temple University in Philadelphia, Pennsylvania, and funded by the Center for Substance Abuse Prevention, U.S. Department of Health and Human Services. Because of its demonstrated success, Across Ages has been replicated within Philadelphia and other sites throughout the United States.

Each school year, the Across Ages project targets approximately 180 sixth grade students who have experienced repeated school failure, high rates of absenteeism from school, and serious behavior problems. Most of these students are poor and live in neighborhoods characterized by high unemployment and drug-related crime. Previous research indicates that each of these factors contributes to an increased risk of substance abuse among young adolescents (Hawkins, 1988; Hawkins, Lishner, Jenson, & Catalano, 1987).

The primary goals of the Across Ages program are to decrease the incidence of alcohol, tobacco, and other drug (ATOD) use and to build resistance to drug abuse in youth by: (a) increasing knowledge of health/substance abuse issues and fostering healthy attitudes, intentions, and behaviors regarding ATOD use; (b) increasing knowledge of and improving attitudes toward older adults; (c) improving school attendance, academic achievement, and in-school behavior; (d) increasing problem-solving skills and feelings of self-worth; (e) enhancing parenting and communication skills and educational participation among the care-givers of targeted youth; (f) promoting more positive classroom environments that foster personal growth and resistance to ATOD use; and (g) developing collaborative school-community partnerships that facilitate project activities and support targeted youth's connection to positive adult and community norms.

The program's objectives also include helping elders to maintain an active role in their communities, enhancing their feelings of self-worth and providing an opportunity to pass on the knowledge they have accumulated over a lifetime.

The following summarizes the previous research relating to each of the Across Ages program components: Youth, mentoring, elders as mentors, community service, problem-solving curriculum, parent-child relationship, and intergenerational mentoring and drug abuse prevention.

## PREVIOUS RESEARCH

*Youth behavior.* Surveys in Pennsylvania indicate an increase in "gateway" drug use by students between the sixth and ninth grades (The Governor's Plan for a Drug Free Pennsylvania). "Gateway" drugs, which include tobacco, alcohol, marijuana, and crack-cocaine, serve as the most common point of initiation for potential addiction. Previous research suggests that life-long patterns of abuse can develop from even the most "casual" early use of such substances (Kandel, 1982).

Although all young adolescents are vulnerable, those at greatest risk for drug use are from low-income households. They are most likely to face physical danger in their daily lives, to spend large amounts of time without adult supervision, and to attend schools which are understaffed, poorly equipped and overcrowded, with no counselors or resource teachers. The students who are selected for the Across Ages program in many ways typify what we would consider to be "at risk" youth (i.e., at increased risk to engage in a number of anti-social behaviors, including early initiation into substance abuse). Approximately 85% of the students at each of the participating schools live at or below the poverty level, and most are eligible for federal assistance in the form of meals and support services at school. In each school, 25-30% of the students are absent on any given day, and student suspensions run as high as 500-600 per year. Only 15-20% of the students score at or above the national average on standardized tests of basic achievement. Criminal activities as reported by school officials are frequent and include weapons offenses, personal assault, indecent exposure, selling and using of illegal substances, and shootings. It has been estimated that 25-35% of the students use drugs.

*Mentoring.* "Mentoring" refers to a relationship between a more experienced person and a younger person that involves mutual caring, commitment, and trust (Flaxman, Ascher, & Harrington, 1988). In a study that assessed the efficacy of the Big Brothers/Big Sisters program, researchers found that youths who participated in this type of mentoring relationship were less likely to report initiation of drug and alcohol use and more likely to show improvement in academic performance and school attendance when compared to youths who did not participate in the program (Tierney, Grossman, & Resch, 1995). Studies such as this suggest that mentoring can be used as part of a viable prevention strategy. As a result, mentoring has garnered increasing attention from practitioners, policy-makers, researchers, foundations, and others interested in the future of our youth (Freedman, 1988).

*Elders as mentors.* America's older adults are an untapped resource for helping youth in need. Over 28 million Americans are currently over the age of 65 years (approximately 12% of the population), and this number is expected to double by the year 2030 (U.S. Bureau of the Census, 1992). Due to improved health, increased longevity, and early retirement, older adults have more time to devote to new pursuits. Through an evaluation of a national, multi-site, intergenerational mentoring initiative called "Linking Lifetimes," Henkin, Rogers, and Lyons (1992) found that youths who were matched with an older mentor showed improvements in school-related behavior (i.e., school performance, behavior, attitudes, and attendance), as well as in self-confidence and communications skills as reported by mentors and program coordinators. For young people who lack a future orientation and who perceive few opportunities, an older adult may serve as a model of strength and perseverance in the face of adversity. Newman, Vasudev, and Onawola (1985) found that older adult volunteers who worked with students in the classroom reported having gained a new sense of purpose. Also, volunteering in the classroom seemed to provide these elders with a way of structuring their time, an issue of some importance to many older adults whose days no longer are filled with work outside the home or family responsibilities.

*Community service.* One factor that may contribute to enhanced resiliency in youth is participation in work that benefits others in direct and personal ways. A strong community-service program is one that engages students in tasks that both the larger community and the students regard as being worthwhile and that challenges them to reflect on the meaning of their experience (Conrad & Hedin, 1990). In addition to gaining valuable skills, students who engage in service-learning activities may experience a heightened sense of personal responsibility (Lewis, 1988). In their survey of 27 variations of experiential learning programs, Conrad and Hedin (1982) found that students showed significant increases in self-esteem, personal and social responsibility, as well as improved attitudes toward adults, more interest in career exploration, and better problem-solving skills.

*Problem-solving curriculum.* In their study of delinquent youths, Hawkins, Lishner, Jenson, and Catalano (1987) found that when youths develop the awareness and skills to set positive goals they may be better able to resist negative peer pressure and possible substance use/abuse. Teaching models that emphasize critical thinking and problem-solving skills, such as the Positive Youth Development Curriculum (PYDC) (Weissberg, Caplan, & Bennetto, 1988) have been successfully implemented and tested in inner-city environments (Caplan, Jacoby, Weissberg, & Grady, 1988; Weissberg, Caplan, & Sivo, 1987). The purposes of implementing the PYDC in the classroom are to enhance students' capacity to work with their peers, teachers, and parents, and to help them make healthy, informed decisions regarding drug use.

*Parent-child relationship.* It has been claimed that fundamental changes in family life have undermined Americans' capacity to raise physically and emotionally healthy children (Kumpfter & DeMarsh, 1985). Strengthening the bonds between parents and children is a prevention strategy that has enormous potential for reversing some of the effects of despair and alienation, but it is also one of the most challenging to implement (Hawkins, 1988; Kumpfter, 1987).

*Intergenerational mentoring and drug-abuse prevention.* A growing body of research suggests that the most successful drug prevention programs are those focused on the many risk/resiliency factors that increase youths' susceptibility to substance abuse (Coie, Watt, West, Hawkins, Asarnow, Markman, Ramey, Shure, & Long, 1993; Jessor, 1993). From our review of the literature, it appears that intergenerational mentoring may be an under-utilized but effective prevention strategy when used concurrently with other program components such as community service, services for parents, and a strong drug-prevention curriculum. In addition to helping to build resistance to drug use among "at-risk" youth, mentoring may provide older adults with a sense of productivity that might otherwise be missing from their lives. However, it appears that to date there has been no empirical research to test the hypothesis that mentoring contributes significantly to program effectiveness. Also, there is little information available regarding the typical characteristics of mentors, how effective mentoring-relationships are built, or how mentoring may influence student outcomes. The evaluation of Across Ages was an opportunity to explore the benefits of a multi-modal approach structured around intergenerational mentoring.

## PROGRAM DESCRIPTION

The Across Ages program consists of four major components: (a) utilizing older adults (55+) as mentors for youth, (b) engaging students in community-service activities, (c) providing a classroom-based, life-skills curriculum, and (d) offering activities and support for parents and families. Descriptions of each program component are provided below.

*Mentors.* Across Ages mentors must be at least 55 years old. Mentors are recruited at churches, senior centers, community groups, retirees' organizations, and social clubs. Many mentors themselves recruit friends and relatives to the program. Public-service announcements and other electronic media are also used in the recruitment process.

*Selection and training.* Individuals who are interested in becoming mentors in the Across Ages program must go through a rigorous selection process. They must submit a written application and must receive clearance on criminal and child-abuse background checks. Project staff conduct interviews with each applicant and personal references are contacted. In addition, applicants must successfully complete a two-day, pre-service training session conducted by project staff. Pre-service training focuses on: (a) raising awareness about issues affecting youth, (b) enhancing listening and communication skills, (c) setting goals, (d) building relationships with family members and school personnel, (e) developing strategies for beginning relationships with students, and (f) understanding program parameters. At the conclusion of training, successful applicants are admitted to the program and are matched with one or two students.

*Support and responsibilities.* Throughout the year, mentors receive constant supervision and support from project staff. Monthly in-service meetings focus on solving problems that may arise with students or their parents. A stipend of $60 a month is given to mentors to offset their expenses.

Mentors are expected to spend a minimum of four hours a week with their "mentees" during the school year and summer. Throughout the process, emphasis is placed on implementing communication and on building trust. Mentors and mentees engage in a variety of activities, which include helping with homework or class projects, accompanying the students on school trips, attending sporting or cultural events, and participating in community service activities.

*Community service.* All of the students in the participating classes have two community-service experiences during the school year. Across Ages students, often accompanied by their mentors, make biweekly, 1 hour visits to frail, elderly residents in nearby nursing homes. Prior to the visits, students receive 6 hours (1.5 hours per week for 4 weeks) of training in aging and lifespan development issues. It seems likely that this process might help them to better understand the aging process and to be more sensitive to issues associated with advanced age and ill health. Visits are carefully planned and structured so as to maximize the benefits for both students and adults. Students and home residents spend time doing projects together, playing modified versions of soccer and bowling, and sharing religious or cultural traditions. Students keep journals and discuss their experiences following each session.

In addition to visiting nursing homes, students develop an environmental project that benefits the larger community. Students might plant trees, clean up a neighborhood, or develop a community garden. Environmental projects require four hours of training, and students spend 1 hour a week on their project, for 8 weeks in all.

*Classroom-based life skills curriculum.* A third component of the project is the promotion of social competence in youths. For this, Across Ages uses the PYDC (Weissberg, Caplan, & Bennetto, 1988). The PYDC is taught to students twice a week for 45 minutes per session.

Teachers receive training from a New Haven School District consultant on the theory and implementation of the PYDC. They are asked to teach the material twice a week for 45 minutes per session. There are a total of 26 lessons, and it takes from 15-25 weeks to complete the program. Materials, such as handouts for the students, are provided by the project staff who are also available for technical assistance to the teachers.

*Parental support and family involvement.* The Across Ages program helps families in two ways: It provides opportunities for parents and other family members to participate in workshops and activities with their children, and it increases their children's access to school and community resources through involvement with an older mentor. Project-sponsored workshops and activities are held one Saturday each month in a community center or church near the schools where the program has been implemented. The focus of each meeting is determined by the participants (i.e., program staff, mentors, parents, and students). Workshops address such topics as accessing community resources and understanding adolescent sexuality. Examples of activities include student talent shows, African Dance recitals, and storytelling. Lunch is served and transportation is provided. In addition, Across Ages sponsors trips for family members to sporting and cultural events.

## DATA BASE AND HYPOTHESES

In this paper we are reporting the results of outcome data on the effectiveness of the Across Ages program that were collected during the academic years 1992-1994 (LoSciuto, Rajala, Townsend, & Taylor, 1996). Process data collected across a 4-year period (1992-1995) are also examined. Analyses were done on outcome data to examine the effects of the intervention as measured by student self-reports on a number of psycho-social scales and school attendance records. Outcome data also were used to investigate the specific effects of level or intensity of mentor involvement on outcome measures. Process data that were collected using evaluation forms and dyadic interviews with program staff, mentors, teachers, and parents also were utilized in the evaluation. The goals of the process data collection were to: (a) identify the hallmarks of a successful mentoring relationship (i.e., those in which mentors and mentees spent more than the required 20 hours a month and were sustained over the one-year minimum period), (b) develop a profile of participating mentors, (c) examine mentors' motivation for participating in the program, and (d) evaluate how the program affects school performance.

The main hypothesis for the outcome evaluation was that the multi-faceted intervention provided by Across Ages would result in significant positive outcomes for all students participating in the two experimental groups as compared with a control group. One experimental group received all four program components, including mentoring (Mentoring Group) whereas the other received only the PYDC, community service, and parental involvement components (Program Group). We further hypothesized that there would be, on average, greater positive program effects for students in the Mentoring Group as compared to those in the Program Group.

## METHOD

### Evaluation Design

A randomized, pretest-posttest control group design (Campbell & Stanley, 1966) was used for the outcome evaluation. It involved the measurement of alcohol, drug, and tobacco use as well as intermediate outcomes (knowledge, attitudes, and behaviors) for sixth-grade students.

Three classes at each school were selected from the available pool of sixth grade classes at three public, middle schools. (Special education or remedial classes were excluded.) Selected classes from each school were randomly assigned to one of three groups. The groups differed in the number of program components that were administered to students:

1. The control group did not receive any program components, but completed both pretest and posttest measures.

2. The program group participated in the PYDC, performed community service, and participated in parent workshops and family activities.
3. The mentoring group participated in the PYDC, performed community service, participated in parent workshops and family activities, and received older adult mentoring.

## *Participants*

Participants were selected from middle schools in north and northwest Philadelphia. A total of 729 students completed the pretest, but the final sample for the evaluation consisted of those 562 students who completed both pretest and posttest, yielding an overall attrition rate of 22.9%. Attrition rates of this magnitude are not unusual in studies of this nature as it is common for students to change classrooms, schools, and school districts. Preliminary attrition analyses suggested that students who completed both measures did not differ significantly in demographic or pretest-outcome measure scores from those who did not complete the posttest.

An approximately equal number of students in each of the experimental and control groups completed both pretest and posttest measures. The sample size of each group, for each program year, is shown in Table 1. Fifty-three percent of the final sample were female. Fifty-two percent of the students identified themselves as *African-American*, 16% as *White*, 9% as *Asian-American*, 9% as *Hispanic*, and 14% as *Other*. An examination of the data showed that the experimental and control groups at each school were similar to each other on the demographic indicators used. As random assignment was used, it was unlikely that program groups differed significantly in terms of SES, absenteeism, suspensions, school achievement, behavioral problems, or incidence of drug abuse.

TABLE 1. Sample Size for Groups by Evaluation Year

| Groups | 1991-1992 | 1992-1993 | 1993-1994 | Total |
|---|---|---|---|---|
| Control | 67 | 63 | 59 | 189 |
| Program | 68 | 58 | 67 | 193 |
| Mentoring | 62 | 58 | 60 | 180 |

## Measures

### Level of Mentoring

Mentor activity logs and mentor-youth goal plans were reviewed by program staff members to assess the "level" or degree of intensity of each mentor-student relationship. Interviews with students were also conducted. Mentors who were rated by program staff members as being "exceptional" mentors were those: (a) who spent more than 8 hours a week with their "mentee," (b) who were involved in a wide variety of mutually planned activities, and (c) who were often available to the youth under unusual circumstances such as testifying in court on the youth's behalf or finding help for a drug-addicted parent. "Average" mentors spent the required 4 to 6 hours a week with their mentee and were involved in a variety of planned activities. "Marginal" mentoring relationships were defined as those in which mentor and mentee engaged only in project or school-sponsored activities and interacted for less than four hours a week. These three levels of mentoring were examined for their relative impact on the outcome measures used in the evaluation.

### Outcome Evaluation

The evaluation battery was based on previous research on the efficacy of the PYDC as well as on the unique goals and objectives of the Across Ages program. The pretest and posttest batteries of 11 scales were identical. The battery contained several extant scales that were adapted for use in this evaluation. Generally, this meant that some questions were selected from the original scales and/or individual questions were modified to make them better-suited for use with this sample.

*Reactions to situations involving drug use.* This scale involves two hypothetical dilemmas (Caplan, Weissberg, Bersoff, Ezekowitz, & Wells, 1986). It asks respondents to choose 5 from a total of 10 possible ways of responding to peer pressure to try cigarettes and alcohol.

*Reactions to stress or anxiety.* This is an 8 item measure in which respondents are asked to report the frequency with which they engage in adaptive behaviors when they feel stressed or anxious (Caplan, Weissberg, Grober, & Sivo, 1992).

*Self-perception profile for children.* This is a 15-item scale that assesses children's self-perceptions of personal competency (Harter, 1985). The subscales adapted for this study were the *Behavioral Conduct* subscale (i.e., the degree to which children like how they behave, behave as they should, and avoid trouble), and the *Self-Worth* subscale (i.e., how much the child likes him/herself as a person).

*Measure of substance abuse.* This is a self-report measure of the frequency of specific substance abuse during the previous two months (Caplan et al., 1992).

*Knowledge about older people.* This is a 10-item scale that measures students' knowledge about aging and older people (Palmore, 1977).

*Rand well-being scale.* This 12-item scale measures self-reported general mood and emotional state (Veit & Ware, 1983). Respondents indicate how often they experienced feelings of loneliness, restlessness, and sadness in the previous 30 days.

*Problem-solving efficacy.* This 4-item scale asks respondents to rate the perceived helpfulness of four specific problem-solving strategies for use when dealing with difficult tasks (Caplan et al., 1992).

*Knowledge about substance abuse.* This is a 14-item scale that measures respondents' knowledge about the effects of various drugs (Caplan et al., 1992).

In addition, the battery contained the following scales designed specifically for this evaluation (LoSciuto, Rjala, Townsend, & Taylor, 1996):

- *Attitudes toward school, elders, and the future.* An 11-item Likert scale.
- *Attitudes toward older people.* A six-item Likert scale.
- *Attitudes and knowledge about community service.* An 8-item true/false scale.

The evaluation battery was identical across all 3 program years for which data were combined.

## Procedure

The pretests were administered to students at the beginning of the school year prior to the implementation of the program interventions. The posttest battery was administered at the conclusion of the school year. The battery took approximately 45 minutes to complete. For ease in administration, the survey was read aloud to each class. An additional program staff member was present in the class to clarify terms and answer questions. The administration procedure for the test battery was the same across all three program years.

## Process Evaluation

The conceptual framework for the process evaluation is consistent with the models described by King, Morris, and Fitz-Gibbon (1987), and Scheirer (1987). The process evaluation provides valuable information about the nature, progression, and intensity of the mentor-youth relationships as well as data concerning the satisfaction of parents, students, and teachers. The measurement of process variables involved (a) exploring the mentor-youth relationship, (b) monitoring activities for families, (c) assessing the impact of the program on the school and classroom "climate," and (d) tracking community partnerships.

Process data were collected primarily from interviews with project participants (mentors, parents, teachers, and community representatives), from focus groups with students, and from records maintained by project staff. Demographic information about mentors from application forms was used to form a "portrait" of the typical individual who volunteers as a mentor. Mentor activity logs, tracking logs, and mentor-youth goal plans (maintained by program staff and mentors, respectively) were examined to determine the activities of mentoring pairs and the extent of the mentor's involvement in the relationship. Student records obtained from school officials, including documentation of school attendance, grades, and records of disciplinary action also were examined to determine if the effects of Across Ages might be reflected in classroom behavior. Process data were also used to identify difficulties that arose during program implementation.

## RESULTS

### Outcome Data

Separate analyses of covariance (ANCOVA) were performed to test the overall hypothesis that students in both of the experimental groups would demonstrate more positive changes on the posttest measures than those in the control group. This statistical procedure was selected because it allows the pretest scores of participants to be held constant (i.e., pre-test scores were used as a covariate), thereby controlling for any potential differences between both the experimental and control groups before the intervention. Focused contrast analyses were used to examine pairwise group differences. These focused analyses were employed rather than diffuse omnibus procedures to test a priori predictions regarding the expected pattern of results. In instances where a priori hypotheses can be made, contrasts provide more statistical power than omnibus tests for detecting mean differences (Rosenthal & Rosnow, 1991). Table 2 presents the means on the eleven scales for

TABLE 2. Mean Scale Scores of Students from Three Experimental Groups

| Scale | Mean Scores[a] | | |
|---|---|---|---|
| | Group C | Group P | Group M |
| *Attitudes toward school, future, and elders | 2.92 | 2.87 | 3.02 |
| *Attitudes toward older people | 2.51 | 2.58 | 2.71 |
| *Rand well-being scale | 2.35 | 2.35 | 2.47 |
| *Facts on aging | .33 | .38 | .33 |
| *Reactions to situations involving ATD use | 6.82 | 6.87 | 7.15 |
| *Attitudes toward community service | .46 | .50 | .53 |
| *Frequency of substance use[b] | .12 | .17 | .12 |
| Reactions to stress | 1.82 | 1.78 | 1.88 |
| Self-perception | 1.72 | 1.74 | 1.73 |
| ATD knowledge | .53 | .54 | .55 |
| Problem-solving efficacy | 2.58 | 2.41 | 2.60 |

Note: Three years of combined data are reported in this table. Pairwise contrast values for scales preceded by an asterisk are included in Results section.
[a]C = Control group; P = Program Group; M = Mentoring Group
[b]Lower scores are considered "better" for this measure.

each of the three groups combined over three years of data collection. The listed means have been adjusted for the covariates.

Seven of the eleven scales (those preceded by asterisks in Table 2) indicate significant (.05 level) or marginally significant (.10 level) differences among groups. Of these seven, the Mentoring group scored significantly better than the Control group on the following four measures: *Attitudes Toward School, Future, and Elders*, $F(1, 316) = 4.34, p = .038$; *Attitudes Toward Older People*, $F(1, 208) = 8.09, p < .005$; *Attitudes Toward Community Service*, $F(1, 208) = 5.10, p < .025$; and *Reactions to Situations Involving Drug Use*, $F(1, 217) = 4.17, p < .042$. The Mentoring group also scored marginally better than the Curriculum group on the *Rand Well-Being* Scale, $F(1, 310) = 3.62, p < .058$. Finally, students in the Mentoring group scored significantly better than students in the Curriculum group on two measures: *Attitudes Toward School, Future, and Elders*, $F(1, 317) = 9.29, p < .002$, and *Attitudes Toward Older People*, $F(1, 317) = 6.36, p < .012$, and marginally better on the *Frequency of Substance Use* measure, $F(1, 315) = 3.67, p < .056$.

The Program group showed significantly greater improvements than the Control group, $F(1, 368) = 5.32, p < .022$ and the Mentoring group $F(1, 313) = 3.66, p < .057$ on the *Knowledge About Older People* scale. One unexpected finding concerning the Program group were their scores on the drug use scale: the Program group indicated a small but statistically significant increase in *Frequency of Substance Use* relative to the Mentoring group and the Control group, $F(1, 315) = 3.67, p < .056$. Those scales in Table 2 not preceded by an asterisk did not demonstrate significant differences in any pairwise contrast analyses.

*Across Ages and school attendance.* Of particular interest to educators and researchers is school attendance, with its obvious implications for school achievement. Students in the Mentoring group had significantly fewer days absent than those in the other two groups, $F(2, 447) = 4.58, p < .01$. Of further interest was whether the level of mentor involvement had any effect on days absent within the Mentoring group. Results showed that students who were perceived by staff as being highly involved with their mentors were absent significantly less often than those whose mentors were involved at an average or marginal level, $F(2, 138) = 25.03, p < .001$.

*Levels of mentoring and performance on outcome measures.* To further explore the effects of levels of mentoring, 11 separate ANCO-VAs were performed on the data from the 11 outcome measures. For these analyses, the scores from children with marginal and average levels of mentoring were combined and compared to the scores of children receiving exceptional mentoring. Results of these analyses are presented in Table 3. Means listed in the table are the adjusted means from the focused ANCOVAs.

When compared to youths who received marginal or average mentoring, youths who received exceptional mentoring showed significant positive improvements on 4 of the 11 measures: (a) *Attitudes Towards School, Future, and Elders*, (b) *Attitudes Toward Older People*, (c) *Reactions to Situations Involving Drug Use*, and (d) *Knowledge About Substance Abuse*. The non-significant differences found for the remaining seven measures were in the expected direction.

*Process Data*

*Mentor profile.* The "typical" mentor was an African-American, high-school graduate between the ages of 65 and 75 years, who held a skilled or semi-skilled position during his or her working years. The majority of mentors were grandparents.

According to self-reports, the major reason that these older adults decided to become mentors was for the opportunity to share with a young person the knowledge, skills, and wisdom learned over a lifetime. Most had been retired for six months to a year and had not found

TABLE 3. ANCOVA for Levels of Mentoring on Outcome Measures

| Scale | Marginal & Average Mentoring | Exceptional Mentoring | $F$ | $p$ |
|---|---|---|---|---|
| Attitudes toward school, future, and elders | 2.78 | 3.09 | 4.26 | .041 |
| Attitudes toward older people | 2.64 | 2.89 | 5.03 | .027 |
| Reactions to situations involving drug use | 7.21 | 7.48 | 5.83 | .018 |
| Knowledge about substance abuse | .50 | .54 | 5.78 | .018 |

Note: Three years of combined data are reported in this table.

retirement–or the freedom it brings–as fulfilling as they had antici-pated. Many reported that their own children and grandchildren do not appreciate or value their life experiences as much as do their mentees. Mentors also cited having a reason to get up in the morning as being critical to maintaining their physical and mental health. These self-re-port data suggest that the need to be appreciated and productive is common in older adults who volunteer as mentors.

*Components of effective mentoring relationships.* It seems axiomat-ic that for a mentor's relationship with a student to result in positive outcomes for that student, an effective relationship must be developed. Effective relationships are defined as those in which both members are satisfied and which are sustained over time.

In an evaluation of Linking Lifetimes, a national intergenerational mentoring program, Styles and Morrow (1992) found that it was the participants' styles of interaction, rather than the type of activity that the pairs engaged in per se that determined reported satisfaction with the relationship. Satisfied matches were characterized as "youth-driv-en" (p. 29) in their content and timing. Participants were more satis-fied in matches in which the elder was able to identify and address the youth's needs in ways of which the youth approved. It was the youth who set the pace for information disclosure and trust-building between the pair.

Interview data from our study suggested that the mentors who nur-tured, coached, and encouraged their mentees, engaged in mutual collaborative problem-solving, and worked cooperatively with family members whenever possible were more likely to be satisfied with the mentoring experience than those who did not. They were also more successful in sustaining the relationship past their original commit-ment of one year. Helping the children set realistic, attainable goals was another predictor of satisfaction and success for mentors, because, presumably, both the mentor and the mentee could see measurable progress.

Some mentors were unable to form an effective partnership with their mentees because they failed to consider the youth's interests or perspective. For example, mentors who restricted the ways in which they worked with the children (e.g., concentrating only on school work or school-related activities) or who tended to lecture and to insist on their way of doing things were unsuccessful in maintaining a mean-ingful relationship with their mentee.

Despite some difficulties, mentors generally were eager to learn from their mistakes and to try again. In some instances, the pair was able to continue because the mentor was willing to try some activities that were interesting and pleasurable for both of them. Training provided by project staff emphasized the importance of setting realistic expectations and goals and taught mentors how to work with the youths to plan their shared activities. An examination of interview data suggested that mentor attrition diminished when mentors received support from project staff.

*School performance.* Of particular interest to educators and researchers in a school-based initiative is the extent to which the program has an effect on school performance. For many students in Across Ages, the transition to middle school brought profound changes in achievement and classroom behavior. School-related problems were demonstrated in poor grades, low attendance, disruptive behavior, and generally negative attitudes. Mentors seemed to play an important role in helping their mentees succeed in school.

## DISCUSSION

### Outcome Measures

In general, the results of this study provided support for our hypotheses regarding the efficacy of the Across Ages program. For students exposed to both mentoring and the PYDC, the benefits of the program took the form of significantly more pro-social attitudes towards school, elders, and their own future as well as improved attitudes about older adults, more healthful reactions to situations involving drug use, more positive attitudes about community service, and a marginally-improved sense of well-being.

We found some evidence to suggest that students in the Mentoring group gained additional, if modest, benefits from their experience with mentoring over and above that which was afforded by the Program alone. This evidence, in the form of improved attitudes about school, future, and elders, and a significant reduction in absenteeism, illustrates the potential of the Mentoring component as a means of improving the lives of "at risk" youth.

One unanticipated finding was the effect of the intervention on self-reported rates of substance abuse. The Program group reported a small but statistically significant increase in drug use. Given that we hypothesized that the program in general, and mentoring in particular, would help reduce substance abuse, this finding, obviously, is of concern. Why did the reported rate of substance abuse not go down for students who had had the benefit of the mentoring? And why should the Program, which appears to be beneficial to participants in so many other respects, cause this slight increase in reported drug use?

We speculate that the small increase in self-reported drug-use among students in the Program group may be an artifact of our research methodology. We believe that this finding may be a reflection of students' relative honesty in reporting drug use. Students in the Program group were given ample opportunities to talk about substance abuse with program staff as part of the PYDC, and we believe that students in this group may have assumed through their participation in the program that they could reveal information about their drug consumption without adverse consequences. This experience may have encouraged students in the Program group to be more honest when responding to questions about drug use in the posttest.

Students in the Mentoring group also had the benefit of these "rehearsals." That is, students in the Mentoring group received the same programmatic intervention as students in the Program group, along with the added benefit of mentoring. However, their rates of drug use were comparable with those of non-participants. This suggests that students who received mentoring may have decreased their drug usage and, in addition, displayed the "honesty effect" manifested by students who received all of the non-mentoring program components. Of course, this explanation is merely speculative. Until research is conducted that examines the impact of mentoring independent of all other program components, the true effects will remain elusive.

Other evidence suggests that differences between groups may have been even more in line with our original hypotheses had the mentoring component of the program been intensified. Analyses concerning level of mentoring provide some insight into the potential of mentoring as a drug-prevention strategy. Results indicated that students who received "exceptional" mentoring attended school more frequently than students in the Program and the Control groups. In addition, students who received "exceptional" mentoring demonstrated more pro-social attitudes, better reactions to situations involving drug use, and more knowledge about substance abuse. Our general recommendation, therefore, is that the mentoring component be intensified so that all students receive "exceptional" rather than "average" or "marginal" mentoring.

### Process Data

To be effective, mentors must dedicate time and attention to their mentees. Those students who spent at least 8 hours a week with their mentors, double the minimum of 4 hours required by the project, seemed to fare better than those who spent less time. As Styles and Morrow (1992) contended, the content of the relationship is also critical to the satisfaction and longevity of the relationship. The mentor's ability to listen, to plan collaboratively, and to respect the mentee seemed to have an impact on the success of the relationship. Developing a sustained, trusting relationship takes time, and mentors who were able to make that commitment seemed to have benefited as much as the youth.

Retaining and supporting strong, active mentors takes time and attention on the part of program staff. Adequate training, regular in-service meetings, telephone contact with staff and access to resources for the mentees all contribute to maintaining a pool of mentors who are competent, confident and dedicated. Across Ages is ambitious in its aims and its scope, serving almost 200 students each project year, but only half receive mentors.

One of the risks involved in a program that relies on older volunteers is the possibility that mentors or their family members will become ill and they may be unable to fulfill their obligation to their mentee. Some Across Ages mentors have had to drop out for a period of time, usually because of the poor health of a spouse. Our results suggested, however, that despite these occasional setbacks, intergenerational mentoring is an intervention worthy of replication and further study.

### Implications for Program Administrators

To be effective, prevention efforts must unite youth and adults in developing positive coping strategies for resisting alcohol, tobacco, and other drugs and for dealing with the other stressors which may make students more susceptible to failure. Our findings suggest that older mentors can play a vital role in helping "at-risk" youth to stay in school and, ultimately, to become responsible adults. In the process, older adults may find the means for serving their communities and for increasing their feelings of self-worth.

Given that the program has not been replicated with populations markedly different from those involved in the our study, we are unable to make unqualified claims regarding the generalizability of these findings. However, longitudinal follow-up studies of other similar drug-abuse prevention programs in a variety of populations have confirmed the apparent efficacy of this general approach. For example, Botvin, Baker, Dusenbury, Botvin, and Diaz (1995) demonstrated long-term positive gains from school-based life skills curricula among populations ranging from suburban, white, and middle-class to urban, minority groups.

The results of our evaluation indicated clearly that Across Ages, and mentoring in particular, had a significant positive impact on many of the children. Through their involvement in the program, many of the children acquired more positive attitudes about their schools and their futures. In general, these children gained a greater understanding of older adults and more pro-social attitudes about the aged. As well, they learned new skills that may help them to react in safer, more healthful ways to situations involving drug use, and their sense of well-being was somewhat improved. School attendance also increased significantly.

The impact of Across Ages goes beyond the children, however. The project also helped an extraordinary group of older volunteers to feel more productive, to experience a greater sense of purpose, and to become more connected to their community. The schools involved in the project may have become more nurturing places, and the teachers seem more enthusiastic. Across Ages' intergenerational approach has mobilized human resources that are often neglected, and surely, this strengthens the ties between generations.

# REFERENCES

Botvin, G. S., Baker, E., Dusenbury, L., Botvin, E. M., & Diaz, T. (1995). Long-term follow-up results of a randomized drug abuse prevention trial in a white middle-class population. *Journal of the American Medical Association, 273*(14), 1106-1112.

Campbell, D. T. & Stanley, J. C. (1966). *Experimental and quasi-experimental design for research.* Chicago: Rand-McNally.

Caplan, M., Jacoby, C., Weissberg, R. P., & Grady, K. (1988). *The positive youth development program: A substance use prevention program for young adolescents.* New Haven, CT: Yale University.

Caplan, M., Weissberg, R. P., Bersoff, D. M., Ezekowitz, W., & Wells, M. L. (1986). *The middle school Alternative Solutions Test (AST): Scoring manual.* New Haven, CT: Yale University.

Caplan, M., Weissberg, R. P., Grober, J. S., & Sivo, P. J. (1992). Social competence promotion with inner-city and suburban young adolescents: Effects on social adjustment and alcohol use. *Journal of Consulting and Clinical Psychology, 60,* 56-63.

Coie, J. D., Watt, N. F., West, S. G., Hawkins, J. D., Asarnow, J. R., Markman, H. J., Ramey, S. L., Shure, M. B., & Long, B. (1993). The science of prevention: A conceptual framework and some directions for a national research program. *American Psychologist, 48,* 1013-1022.

Conrad, C. & Hedin, D. (1990). Rationale: Selling the youth service program. In. J. C. Kendall (Ed.), *Combining Service and Learning. A Resource Book for Community and Public Service.* Raleigh, NC.

Conrad, C. & Hedin, D., (1982). *Experiential Education Evaluation Project.* St. Paul, MN: Center for Youth Development, University of Minnesota.

Flaxman, E., Ascher, C., & Harrington, C. (1988). *Mentoring programs and practices: An analysis of the literature.* New York: Teachers College, Columbia University, Institute for Urban and Minority Education.

Freedman, M. (1988). *Partners in growth: Elder mentors and at-risk youth.* Philadelphia, PA: Public/Private Ventures.

*Governor's Plan for a Drug-Free Pennsylvania.* (1989). Harrisburg, PA: PA Department of Health.

Harter, S. (1985). *Manual for the self-perception profile for children.* Denver, CO: University of Denver Press.

Hawkins, J. D. (1988). *Risk and protective factors for adolescent substance abuse: Implications for prevention.* Seattle, WA: University of Washington.

Hawkins, J. D., Lishner, D. M., Jenson, J. M., & Catalano, R. J. (1987). Delinquents and drugs: What the evidence suggests about prevention. In B. S. Brown and A. R. Mills (Eds.), *Youth at risk in substance abuse.* DHHS Pub. No. (ADM) 83-1537. Washington, DC: U.S. Government Printing Office.

Henkin, N., Rogers, A., & Lyons, M. (1992). *Linking lifetimes: A national mentoring initiative summary report.* Philadelphia, PA; Center for Intergenerational Learning, Temple University.

Jessor, R. (1993) Successful adolescent development among youth in high-risk settings. *American Psychologist, 48,* 117-126.

Kandel, D. B. (1982). Epidemiological and psychosocial perspectives on adolescent drug use. *Journal of American Academic Clinical Psychiatry, 21*(4), 328-347.

King, J. A., Morris, L. L., & Fitz-Gibbon, C. T. (1987). *How to assess program implementation.* Newbury Park, CA: Sage.

Kumpfter, K. L. (1987). Etiology and prevention of vulnerability to chemical dependency in children of substance abusers. In B. S. Brown & A. R. Mills (Eds.), *Youth at high risk for substance abuse.* National Institute on Drug Abuse, DHHS Pub.

No. (ADM) 87-1537 (pp. 117-151). Washington, DC: U. S. Government Printing Office.

Kumpfter, K., & DeMarsh, J. (1985). Genetic and family environmental influences on children of substance abusers. *Journal of Children in Contemporary Society, 3*(4), 117-151.

Lewis, A. C. (1988). Facts and faith: A status report on youth service. In *Youth and America's future* (series). Washington, DC : The William T. Grant Foundation Commission on Work, Family, and Citizenship.

LoSciuto, L., Rajala, A., Townsend, T., & Taylor, A. (1996). An outcome evaluation of Across Ages: An intergenerational mentoring approach to drug prevention. *Journal of Adolescent Research,* 116-129.

Newman, S., Vasudev, J. B., & Onawola, R. (1985). Older volunteers' perceptions of impacts of volunteering on their psychological well-being. *Journal of Applied Gerontology, 4*(2), 123-127.

Palmore, E. (1977). Facts on aging: A short quiz. *The Gerontologist, 17,* 315-320.

Rosenthal, R., & Rosnow, R. (1991). *Essentials of behavioral research: Methods and data analysis.* New York: McGraw Hill.

Scheirer, M. A. (1987). Program theory and implementation theory: Implications for evaluators. In L. Bickman (Ed.), *Using program theory in evaluation. New Directions* (pp. 495-501). San Francisco: Jossey-Bass.

Styles, M., & Morrow, C. (1992). *Understanding how youth and elders form relationships: A study of four Linking Lifetimes programs.* Philadelphia, PA: Public/Private Ventures.

Tierney, J. T., Grossman, J. B., & Resch, N. (1995). *Making a difference: An impact study.* Philadelphia, PA: Public/Private Ventures.

U. S. Bureau of the Census. (1992). *Projections of the Populations of the United States by age, race and sex. 1983-2080.* Current Population Report Series P-25. May. Washington, DC: G. Spencer.

Veit, C. T., & Ware, J. E. (1983). The structure of psychological distress and general well-being in the general population. *Journal of Consulting and Clinical Psychology, 51,* 730-742.

Weissberg, R. P., Caplan, M., & Bennetto, L. (1988). *The Yale-New Haven social problem-solving program for young adolescents.* New Haven, CT: Yale University.

Weissberg, R. P., Caplan, M., & Sivo, P. J. (1987). A new conceptual framework for establishing school-based social competence promotion programs. In L. A. Bond & B. E. Compas (Eds.), *Primary prevention and promotion in the schools* (pp. 52-64). Newbury Park, CA: Sage.

# Predictors of the Likelihood to Provide Intergenerational Activities in Child and Adult Day Care Centers

Shirley S. Travis
Andrew J. Stremmel

**SUMMARY.** This study examined the relative contribution of various factors to the likely provision of intergenerational activities in child and adult day care settings. Two hundred and twenty-six administrators rated their: (a) current frequency of contact with children and older adults; (b) current frequency of intergenerational activities in their settings; (c) attitudes toward intergenerational exchanges, using the Intergenerational Exchanges Attitudes Scale; and (d) self-reported likelihood to provide intergenerational activities in the future. As was predicted, attitudes toward intergenerational exchanges accounted for significantly more ($p < .0001$) of the overall variance in likelihood scores (12.8%) than did either current intergenerational program activity (3.7%) or current intergenerational contact (2.0%). *[Article copies available for a fee from The Haworth Document Delivery Service: 1-800-342-9678. E-mail address: getinfo@haworthpressinc.com <Website: http://www.haworthpressinc.com>]*

---

Shirley S. Travis is affiliated with the University of Oklahoma College of Nursing, P. O. Box 26901, Oklahoma City, OK 73190. Andrew J. Stremmel is affiliated with the Department of Family and Child Development, Virginia Polytechnic Institute and State University, Blacksburg, VA 24061-0416.

The authors wish to thank Dr. Patti Kelly-Harrison for her management of the project data.

This research was supported by a grant from the College of Human Resources, Virginia Polytechnic Institute and State University, Blacksburg, VA.

[Haworth co-indexing entry note]: "Predictors of the Likelihood to Provide Intergenerational Activities in Child and Adult Day Care Centers." Travis, Shirley S. and Andrew J. Stremmel. Co-published simultaneously in *Child & Youth Services* (The Haworth Press, Inc.) Vol. 20, No. 1/2, 1999, pp. 101-114; and: *Intergenerational Programs: Understanding What We Have Created* (ed: Valerie S. Kuehne) The Haworth Press, Inc., 1999, pp. 101-114. Single or multiple copies of this article are available for a fee from The Haworth Document Delivery Service [1-800-342-9678, 9:00 a.m. - 5:00 p.m. (EST). E-mail address: getinfo@haworth pressinc.com].

**KEYWORDS.** Adult day care, child care, intergenerational research programs, administration

Bringing young children and frail or impaired elders together in nursing home settings has been popular for a number of years, possibly because these exchanges are seen as an opportunity for developing mutual respect, sharing knowledge, and developing meaningful relationships between the generations (Newman, 1989; Paul, 1988; Reville, 1989; Ventura-Merkel, Liederman, & Ossofsky, 1989; Ziemba, Roop, & Wittenberg, 1988). More recently, community-based, long-term care options, such as adult day-services, have been available as alternative settings for intergenerational programming (Travis, Stremmel, & Duprey, 1993). Yet despite a growing knowledge-base about the potential benefits of intergenerational programs, many adult and child care centers have not yet implemented any intergenerational programming (Stremmel, Travis, Kelly-Harrison, & Hensley, 1994).

To our knowledge, there is no existing conceptual model for understanding the programming intentions of center administrators, who play key decision-making roles regarding the kinds of activities that are offered in their day care settings. The present study employed Fishbein's behavioral intention model (Fishbein, 1967; Fishbein & Ajzen, 1975) to examine the factors related to the self-reported likelihood that child and adult day care administrators would provide intergenerational activities. The data were collected from a large statewide survey of child and adult day care administrators in Virginia. The present study was an extension of previous work by the authors that focused on the characteristics of child and adult day-care professionals (Travis et al., 1993). The previous study also described (a) the perceived benefits and consequences of intergenerational programming in day care settings for administrators (Stremmel et al., 1994), (b) the development of an instrument for measuring attitudes toward intergenerational exchanges (Stremmel, Travis, & Kelly-Harrison, 1996), (c) the general characteristics of current intergenerational programming in day care settings (Travis, Stremmel, & Kelly-Harrison, 1996), and (d) some of the factors that may affect administrators' attitudes toward intergenerational exchanges (Travis, Stremmel, & Kelly-Harrison, 1997).

## PRELIMINARY STUDIES
## AND REVIEW OF RELEVANT LITERATURE

From a review of the relevant literature and our own earlier work, four sets of variables were identified as being conceptually and logically associated with the self-reported likelihood of providing intergenerational opportunities: (a) background characteristics (age, education, gender), (b) contact variables (i.e., frequency of meaningful contact with children and with elders, (c) current exposure to intergenerational programming, and (d) attitudes toward intergenerational exchanges.

Prior to the present study, there were no instruments for measuring attitudes toward intergenerational exchanges. We developed the Intergenerational Exchanges Attitude Scale (IEAS) (Stremmel et al., 1996) for use with child and adult day care administrators. Although previous research had looked at generalized attitudes toward older adults and children, we felt that it was important to look at more specific attitudes toward intergenerational exchanges. We believe that the IEAS provides the conceptual and logical link between such attitudes and behavioral intentions. That is, if administrators are going to make the decision to offer intergenerational programming, they first have to believe that the interactions between young children and older adults in day care will be mutually beneficial, nurturing, challenging, and important for human development of the young and old intergenerational partners. The IEAS was designed to measure those attitudes. All subsequent references to measurement of attitudes toward intergenerational exchanges are based on this work.

We were also interested in the potential factors involved in child and adult day care administrators' attitudes toward intergenerational exchanges. We began by searching the attitudinal research in the gerontology and child development literature (e.g., Allen, Allen, & Weekly, 1986; Jantz, Seefeldt, Galper, & Serock, 1997; Kogan, 1961; Mitchell, Wilson, Revicki, & Parker, 1985; Sanders, Montgomery, Pittman, & Balkwell, 1984; Seefeldt, Jantz, Serock, & Bredekamp, 1982; Thomas & Yamamoto, 1975) because no other literature was available that described attitudes toward a specific kind of event such as intergenerational exchanges. The "contact hypothesis" literature examines how meaningful contact among individuals may affect prejudicial attitudes (Amir, 1969; Caspi, 1984; Seefeldt, 1987). In a previous study, we had found that positive intergenerational attitudes were affected by more frequent contact with existing intergenerational programming while meaningful contact with either children or with elders did not have any significant effect on administrators' intergenerational attitudes (Travis et al., 1997). Our findings seemed inconsistent with elder attitudinal research (see reviews by Dooley & Frankel, 1990; Green, 1981; Harris & Fiedler, 1988; Lutsky, 1980), which suggests that advanced age and more education may have positive effects on attitudes toward intergenerational exchanges. In our work, we had found that level of education had no significant effect on respondents' attitudes toward intergenerational exchanges and that younger rather than older day care administrators had more positive attitudes.

From what we had learned about the effect of background and contact variables on attitudes toward intergenerational exchanges, our next step was to explore potential antecedents of child and adult day care administrators' likelihood of providing intergenerational activities in their centers. For this, we employed Fishbein's behavioral intention model (Fishbein, 1967; Fishbein & Ajzen, 1975). According to Fishbein's model, actual behavior is a function of the intention to perform that behavior, which, in turn, is a function of attitudes. Fishbein and Ajzen (1975) proposed that the magnitude of the relationship between intention and behavior depends on the level of specificity of the attitude-behavior link, as well as the degree to which the intention is under the person's control. Therefore administrators, who tend to have control over programming decisions, should be more likely to provide intergenerational activities if they have strong positive attitudes toward the idea of exchanges. Positive attitudes may, in turn, be influenced by personal background characteristics, meaningful contact with the target groups, and current exposure to the desired behaviors.

The logical and empirical connections among the above variables led to a testable regression model. Using a regression model based on Fishbein's notion of behavioral intentions, we estimated the proportion of variance in self-report ratings of the likelihood to provide intergenerational activities that is accounted for by the personal variables, meaningful contact with elders and children, current exposure to intergenerational exchanges, and attitudes toward intergenerational exchanges. It was hypothesized that attitudes toward intergenerational exchanges would account for a greater proportion of variance in the likelihood of providing intergenerational activities than would exposure to intergenerational activities, meaningful contact with children and older adults, and personal variables (i.e., age and education).

## METHOD

### Participants

A comprehensive description of the personal characteristics of the sample has been previously reported (Stremmel et al., 1994). In brief, all respondents were child and adult day care administrators, overseeing agencies that provided care services to their respective clients. The majority of the respondents were female (90%) and white (83%). Child care administrators ranged in age from 20-74 years with an average age of 41 years. They had held their current administrative positions for periods ranging from 2 months to 42 years, with an average tenure of approximately 6 years. In contrast, adult day care administrators were between the ages of 28 and 65 years, with an average of 44 years. These administrators had been in their positions for periods ranging from 3 months to 18 years, averaging about 4.5 years. Approximately 77% of the child care providers and 85% of the adult care providers had at least a 2-year college degree. Twenty-five percent of the child care administrators and almost 30% of the adult care administrators had graduate degrees. The respondents ranged in age from 20 to 74 years, with a mean age of approximately 42 years. Because the administrators from both kinds of centers were comparable on most of the demographic variables, and because of the relatively small sample size of the adult day care administrators, the two groups were collapsed into one for analysis. That there were considerably fewer adult day care center administrators than child care center administrators seems to reflect the newness of adult day care in the state of Virginia.

### Procedure

The data analyzed in the present study were part of a comprehensive survey used to learn more about intergenerational exchanges in day care settings across the state. A total of 336 day care center administrators in Virginia were asked to participate in the study (36 licensed adult day care centers and 300 licensed child care centers). They were selected by way of a stratified random sampling procedure, using guidelines established by Krejcie and Morgan (1970), and stratified by Virginia Department of Social Services' Licensing Regions.

The sampling frame consisted of all child care centers licensed in Virginia at the time of the study (*N*–approximately 1,100). Because few adult day care centers exist in the State relative to the number of child care centers, all adult day services administrators were included in the survey. A multistep mail-survey design by Dillman (1978) was used to enhance response rates. The initial survey was followed up in 6 weeks by two reminder letters at 2-week intervals, and a repeat mailing of the survey instrument to nonrespondents. These procedures resulted in approximately 67% of all administrators (*N* = 226) returning usable questionnaires. Respondents included 94% of the adult day care administrators surveyed and 64% of the child care administrators.

## Materials

*Background (age and education) variables.* As already reported, the average age of respondents was 41 years (child care) and 42 years (adult care). Because 90% of the respondents were female, gender was not included in the data analysis. Response categories for education ranged from less than a high school degree to a graduate degree (1 = some high school, 2 = high school degree, 3 = technical/vocational school, 4 = some college, 5 = 2 year college degree, 6 = 4 year college degree, 7 = some graduate education, 8 = graduate degree).

*Meaningful (child and elder) contact variables.* Respondents were asked how often they had "meaningful contact" (a) with older adults 65 years of age and older, and (b) with a young child under the age of 6, excluding any older adults or young children who lived with them. Therefore, individuals with whom the respondent had meaningful contact might include the respondent's own clients as well as friends, family members, and neighbors. Response categories for both items ranged from "rare meaningful contact" to "daily meaningful contact" (8 = daily, 4 = monthly, 1 = rarely).

*Current exposure to intergenerational exchanges.* Attitudes were measured using the Intergenerational Exchanges Attitudes Scale (IEAS) (Stremmel et al., 1996). The IEAS consists of 24 items with 7 response categories and 5 subscales. When it was first developed, the IEAS was found to have an overall internal consistency reliability of .89. As a measure of predictive validity of the IEAS, we reported a significant, positive relationship between scores of the IEAS and administrators' self-reported likelihood of providing intergenerational programming (*r* = .36, *p* < .01). In addition, each of the IEAS subscales was also positively ($p < .01$) associated with the likelihood construct, as follows: (a) Relationship Between Older Adults and Children, $r = .33$; (b) Children's Perceptions of Older Adults, $r = .25$; (c) Attributes of Children, $r = .31$; (d) Attributes of Older Adults, $r = .25$; and (e) Power-Control, $r = .29$. The 7 response categories for scale items range from strongly agree to strongly disagree. Internal consistencies (coefficient alpha) for each subscale were generally above the .70 minimum suggested by Nunnally (1978), and ranged from .60 (Power/Control) to .86 (Relationships Between Older Children and Older Adults).

The IEAS is scored such that higher scores represent more positive attitudes toward intergenerational exchanges. The total IEAS score ranges theoretically from 24 to 168. Missing data on individual items were assigned the scale midpoint value of 4 (neutral).

*Likelihood of providing intergenerational programming.* The outcome variable was measured by a single question that asked respondents how likely they would be to incorporate intergenerational activities in their day programs if they were provided with adequate resources. The response scale ranged from 1 to 10 (where 1 = not very likely to 10 = very likely).

## RESULTS

Group means were substituted for missing values in all analyses. As shown in Table 1, the reported frequency of meaningful contact with young children was much higher than the reported frequency of meaningful contact with elders. This difference may be due to the larger number of child care centers in the sample relative to adult care centers. Also it seems likely that the child care centers do not facilitate very much meaningful contact with older adults for staff or children in their care. Across both categories, the frequency of current exposure to intergenerational exchanges in the centers tended often to be "rarely" or "very infrequently." Approximately half of all administrators reported "rare" planned intergenerational activities. Intercorrelations among the predictor variables and the likelihood of providing intergenerational programs are shown in Table 2.

Hierarchical regression was used to assess the contributions of meaningful contact, current intergenerational exposure, and attitudes toward intergenerational exchanges to the prediction of the self-re-

TABLE 1. Means, Standard Deviations, and Range of Scores for Background Variables, Contact Variables, Current Intergenerational Exposure, Attitudes and Likelihood of Providing Intergenerational Activities

| Variable | M | SD | Range | N |
|---|---|---|---|---|
| Background Variables | | | | |
|    Age | 41.68 | 10.72 | 20-74 | 222 |
|    Education | 6.11 | 1.56 | 2-8 | 222 |
| Contact Variables | | | | |
|    Elder Contact | 5.65 | 2.09 | 1-8 | 218 |
|    Child Contact | 7.55 | 1.16 | 1-8 | 224 |
| Current Exposure | 1.27 | 1.38 | 0-5 | 211 |
| Attitudes Toward Intergenerational Exchanges | 121.56 | 14.37 | 79-168 | 226 |
| Likelihood of Providing Intergenerational Activities | 6.71 | 3.06 | 1-10 | 225 |

ported likelihood of providing intergenerational activities in day care settings. The background variables (education followed by age) were entered first as control variables, followed in separate succeeding steps by the contact variables (elder contact followed by child contact) (step 2), current intergenerational exposure (step 3), and attitude toward intergenerational exchanges (step 4). The order of entry for the variables was based on the assumption that if attitudes toward intergenerational exchanges were linked directly to the self-reported likelihood of providing intergenerational activities, attitudes would account for a significant proportion of variance in likelihood beyond that of exposure and meaningful contact. Significant increments in the squared multiple correlation ($R^2$) indicate the independent contribution of specific predictor variables to prediction of scores on the likelihood variable.

Table 3 displays the unstandardized regression coefficients ($B$), standardized regression coefficients ($\beta$), change-$R^2$ for each step of the analysis, model $R^2$, Adjusted $R^2$, and R. After step 4, with all the predictor variables in the equation, $R = .50$, $F(6,219) = 12.33$, $p < .0001$. As indicated by the change in $R^2$ after each step, 6.8% of the variability in likelihood to provide intergenerational activities was predicted by the background variables. Meaningful contact contrib-

TABLE 2. Intercorrelations Among Predictor Variables and Likelihood of Providing Intergenerational Opportunities

| Variable | Age | Education | Elder Contact | Child Contact | Current Exposure | Attitudes | Likelihood |
|---|---|---|---|---|---|---|---|
| Age | | | | | | | |
| Education | .116* | | | | | | |
| Elder Contact | .173** | .0.85 | | | | | |
| Child Contact | −.159** | −.122* | −.081 | | | | |
| Current Exposure | −.025 | .031 | .185** | −.109* | | | |
| Attitudes Toward Intergenerational Exchanges | −.137* | .093 | .047 | .006 | .197*** | | |
| Likelihood of Providing Intergenerational Activities | −.135* | .206*** | .127* | −.031 | .226*** | .432*** | |

$*p < .05$; $** p < .01$; $***p < .001$

TABLE 3. Summary of Hierarchical Regression Analysis for Variables Predicting Likelihood of Providing Intergenerational Activities (N = 226)

| Step | Variables | B | SE B | β |
|---|---|---|---|---|
| 1 | Education | .445 | .129 | .225*** |
| | Age | −.046 | .019 | −.160** |
| 2 | Elder Contact | .206 | .097 | .139* |
| | Child Contact | −.062 | .173 | −.024 |
| 3 | Current Exposure | .449 | .148 | .196** |
| 4 | Attitude Score | .079 | .013 | .371*** |

Note: $R^2 = .068$ for Step 1; Change $R^2 = .020$ for Step 2; Change $R^2 = .037$ for Step 3; Change $R^2 = .128$ for Step 4.
$R^2 = .253$; Adjusted $R^2 = .232$; R Multiple = .503
$F(6,219) = 12.33, p < .0001$
$*p < .05$; $**p < .01$; $***p < .001$

uted another 2%, current exposure to intergenerational exchanges another 3.7%, and attitude toward intergenerational exchanges another 12.8% of variability in likelihood scores. Altogether, 25.3% (23.2% adjusted) of the variability in the reported likelihood of providing intergenerational activities was predicted by knowing scores on these 6 variables.

## DISCUSSION

The present study examined the relative contribution of specific demographic and perceptual variables to predicting the self-ratings of the likelihood of providing intergenerational programming by adult and day care center administrators. As hypothesized, administrators' attitudes toward intergenerational exchanges were found to be the most significant contributor to the likelihood outcome variable, as compared to the other predictor variables used in the regression equation. As there is some evidence that attitudes are an important predictor of intentions, it seems reasonable to expect that administrators must feel positive about the concept of intergenerational exchanges before they are likely to implement intergenerational programs in their care settings.

The results showed also that a younger chronological age, increased levels of education, greater current exposure to intergenerational exchanges, and more exposure to meaningful contact with elders each contributed significantly to the prediction of self-reported likelihood of intergenerational exchanges. When the contributions of these variables are considered as a whole, they accounted for as much of the explained variance in the likelihood variable as did the attitude variable when it was entered last in the equation. For those who would like to see more intergenerational programming in child and adult day care centers, these findings suggest that tackling administrators' attitudes toward intergenerational exchanges may be an important first step. Because it may be easier to influence attitudes *before* rather than *after* they are formed, it may be best to intervene during the training of child and adult day care administrators.

At the present time, little is known about factors that predict child and adult day care administrators' attitudes toward intergenerational exchanges. In a previous study, we found that increased exposure to children and elders who are participating in successful intergenerational programs influence administrators' attitudes in a positive direction (Travis et al., 1997). Therefore, coordinators planning a gerontology and child development program aimed at promoting positive attitudes toward intergenerational exchanges should carefully select practicum experiences for students. Where few existing programs are available, educators may need to develop their own intergenerational programs, either in partnership with child and adult day care centers in nearby communities or in their own child development lab-schools and adult day care centers. A handful of programmers have implemented contemporary models of intergenerational day care.

Though it may be more difficult to facilitate attitudinal change among older and more experienced providers as compared to those younger, it may be worth trying to correct any of their misconceptions about the effects of bringing young children and older adults in adult care together for intergenerational exchanges (Stremmel et al., 1994). Specific misconceptions, such as questions about infection control and safety can be changed through educational interventions. Such interventions also may be designed to provide the knowledge and skills necessary to develop successful intergenerational programs. Professional organizations that support intergenerational models of care seem to be effective vehicles for providing intergenerational education experience to their members.

Although the results of the present study showed that meaningful contact with elders and current exposure to intergenerational exchanges were important factors in predicting administrators' reported likelihood of providing intergenerational programming, their relative contributions were fairly small. Further, both of these findings may be limited in their generalizability. With respect to the contact variable, respondents were not asked about negative contact with children and elders. It seems possible that a high frequency (or high intensity) of negative contact may moderate or override the effects of meaningful (positive) contact on an administrator's decision to provide intergenerational programming. A measure that assesses both positive and negative contact with children and with elders would be more balanced and could provide a more complete picture of the relationship between contact and reported likelihood of providing intergenerational programming.

With respect to the question about current intergenerational exchanges in their care setting, respondents were not asked about naturally-occurring exchanges that might occur between foster grandparents, senior volunteers, or other aged individuals (center cooks or housekeepers) and the children in the care setting. It may be worth examining the potential effects of these subtle and often invisible points of contact on administrators' attitudes and their likelihood of providing intergenerational activities.

The current high level of geographic mobility of American families often serves to separate the generations and reduce the opportunities for important and meaningful intergenerational exchanges. If, as many believe, bringing the young and the old together is important to a society for the transfer of history, knowledge, values, and beliefs, it seems to follow that professionals should be looking for ways and places to facilitate those exchanges. Assuming that the environmental ingredients (resources) are available and the facilitators (center administrators) are willing, child and adult day environments can be important settings for mutually beneficial intergenerational exchanges.

In conclusion, although there has been a steady increase in the literature about intergenerational programming, the vast majority of this information is anecdotal in nature. The purpose of the survey was to develop an empirical foundation for those involved in intergenerational program-planning and decision-making in child and adult day settings. The measures used, such as the Intergenerational Exchanges Attitudes Scale, need to be used in further studies to establish their validity. Despite the limitations of the present findings, it is hoped that they serve as a springboard for additional research on factors that may influence the provision of intergenerational activities in child and adult day care centers.

## REFERENCES

Allen, S.M., Allen, J.G., & Weekly, J. (1986). The impact of a practicum on aging and reminiscence on gifted students' attitudes toward the elderly. *Rooper Review, 9*, 90-94.

Amir, Y. (1969). Contact hypothesis in ethnic relations. *Psychological Bulletin, 71*, 319-342.

Caspi, A. (1984). Contact hypothesis and inter-age attitudes: A field study of cross-age contact. *Social Psychology Quarterly, 47*, 74-80.

Dillman, D. (1978). *Mail and telephone surveys.* New York: Wiley.

Dooley, S., & Frankel, B.G. (1990). Improving attitudes toward elderly people: Evaluation of an intervention program for adolescents. *Canadian Journal of Aging, 9*, 400-409.

Fishbein, M. (1967). Attitude and the prediction of behavior. In M. Fishbein (Ed.), *Readings in attitude theory and measurement* (pp. 477-492). New York: Wiley.

Fishbein, M., & Ajzen, I. (1975). *Belief, attitudes, intention, and behavior.* Reading, MA: Addison-Wesley.

Green, S.K. (1981). Attitudes and perceptions about the elderly: Current and future perspectives. *International Journal of Aging and Human Development, 13,* 99-119.

Harris, J., & Fiedler, C.M. (1988). Preadolescent attitudes toward the elderly: An analysis of race, gender and contact variables. *Adolescence, 23,* 335-340.

Jantz, R.K., Seefeldt, C., Galper, A., & Serock, K. (1977). Children's attitudes toward the elderly. *Social Education, 41,* 518-523.

Kogan, N. (1961). Attitudes toward old people: The development of a scale and an examination of correlates. *Journal of Abnormal and Social Psychology, 62,* 44-54.

Krejcie, R.V., & Morgan, D.W. (1970). Determining sample size for research activities. *Educational and Psychological Measurement, 30,* 607-610.

Lutsky, N.S. (1980). Attitudes toward old age and elderly persons. In C. Eisdorfer (Ed.), *Annual review of gerontology and geriatrics* (pp. 287-336). New York: Springer.

Mitchell, J., Wilson, K., Revicki, D., & Parker, L. (1985). Children's perceptions of aging: A multidimensional approach to differences by age, sex, and race. *The Gerontologist, 25,* 182-187.

Newman, S. (1989). A history of intergenerational programs. In S. Newman and S. Brummel (Eds.), *Intergenerational programs: Imperatives, impacts, trends* (pp. 1-16). New York: The Haworth Press, Inc.

Nunnaly, J.C. (1978). *Psychometric Theory.* New York: McGraw-Hill.

Paul, G. (1988, January/February). Don't be afraid of children's projects. *Nursing Homes,* 33-34.

ReVille, S. (1989). Young adulthood to old age: Looking at intergenerational possibilities from a human development perspective. In S. Newman and S. Brummel (Eds.), *Intergenerational programs: Imperatives, impacts, trends* (pp. 173-180). New York: The Haworth Press, Inc.

Sanders, G.F., Montgomery, J.E., Pittman, J.F., & Balkwell, C. (1984). Youth's attitudes toward the elderly. *Journal of Applied Gerontology, 3,* 59-70.

Seefeldt, C. (1987). The effects of preschoolers' visits to a nursing home. *The Gerontologist, 27,* 228-232.

Seefeldt, C., Jantz, R.K., Serock, K., & Bredekamp, S. (1982). Elderly persons' attitudes toward children. *Educational Gerontology, 8,* 493-506.

Stremmel, A.J., Travis, S.S., & Kelly-Harrison, P. (1996). Development of the intergenerational exchanges attitude scale. *Educational Gerontology, 22,* 317-328.

Stremmel, A.J., Travis, S.S., Kelly-Harrison, P., & Hensley, A.D. (1994). The perceived benefits and problems associated with intergenerational exchanges in day care settings. *The Gerontologist, 34,* 513-519.

Thomas, E.C., & Yamamoto, K. (1975). Attitudes toward age: An exploration in school-age children. *International Journal of Aging and Human Development, 6,* 117-129.

Travis, S.S., Stremmel, A.J., & Duprey, P.A. (1993). Child and adult day care professions converging in the 1990s?: Implications for training and research. *Educational Gerontology, 19*, 283-293.

Travis, S.S., Stremmel, A.J., & Kelly-Harrison, P. (1996). Intergenerational programming for young children and dependent elders: Current status and future directions. *Activities, Adaptation, & Aging, 20*, 33-50.

Travis, S.S., Stremmel, A.J., & Kelly-Harrison, P. (1997). Attitudes toward intergenerational exchanges among administrators in child and adult day care centers. *Educational Gerontology, 23*, 775-787.

Ventura-Merkel, C., Liederman, D.S., & Ossofsky, J. (1989). Exemplary intergenerational programs. In S. Newman and S. Brummel (Eds.), *Intergenerational programs: Imperatives, impacts, trends* (pp. 173-180). New York: The Haworth Press, Inc.

Ziemba, J., Roop, K., & Wittenberg, S. (1988). A magic mix: After-school programs in a nursing home. *Children Today, 17*, 9-13.

# SECTION THREE:
# PROCESS-ORIENTED
# INTERGENERATIONAL PROGRAM
# RESEARCH

# Intergenerational Interactions:
# A Descriptive Analysis
# of Elder-Child Interactions
# in a Campus-Based Child Care Center

Heidi L. Angersbach
Stacy Jones-Forster

SUMMARY. The purpose of this study was to examine interactions between elder volunteers and children in a campus-based child care center, using the revised Interaction Analysis Instrument (Newman & Onawola, 1989). Findings from video-taped interactions suggested that intergenerational interactions may be systematically related to the nature of specific program activities. Thus it may be important for program coordinators to consider the kind of intergenerational interactions they want to facilitate when choosing among various intergenerational activities. Additional recommendations are offered to child-care and elder-care organizers who are interested in developing intergenerational programs. [Article copies available for a fee from The Haworth Document Delivery Service: 1-800-342-9678. E-mail address: getinfo@haworthpressinc.com <Website: http://www.haworthpressinc.com>]

KEYWORDS. Intergenerational research, interactions, observation, child care

---

Heidi L. Angersbach is affiliated with Nationwide Studios, Inc., Teddy Bear Portraits, 35-8 Balmoral Court, Freehold, NJ 07728. Stacy Jones-Forster is affiliated with the Woodbridge Township School District, Woodbridge, NJ.

[Haworth co-indexing entry note]: "Intergenerational Interactions; A Descriptive Analysis of Elder-Child Interactions in a Campus-Based Child Care Center." Angersbach, Heidi L. and Stacy Jones-Forster. Co-published simultaneously in *Child & Youth Services* (The Haworth Press, Inc.) Vol. 20, No. 1/2, 1999, pp. 117-128; and: *Intergenerational Programs: Understanding What We Have Created* (ed: Valerie S. Kuehne) The Haworth Press, Inc., 1999, pp. 117-128. Single or multiple copies of this article are available for a fee from The Haworth Document Delivery Service [1-800-342-9678, 9:00 a.m. - 5:00 p.m. (EST). E-mail address: getinfo@haworthpressinc.com].

The present investigation focused on interactions between young children and older adults. Few studies have focused exclusively on the nature of intergenerational interactions. In one of the few that did, Kuehne (1988) examined interactions among participants in adult and child day-care settings, and found that the interactions were generally positive. That is, 9 of the 11 categories of observed interactions were rated as being positive in nature. Kuehne concluded that intergenerational programs may be valuable experiences for participants because of the many positive aspects of these social situations.

In another study, Newman and Ward (1993) studied the interactions between young children and older adults with dementia. They observed that the adults consistently displayed many positive behaviors (extending hands, touching and holding hands) when the children were present which they did not tend to display when the children were not present.

The present study focused on videotaped interactions between young children and elders in a child-care center. On the basis of these taped observations, a frequency count of specific categories of behaviors was recorded on a revised form of the Elder/Child Interaction Analysis Instrument (Newman & Onawola, 1989).

## METHOD

### Participants

Three older adult volunteers (one male, aged 82 years and two females, aged 72 and 81 years) were chosen to participate in a 6 week, 12-session program. All of the volunteers were Caucasian and were thought to be of a middle-class socioeconomic status. Two of them were recruited through personal acquaintances and one through a local church. Prior to their participation in the study, the adult volunteers and the child-care staff participated in a general orientation session led by the researchers.

The 16 children (8 male and 8 female) who participated in the study were enrolled in a campus-based child-care center in Union, New Jersey. The children ranged in age from 4 years and 2 months to 5 years and 1 month and were of either African-American, Caucasian, Eastern Indian, European or Hispanic racial heritage. The income levels of the children's families were thought to range from low- to middle-income. The day care center is located on the main campus of Kean College and has an enrollment of approximately 60 children between the ages of 2 1/2 and 6 years.

## Materials

Several measures were used before, during and after the program. The Elder/Child Interaction Analysis (ECIA) instrument (Newman & Onawola, 1989) was used to record the observed elder-child verbal and non-verbal social interactions during each videotaped session (see Appendix A). The ECIA was created originally to record observations of third and fourth-grade children in an elementary school setting. Newman and Onawola created the behavioral categories and their definitions from interactions that seem to typically occur between adults and children in structured and unstructured situations. The ECIA was modified for use in the present study, which involved very young children in a child-care setting. Specific higher-level activity categories were deleted, such as those pertaining to writing and reading, and interaction categories that were thought to be more developmentally appropriate were added, such as hugging and lap-sitting. The instrument was also changed to accommodate observations of dyadic, small or large group interactions over indefinite periods of time, rather than solely 2 or 3 participants over a 30-second period.

Each volunteer completed a Volunteer Information Sheet at the time of their orientation and once weekly thereafter. The Volunteer Information Sheet consisted of three open-ended questions about what volunteers considered to be enjoyable or frustrating aspects of the program and about what they considered to be significant occurrences during their visits with the children. The authors and the head teacher completed a Daily Evaluation Form on which they described their impression of daily activities and interactions during program sessions.

## Procedures

Program activities during each 2 hour session were structured according to the philosophy of the Child Care Center and to the developmental levels of the children. Wherever possible, the specific interests and skills of the older adult volunteers were integrated into the activities. The adult volunteers were involved with a class of approximately 16 children during each of the 12 sessions.

Activities were either (a) teacher-selected and directed, (b) volunteer-selected and directed, or (c) child-selected or directed. Informal games were also initiated by children and volunteers throughout the program. All activities were recorded (see Appendix B) and classified as being either dyadic, small-group, or large-group. The classroom in which these activities took place contained materials for art, science, music, block-building, writing and reading.

An average of 44% (approximately 52 minutes) of each session was videotaped. Randomly selected videotaped portions were analyzed for the study and often included the "major" parts of the day (greetings, activity times, etc.). The entire length of footage selected (10 hours, 26 minutes) was analyzed and interactions were tallied using the ECIA.

Still-life photographs were also taken of participants' facial expressions and body language. Videotaping and photographing were thought to be generally unobtrusive. The children had been introduced gradually to the presence of a video camera in the classroom for a period of 2 weeks before the program began. The researchers videotaped the interactions from the perimeter of the room, utilizing the camera on a tripod or by hand.

## RESULTS

The ECIA was used to take frequency counts for specific categories of observed behaviors during each videotaped session. Overall, there was a substantial amount of engagement between the adults and children in given activities as well as a high number of positive interactions. The intergenerational program seemed to elicit many different patterns of interactions. Examining these various patterns allows for a greater understanding of the ways in which children and elderly persons may respond to and interact with each other. The observed patterns seemed to be systematically related to the type of activity, the size of the group involved, and the number of children and volunteers who were present.

The following analysis is based on an informal and descriptive examination of these frequency counts. Some parts may be understood best by referring to Appendix B, which includes a list of the activities that took place during each session.

### Teacher-Selected Activities

Activities that were teacher-selected and teacher-directed seemed to involve most of the children and all of the volunteers. Interactions were less frequent in teacher-chosen activities than during volunteer-chosen activities, possibly because the teacher was the main focus and because the activity took place within the context of a large group. Instances of initiating conversation, assistance, encouragement, smiles, and hugs seemed minimal during activities of this sort, for example, during the making of rain sticks and music painting (see Appendix B, session 6).

"Circle time" was a specific large-group activity that allowed for an increased number of interactions (i.e., "lap-sitting" and "looks at"). In 3 out of the 12 sessions, circle time was held to discuss available activities, plans and expectations, and it seemed to set the tone for the day. Both volunteers and children appeared to focus primarily on the appropriate activities and interactions unique to circle time. For example, instances of *lap sitting* occurred seven times in session nine during circle/storytime, but did not occur in session seven, when no large group activity took place. Opportunities for the *children to present things to the volunteers* (often eliciting smiles) also occurred more often during larger group times.

### Volunteer-Selected Activities

Some activities were chosen by a volunteer. The volunteers initiated activities such as wood-painting, cookie-baking, and bingo. When volunteers took the role of leader in the group, interactions such as *elder inviting child into the activity* and *elder answering questions* seemed to increase. These activities were often new to the children (i.e., sawing, quilt making), which may have contributed to the increased level of involvement. These activities elicited many directive commands from the volunteer, who was acting as a "teacher." One volunteer told stories to the class that held the children's interest and attention. They seemed to listen to and observe the volunteer more during this volunteer-selected activity than when activities were child-selected.

A hat-making activity was also volunteer-selected and directed. However, this activity may not have been developmentally appropriate for this age-group, as it required a certain mastery of fine motor skills that are typically found in older children. Perhaps not surprisingly, the majority of children appeared to lose interest during the course of this activity, and wandered from this to other activities. However, the children seemed to thoroughly enjoy the final products: They used the newspaper hats for intense dramatic play for many days. If the volunteer had not been "allowed" to make hats for the children, they would have missed the opportunity to see his talent and to use his work to become "kings of the castle" in the block corner. The volunteer seemed also to derive satisfaction from seeing his hats used so creatively.

Informal games such as "on-the-back-spelling," "sack-of-potatoes," tickling, and "catch your hand" were introduced by a volunteer and were requested often by the children thereafter. These games occurred during other activities and were most often one-on-one. They seemed to elicit nonverbal interactions such as laughing and touching. Relationship-building between the children and the volunteers seemed apparent from an observed increase in conversation and in smiling during and after these spontaneous games. The children frequently asked them to "do sack-of-potatoes" and after one round said, "Do it again!" The volunteers seemed especially pleased to honor the requests of the children throughout the program.

### Child-Selected Activities

Child-selected activities occurred at least once during each session. Manipulatives (puzzles and Lincoln Logs), art materials, and block building were child-initiated activities in which volunteers joined. These interactions were typically small-group or one-on-one interactions. Activities that likely stimulated cognitive activity and creative expression (e.g., counting blocks and creating block towers) seemed to increase the number of questions asked by both children and volunteers to a greater degree than did other types of activities. Recorded instances of looking, touching, encouraging, and initiating conversation occurred more frequently during these activities than during larger group activities.

## Interaction Analysis

As compared to every other category, unique patterns seemed to appear between the interaction categories of *hesitation* and *anger*. Relatively high frequencies of behaviors categorized as *hesitation* took place in the first three sessions on the part of both the children and the volunteers, as indicated by rigid body language (i.e., folded arms) and a lack of initiated conversations. We attributed this to the "newness" of the situation rather than to any other factor. Activities were planned according to the interests of the volunteers. Observed instances of *hesitation* decreased over time, and rose again only during a "messy" activity involving glue. The frequency of *hesitation* behaviors dropped and remained at zero after the third session. This could be interpreted as indicating an increase in the comfort levels of both the children and the volunteers.

Instances of *anger* occurred twice during the program. One incident involved a child who had been disagreeing with another child and who was angry and upset. He moved away from the child toward a small group of volunteers and children playing bingo. A volunteer invited the child into the game and he angrily replied, "No!" The volunteer looked away, and after a while the child decided to join the game. It appeared that the gentle manner of the volunteer dissipated the child's anger. The second instance of *anger* involved a volunteer and a child engaged with play dough. The child was teasing the volunteer by taking small pieces from the volunteer's lump of play dough. After a few minutes, the lump had become a creation of the volunteer's and the child again took a piece. The volunteer appeared angry, stating, "That's mine!" and grabbed it back from the child. Although the child appeared upset, the pair continued to engage in the activity as if nothing had happened.

Some activities seemed characterized by high levels of neutral interactions. For example, there was an especially high frequency of *looks at elder* when one of the volunteers first told a story to the class. High levels of *looks at child* and *looks at elder* were recorded also during bingo and piano-playing activities.

High frequencies of *observing elder* were recorded during the first session of woodworking activities. The activity was new to the children and there were certain things they needed to learn in order to be safe and fully utilize the materials. There were high frequencies of *children being observed* when the volunteers went outside on the playground with the children.

Recorded frequencies of *mutual touching* neither increased nor decreased over time. Although instances of *touching child* and *touching elder* increased during pretzel-making and during the good-bye party in the last session, these behaviors were maintained at a fairly steady level throughout the rest of the program.

The frequency of *presenting things to child* was especially high due to a volunteer handing out candy Valentine hearts to the children. The frequency of *presenting things to elder* was high in another session, when the children invited the volunteers to stay for lunch and name cards were given out during circle time.

Tallies of *encourages child* were notably higher when the volunteer first colored with the children, the first time that bingo was played, and the first time that hammering, drilling, and sawing were done at the woodworking table. Incidents of *children initiating conversation* occurred frequently the first time the volunteers went outside with the children. The children seemed excited to show the volunteers what they were able to do on the playground.

In every session, elders were observed assisting children more frequently than were children seen assisting elders. *Imitation of elders* occurred more often during times at the piano and while playing harmonicas than during any other activity.

Instances of *hugs and lap-sitting* occurred rather infrequently during the first half of the program. Although both of these behaviors increased during the session in which one volunteer returned from vacation, they typically occurred during circle/story time, arrival, and departure. One-on-one interaction peaked notably during the first woodworking time, but otherwise occurred rather regularly throughout the program.

## CONCLUSIONS AND RECOMMENDATIONS

It was our overall impression that specific intergenerational activities were associated with certain kinds of the intergenerational interactions that were observed. To the extent that this is true, it might be best to include a wide range of activities in an intergenerational program, including teacher-selected, volunteer-selected, and child-selected types. We speculate that minimizing, but not eliminating, teacher-selected activities will result in increased levels of positive interactions between children and older adult volunteers. It appeared to us that volunteer-selected activities resulted in particularly strong interest levels among all participants and apparent feelings of "ownership" of the program in the volunteers. Verbal communications such as questioning occurred more frequently during child-selected activities than did any other behavioral category. Although such behaviors may lessen teacher involvement, they seem to create strong bonds between the adult volunteers and the children, and create an atmosphere of light-hearted fun.

Perhaps our most interesting impression from this study was that although we did not use varying group sizes and activity types for the purpose of affecting interactions between participants, this is what we believe did, in fact, occur. It may be that by manipulating group size and/or activity, specific kinds of interactions can be minimized or maximized in various settings and with different populations. In addition, gathering information about the interests and abilities of the volunteers may help the program coordinator to choose activities that maximize participant involvement and enrich the interactions between children and older adults.

Sufficient time must be allowed for children and volunteers to become engaged together in activities. Approximately 45 minutes is reasonable for children 4-5 years old to become intensely engaged, but to not lose interest, according to The National Association for the Education of Young Children. Therefore, teachers must be flexible and be able to alter lesson plans if necessary. It is important to recognize personality differences among participants and to be aware of their apparent comfort levels during various activities. For example, a shy person should not be expected to initiate conversations or to exchange physical gestures any more frequently than what is considered "normal" simply because they are a participant in an intergenerational program. One of the volunteers in the present study was described as a passive observer, yet this individual became involved in activities when encouraged by the children. Researchers must be attuned to the balance of personality differences among prospective participants in order to elicit positive interactions.

We would recommend that the role of the volunteers be clearly defined before the program begins. In the program observed, negative situations might have occurred if, for example, the volunteers had taken the role of the teacher in disciplining children.

In our view, the ECIA provided a sufficient balance of verbal and nonverbal interactions that occur frequently between young children and elder volunteers. It seems important that the ECIA be modified for use with specific combinations of age groups, according to the type and developmental level of interactions that might be reasonably expected.

One of the limitations of the present study is that both the program activities and the range of observed behaviors were chosen by the researchers. Also the small number of older adult volunteers may limit the generalizability of our observations and conclusions. Finally, the informal examination of the data may limit the validity of our conclusions and recommendations.

## REFERENCES

Kuehne, V. (1988). "Younger friends/older friends": A study of intergenerational interactions. *Journal of Classroom Interaction, 24*(1), 14-21.

Newman, S., & Onawola, R. (1989). *The ECIA: Elder/Child Interaction Analysis.* Generations Together, University of Pittsburgh Center for Social and Urban Research, Pittsburgh, PA. Unpublished Manuscript.

Newman, S., & Ward, C. (1993). An observational study of intergenerational activities and behavior change in dementing elders at adult day care centers. *International Aging and Human Development, 36*(4), 253-265.

## APPENDIX A

### Definitions of Elder/Child Interaction Categories

Elder/Child Behavior:

*Smiles at child/elder:* Facial expressions characterized by an upward curving of the corners of the mouth indicating pleasure, favor, or approval.

*Looks at child/elder:* To direct one's attention toward someone using the sense of sight. A glance lasting a few seconds.

*Observes child/elder:* To notice, perceive, or pay special attention to someone, lasting longer than a glance.

*Touches child/elder:* To be or come into contact with, in a kind manner, through the use of hands (i.e., a pat on the shoulder).

*Presents thing to child/elder:* An offering of an object to someone (i.e., volunteer gives napkin to child).

*Hesitation:* The act of being reluctant toward or uncertain about an interaction, activity, or suggestion; displayed verbally or physically; may result in refusal or acceptance (i.e., child backs off when asked to dance).

*Encourages child/elder:* To instill a desire to continue an activity, conversation, or behavior (i.e., "you can do it . . . " or "and then . . . ").

*Expresses disinterest:* Callous or indifferent behavior toward someone expressed verbally or nonverbally; result is always negative (i.e., child says no to elder).

*Anger toward child/elder:* Indignant behavior toward someone; expressed verbally or nonverbally (i.e., volunteer says, "That's mine!" and grabs play dough from child).

*Leads activity:* To guide or direct an activity in any size group (i.e., volunteer reads to children).

*Invites child/elder into activity:* To request the presence or participation of someone verbally or nonverbally (i.e., child leads volunteer by hand to electronics table).

*Initiates conversation:* To start a discussion with someone by talking first (i.e., "Hey, Bill . . ." ).

*Asks question:* To use words in seeking an answer.

*Answers question:* To reply using words.

*Assists child/elder:* To offer help in achieving a desired goal (i.e., volunteer helps child write her name).

*Uses directive commands:* A straightforward demand verbalized by the volunteers to elicit or prevent a behavior of a child (i.e., "Put your goggles on.").

## APPENDIX A (continued)

*Imitates elder:* To follow the example of a volunteer with words or actions (i.e., the child retells a story told by volunteer).

Mutual Behaviors:

*Hugs:* To put arms around and hold closely.

*Lap sitting:* A child resting upon a volunteer when the volunteer is seated.

*Consoles:* To make a child feel less sad by comforting (i.e., volunteer using tissue to wipe a child's tears).

*One-on-one interaction:* Child and elder are involved apart from the group for more than a few minutes.

*Small group activity:* Interactions involving less than half of the children present in the class and one to three volunteers.

*Large group activity:* Interactions involving more than half of the children present in the class and 1 to 3 volunteers.

## APPENDIX B

### Activities Listed by Session #

| | | | |
|---|---|---|---|
| Session #1: | Cake baking<br>Electronics<br>Circle time/story<br>Dancing | Session #7: | Woodshop<br>Mask Making<br>Alphabet Bingo<br>Music |
| Session #2: | Coloring<br>Story<br>Piano/dancing<br>Electronics | Session #8: | Circle time<br>Quilt Making<br>Woodshop<br>Bingo<br>Outside |
| Session #3: | Collage pictures<br>Dancing<br>Storytime | Session #9: | Cookie Baking<br>Painting<br>Story<br>Coloring<br>Lunch |
| Session #4: | Hatmaking<br>Painting<br>Coloring/cutting<br>Circle time/story<br>Manipulatives | Session #10: | Electronics<br>Quilt Making<br>Playdough<br>Blocks |
| Session #5: | Woodworking<br>Music<br>Art<br>Story | Session #11: | Blocks<br>Bingo<br>Puzzles<br>Quilt Making |
| Session #6: | Music Painting<br>Rainsticks<br>Harmonicas<br>Bubbles | Session #12: | Pretzel Making<br>Popcorn Making<br>Art/gluing<br>Good-bye Party |

# Elder-Child Interaction Analysis:
## An Observation Instrument
## for Classrooms Involving Older Adults
## as Mentors, Tutors, or Resource Persons

Sally Newman
Gregory A. Morris
Heidi Streetman

**SUMMARY.** This study reports on the interactions of 60 children and 12 older adults in a school-based mentoring program, as well as four teachers' perceptions of the relationship between such interactions and the children's subsequent classroom behavior. Dyadic interactions were assessed using the Elder-Child Interaction Analysis instrument (Newman & Onawola, 1989). The authors concluded from recorded observations that, overall, the elders and the children had interacted with each other in a positive and constructive manner. The teachers interviewed perceived that the mentoring interactions were followed by an increase in students' self-management skills, interest in school work, and by improved peer relationships. *[Article copies available for a fee from The Haworth Document Delivery Service: 1-800-342-9678. E-mail address: getinfo@haworthpressinc.com <Website: http://www.haworthpressinc.com>]*

Sally Newman is affiliated with Generations Together, University of Pittsburgh Center for Social and Urban Research, 121 University Place, Suite 300, Pittsburgh, PA 15260. Gregory A. Morris is affiliated with the School of Education, University of Pittsburgh 4016 Forbes Quadrangle, Pittsburgh, PA 15260. Heidi Streetman was affiliated with Generations Together, University of Pittsburgh, at the time this paper was written.

[Haworth co-indexing entry note]: "Elder-Child Interaction Analysis: An Observation Instrument for Classrooms Involving Older Adults as Mentors, Tutors, or Resource Persons." Newman, sally, Gregory A. Morris, and Heidi Streetman. Co-published simultaneously in *Child & Youth Services* (The Haworth Press, Inc.) Vol. 20, No. 1/2, 1999, pp. 129-145; and: *Intergenerational Programs: Understanding What We Have Created* (ed: Valerie S. Kuehne) The Haworth Press, Inc., 1999, pp. 129-145. Single or multiple copies of this article are available for a fee from The Haworth Document Delivery Service [1-800-342-9678, 9:00 a.m. - 5:00 p.m. (EST). E-mail address: getinfo@haworthpressinc.com].

*129*

**KEYWORDS.** Intergenerational, research, interaction, observation, school

Throughout history, older adults have often assumed the roles of nurturer and teacher of their grandchildren. They brought to these roles many qualities that had been developed during their lifespan. Today, unfortunately, many older persons are deprived of the opportunity to pass on their wisdom, knowledge and skills because America is now what Kalish (1969) called an age-segregated society.

To help restore this interdependence among generations, intergenerational programs have been established in schools throughout the United States. During the last 20 years, many older adults have participated in school-based mentoring programs designed to support the growth and learning of children and youth. Informal assessments of the programs have shown a generally positive impact on both the participating youth and elders (e.g., Freedman, 1994). Both teachers and mentors have reported their perceptions of improvement in the attitudes, behaviors, and academic performance in students as well as positive changes in attitudes, productivity, and reported life-satisfaction in the mentors themselves. However, there have been no published studies of the nature of specific elder-child interactions in school settings or the relationships between these interactions and subsequent child behavior and academic performance. This study was an examination of these interactions and their perceived effect on children's behaviors.

## *WHAT IS MENTORING?*

In the context of social programs, mentoring is defined as a social intervention to address the needs of youth (Henkin, Perez-Randal, & Rogers, 1993). "Mentors teach, challenge, and support a young person while serving as a role model and companion" (Henkin et al., 1993, p. ii). In the context of this study, mentoring refers to the interaction between children in schools and elder volunteers who assist them, either in after-school tutoring programs or in regular classrooms under the guidance of and in concert with the classroom teachers.

## WHAT DOES MENTORING ACCOMPLISH? WHY ARE PEOPLE DOING IT?

Intergenerational mentoring has become a popular component of educational systems in many communities in the United States. At a time when the nuclear family seems threatened and elderly people are often isolated from mainstream society, an increasing number of older adults are assisting in schools as mentors. They may serve as positive role models for and supports of children's academic and social growth. School systems may benefit from intergenerational mentoring programs by an increase in human resources that is cost-effective and may help improve student performance. Individual school staff members may benefit professionally from supportive interactions with older adults. Lyons (1985) suggested that many "teachers are young people teaching still younger people" and thus "suffer age segregation. Older people may serve as additional resources to whom the teachers can turn, and offer personal perspectives that are based on years of personal experience" (p. 5).

## HOW DOES MENTORING AFFECT ELEMENTARY-AGED CHILDREN?

Research has shown that mentoring may offer a variety of benefits to the younger participants in an intergenerational program. For example, mentor relationships "can build a young person's skills and self-reliance," and "mentors can help youth learn when and how to access and utilize adult relationships" (Henkin et al., 1993, p. ii). Children may recognize that "both older and younger people have something to offer." They may also learn to work with people who are different from themselves and to view others as vital to their lives.

Through their participation in an intergenerational program, children may benefit from the individualized attention and affection provided by mentors, may find joy and comfort in a relationship with a grandparent figure, and may learn more about the aging process. Often, children reap plentiful praise and encouragement from their mentors, who may eventually become reliable confidants and helpmates.

## HOW DOES MENTORING AFFECT THE OLDER VOLUNTEERS?

Surveys by Newman (1982) and Newman and Larimer (1995) of 555 senior citizen school volunteers in western Pennsylvania reported that mentoring had positively affected the mentors' reported self-esteem and health. The seniors also reported learning new skills, having fun and feeling that their mentoring work was "productive and rewarding" (p. 4). Mentoring may also alleviate some of the isolation that many seniors experience. Through mentoring, older adults have the opportunity to pass on knowledge and skills that they have found useful in their lives, and may experience feelings of satisfaction from contributing in a positive way to children's development.

Thus, both elders and children who participate in mentoring may benefit through enhanced self-esteem, the acquisition of new skills and an increased sense of connection to society at large. Moreover, they often develop relationships that create joy and otherwise enhance the overall quality of their lives.

## RATIONALE FOR THE STUDY

Although some researchers have begun to examine the benefits of mentoring for older and younger participants, there are no published studies about the specific interactions that occur between the elders and children during the mentoring process. In the present study, which was conducted by *Generations Together* at the University of Pittsburgh's Center for Social and Urban Research, we examined some of the specific interactions and perceived outcomes of intergenerational mentoring in selected school settings. The study was designed to examine the relationship between the interactions of children and elders involved in a mentoring program and teachers' perceptions of the children's subsequent academic performance and social behaviors. The data were collected in schools in which intergenerational mentoring programs had been in place for some time. Older volunteers were trained to work with the children in the classroom or in after-school mentoring programs.

There were two components to the present study. The first consisted of observing mentor-mentee interactions in three school sites during two 45-minute visits to each site and using the Elder/Child Interaction Analysis instrument (ECIA) to analyze the recordings taken. To meet the requirements of a state-funded program, the data were collected in the autumn term. The second component involved interviewing the teachers whose students were participants in intergenerational mentoring. The interviews took place in the spring term after the observational sessions.

## METHOD

### Participants

The study was conducted during the 1995-1996 school year at three elementary schools in Allegheny County, western Pennsylvania. All of the participating schools had been identified through a demonstration project funded by the Pennsylvania Department of Education. The project looked for three ethnically diverse elementary schools that were located in low socioeconomic communities. Older adults were recruited as volunteer mentors from the same communities as the students and were of similar socioeconomic and racial backgrounds.

One school is located in the Hill District, an inner-city community near downtown Pittsburgh. The other two are in McKees Rocks and Glassport, both formerly thriving communities within 15 miles of Pittsburgh. Each school has an enrollment of approximately 350 students who range in age from 5-10 years and whose families may be considered to be of low socioeconomic status. All of the students at the Pittsburgh school at the time were African-American. Fifteen percent of the Glassport students were African-American and the remaining 85% were Caucasian. The McKees Rocks student body was 35% African-American and 65% Caucasian.

Sixty children participated in the study and all were in the third and fourth grades of school (8-9 years of age). Students were selected for participation if their teachers thought they might benefit from mentoring, if there was an available mentor, and if the teacher was interested in participating in the study. Twelve adults over 60 years of age were recruited as volunteer mentors from the communities in which the participating schools were located. All of the volunteers were trained for mentoring by *Generations Together* and received a small stipend for their work with students. The teacher's role was to identify students as potential participants, to provide mentors with tutoring materials, and to meet with the mentors and other teachers to discuss student progress.

The mentoring activities took place either in classrooms in which mentors assisted teachers with regular classroom activities or in supervised, after-school mentor/tutoring programs. A total of four teachers volunteered to participate in the study. For two of the participating teachers, data consisted of observations recorded during classroom activities, whereas for the remaining two teachers, observations were taken during after-school mentoring activities in which they were involved.

## Materials

*Observation.* In the 1960s, Flanders developed an *Interaction Analysis* instrument (Flanders, 1970) to record the verbal behaviors of teachers and their students in a classroom setting. The Interaction Analysis provided for a "cause-effect analysis of classroom verbal behavior" found in the learning process (Amidon & Hough, 1967, p. 118). Flanders established an important and useful protocol for recording observed behaviors of teachers and students and for using the Interaction Analysis to interpret these behaviors.

Subsequently, the first author modified the Interaction Analysis and created an expanded measure with new components, the Elder-Child Interaction Analysis (ECIA), to observe both verbal and non-verbal interactions between older adults and children in school settings (Newman & Onawola, 1985). The ECIA was designed for recording specific aspects of the observed interactions between elder mentors and their students in elementary kindergarten through sixth grade settings. The 32 behavioral items of the ECIA are considered typical of interactions between older adults and children. The items are organized into verbal/nonverbal and social/academic categories. Non-verbal behaviors were included because previous observations indicated that many of these, such as smiling and touching, seem frequently to be involved in the learning process. Interrater reliability for ECIA categories ranged from 75% to 100%, with an overall rate of agreement of 84%.

The ECIA was modified for use in the present study. The modified version consists of 40 behavioral items, 14 of which refer to a child's behavior paired with a reciprocal behavior by an elder. Items were selected from simulated student-teacher interactions on videotape and from the results of field testing. The simulations consisted of four 5-minute videotaped interactions between teachers, students, and elders in two of the fourth-grade classes not included in the present study. The simulated interactions were videotaped in classrooms at the Sto-Rox School and the Glassport School one month prior to the present study. ECIA items selected through this process included *student touches elder* paired with *elder touches student*, and *student exhibits frustration* with *elder expresses displeasure*.

The modifications made to the ECIA for the present study were intended to further clarify the behavioral categories and to allow recording of simultaneous behaviors observed in mentor-mentee interactions. Each verbal and non-verbal behavior is listed on a grid line, with the elders' behaviors on the left and those of the children on the right. The grid includes five cells, each representing 1-minute intervals, enabling observations of 1-minute spans to be recorded over the course of 5 minutes. The margins are broad around the grid and space is left at the bottom of the instrument for the recording of notes and other relevant information (see Appendix A).

The behaviors recorded by the modified ECIA represent patterns that typically occur in intergenerational interactions. For example, an elder might be observed asking a child a question. The child might, in turn, be observed answering a question. The situation might also occur in the reverse, with the child asking the elder the question, and so forth. Therefore, the lists of observable behaviors for children and elders often mirror one another or are often reciprocal.

*Teacher Interviews.* Newman and Larimer (1995) found that many teachers perceived that interactions between children and elder mentors contributed to a more positive classroom climate as well as to improvements in the children's academic performance, communication skills, general observed behavior, and apparent feeling of acceptance. The observational data collected in the present study suggests that specific, positive behaviors categorized by the ECIA may occur in mentor-mentee interactions on a relatively frequent basis. The authors of the present study were interested in whether teachers perceived a relationship between these frequently-occurring positive behaviors and specific positive classroom outcomes for the children who had participated in the mentoring program. To examine this possibility, a questionnaire was developed, post-hoc, for interviewing the participating teachers. The teacher interview questionnaire has seven questions and was designed to assess teachers' perceptions of the impact of mentoring on a range of student behaviors (see Appendix B).

## Procedure

*Observation.* The observers were two trained education specialists whose experience included previous work as classroom teachers. One was a member of the faculty at the University of Pittsburgh and the other a recent PhD graduate. Both observers were trained to use the ECIA and were directly involved in its modification for the present study.

Volunteer coordinators at each of the participating schools arranged appointments for observational visits. Each site was visited twice during the period between October and January, the first semester of the school year. Scheduling of sessions was determined by the school calendar and the availability of participants. Each of the 12 mentors was observed at least once during the two site visits, each of which lasted approximately 30 minutes. Each observation focused on the mentors' interaction with a different student.

For two of the participating schools, the observational setting was the school cafeteria, where children met with elders for mentoring/tutoring activities at the end of the school day. For the other two schools, observations were recorded in classrooms in which elders assisted teachers as they conducted classroom activities. Observations were recorded directly onto the ECIA instrument.

Observers were seated 10-20 feet away from the participants. Observation periods were carefully timed and recorded during five 1-minute intervals. Recorded observations were indicated by a checkmark on the ECIA grid, in the box designated for the 1-minute interval in which the specific behavior was observed. Although both observers were present in the same classroom or cafeteria simultaneously, one was not necessarily observing the same elder-child pair at the same point in time as the other.

*Interviews.* Structured teacher interviews were conducted at two of the schools, with four teachers whose students had participated in the present study. For two of the teachers, elders had assisted in their classrooms whereas for each of the other two, one student had received after-school mentoring. The teachers were interviewed in one-on-one, 15-minute sessions. Notes were taken on teacher responses to the questions during the interviews.

## RESULTS

### *Observation*

The frequency data collected from each observational visit from the three school sites were combined in one data set. Therefore, the recorded observations were not program-specific. Check-marks for specific ECIA items were hand-tallied to calculate the total frequency for each behavioral category. Observed behaviors with a recorded frequency less than 20 were considered *low frequency*. Those with a recorded frequency range of 21-40 were categorized as *medium frequency*, whereas those with a recorded frequency greater than 40 were considered as *high frequency*. Table 1 shows the raw total frequencies for high-frequency items from the ECIA, across all observational sessions and across all three participating schools.

TABLE 1. Most Frequently Occurring Observed Behaviors

| OBSERVED BEHAVIOR | FREQUENCY |
|---|---|
| Elder provides instruction | 158 |
| Elder asks questions | 143 |
| Child responds to instruction | 99 |
| Child answers questions | 96 |
| Elder offers help | 82 |
| Elder reviews students' work | 74 |
| Elder talks calmly to student | 73 |
| Elder encourages student | 51 |
| Elder corrects/positively redirects student's behavior | 47 |
| Student talks spontaneously | 53 |
| Elder talks spontaneously | 44 |

## *Interviews*

Seven questions were used to elicit four teachers' perceptions of the impact of the mentoring experience on specific student behaviors. The first question asked whether students seemed more responsive to student-teacher help and student-student help as the result of intergenerational mentoring. All four teachers reported the perception that their students were more responsive to receiving help. Three of them reported that their students also seemed more likely to offer help to other students. One teacher remarked that this change seemed especially marked in one student, because the child had seemed quite withdrawn prior to participating in the mentoring program.

In response to the second question, all of the teachers shared the perception that the students' homework seemed to have improved as a result of the intergenerational interactions. It appeared to them that homework was more likely to be completed and handed in. As one teacher remarked, the quantity of work completed seemed to have improved along with the quality. All of the teachers perceived that students were more eager to show work to them, which led them to conclude that students were taking more pride in their work. One teacher remarked that the students appeared more apt to correct mistakes in their own work, resulting in apparent improvements in legibility, punctuation, and spelling. Most of the teachers perceived also that students' enthusiasm about school work had improved overall. One teacher observed that his student was "naturally bubbly," making it difficult to conclude whether the apparent enthusiasm had anything to do with the student's mentoring experience.

The third question was whether students seemed more likely to speak quietly after the elder had been in the classroom. Several teachers perceived a greater overall sense of calmness in the classroom when the older adults were present. This would seem to be an important effect for children with extra academic or emotional needs, and where the classroom environment may be typically tense and loud.

The fourth set of questions pertained to the children's apparent responses to mentor encouragement. All of the teachers perceived their students as being more confident and more willing to participate as the result of mentor encouragement. Specific responses included the perceptions that: (a) "students were more consistent in completing tasks and were more cooperative in the classrooms"; (b) "students were more positively assertive and more sociable"; and (c) "the presence and encouragement of the older mentors seemed to create a reduction in student anxiety and increased their belief that they were capable of completing assigned tasks." With regard to sociability, many students were reportedly less abrupt with others and seemed to have learned that there are rewards to having good social skills.

The fifth question asked whether students were exhibiting better self-control and behavior as the result of the mentoring experience. Three teachers reported the perception that students' self-control had improved. One thought that students were more likely to curtail "foolish behavior" after mentoring. One teacher expressed the belief that the children were more likely to be patient and to wait their turns for individualized attention from the mentor or the teacher. The fourth teacher did not respond.

In response to the sixth question, all four teachers reported that with intergenerational tutoring, students seemed more likely to stay on task when given an assignment. One teacher perceived that students would work around the questions they could not answer on their own and wait until either she or the mentor could assist the student. It seemed to her that the presence of the mentor in her classroom may have reassured the children that their needs would be met.

With respect to the seventh question, most of the teachers expressed the impression that students who had received tutoring were exhibiting greater comprehension of homework and in-class assignments. As one teacher said, "[The student] is better able to understand what he is to do and thus, he goes ahead and does whatever the work calls for. He is much more responsible, he has matured in terms of his patterns of approaching the task. He has become very positive."

## CONCLUSIONS AND DISCUSSION

In the present study, we examined teachers' subjective perception of the relationship between frequently-observed behaviors recorded during a session of intergenerational mentoring and children's subsequent academic and social behaviors. The first component of the study consisted of recording the frequency of behavioral categories that previous work has identified as being characteristic of interactions between older adults and children in a classroom setting.

An informal examination of the observational data suggested that the elders and children who participated in intergenerational mentoring activities were highly engaged with one another as well as in their shared tasks.

The elders were often observed guiding the children through their work using questions that seemed aimed at encouraging the child to reason his or her way through homework questions. It appeared also that the elders helped keep the children on task, for example, by reviewing with the children what they had or had not yet accomplished. Students were praised often for their efforts and encouraged to participate in the learning process. The mentors seemed to pay individualized attention to the students, looking at them frequently and responding to their questions and behavior. In general, the nature of recorded observations seemed consistent with the notion that elders support and reinforce the kinds of behaviors that may facilitate improved performance in children's school performance (Weaver, 1994).

Although most of the interaction revolved around school work, there were also many informal conversations, which seemed to suggest that the children and elders were developing friendly, social relationships with one another. It was concluded overall that both elders and children seemed highly involved in the mentoring process and that most of the interactions appeared positive in nature.

For the second component of the study, the teacher interview questionnaire revealed teachers' agreement that elders and children appeared highly engaged with their given tasks during mentoring and engaged with each other in a positive and constructive manner. They expressed the shared belief that mentoring had a positive impact on the children's school-related behaviors and performance. It seemed to most of them that the children were more likely to correct their own mistakes and more likely to assist other children in getting through a given task. Some teachers perceived in their students improved levels of comprehension of classroom and homework assignments. It appeared to the teachers that most of the children's work had improved in terms of quality and quantity. Overall, the teachers' remarks seemed to suggest that students felt reassured that their needs would be met by either the teacher or the mentor, which may have contributed to more positive behavior and greater persistence in completing academic tasks.

It was also perceived that mentoring was related to subsequent improvements in the students' social behaviors. Several teachers thought that the students exhibited more confidence, better social skills, and greater levels of self-control as a result of their mentoring experiences.

The findings of the present study suggest that specific verbal and non-verbal behaviors and interactions observed during intergenerational mentoring may be linked to subsequent improved social behavior and academic performance in students. This seems an exciting possibility with important implications for educators, especially as intergenerational mentoring is currently expanding in K-6 schools across the United States, in response to the "America Reads" national initiative.

At the same time, we acknowledge the limitations of the present study and offer suggestions for future research in this area. For example, more empirical support for these findings might have been obtained with larger numbers and if correlations were computed between teacher interview questions and specific ECIA category frequencies. Also the participating schools in the present study reflected some ethnic and socioeconomic diversity. However, future studies will need more socioeconomic, racial, and ethnic variation than was possible in this study to demonstrate the measure's effectiveness nationally. Thus, future studies, involving intergenerational programs across a wide range of communities and using statistical analyses, are necessary to increase the rigor and generalizability of the present findings.

Future studies might also examine intergenerational mentoring activities over a longer range of time than was done here. This would allow teachers to assess student performance and social behavior using additional measures, such as test scores, written classwork, and the nature of peer relationships. As was done with teachers, both mentors and students could be interviewed to elicit their subjective perceptions of the impact of intergenerational interactions on children's academic performance and social behaviors.

## REFERENCES

Amidon, E., & Hough, J. (Eds.). (1967). *Interaction analysis: Theory, research and application.* Reading, MA: Addison-Wesley Publishing Company.

Flanders, N. (1970). *Analyzing teacher behavior.* Reading, MA: Addison-Wesley.

Freedman, M. (1994). *Seniors in national community services: A report prepared for the Commonwealth Fund's Americans Over 55 at Work Program.* Philadelphia, PA: Public/Private.

Henkin, N., Perez-Randal, C., & Rogers, A. (1993). *Linking Lifetimes: A national intergenerational mentoring initiative*–Program development manual. Philadelphia, PA: Center for Intergenerational Learning, Temple University.

Kalish, R.A. (1969). The old and new as generation gap allies. *The Gerontologist, 9,* 83-89.

Lyons, C. (1985). Older adults in intergenerational programs: The other side of the story. *Beginning, 2*(2), 3-5.

Newman, S. (March, 1982). *The impact of intergenerational programs on children's growth and on older persons' life satisfaction.* Unpublished paper presented at symposium entitled: "Innovations Within Educational Gerontology."

Newman, S., & Larimer, B. (1995). *Senior Citizen School Volunteer Program: Report on cumulative data. 1988-1995.* Pittsburgh, PA: Generations Together.

Newman, S., & Onawola, R. (1989). The ECIA: *Elder/Child Interaction Analysis.* Generations Together, University of Pittsburgh Center for Social and Urban Research, Pittsburgh, PA: Unpublished Manuscript.

Weaver, C. (1994). *Reading process and practice.* Portsmouth, NH: Heinemann.

## APPENDIX A

Generations Together Interaction Analysis Instrument

| ELDER BEHAVIOR | 1st min. | 2nd min. | 3rd min. | 4th min. | 5th min. | CHILD BEHAVIOR |
|---|---|---|---|---|---|---|
| Looks at student | | | | | | |
| | | | | | | Looks at elder |
| Smiles at student | | | | | | |
| | | | | | | Smiles at elder |
| Touches student | | | | | | |
| | | | | | | Touches elder |
| Engages in personal inquiry | | | | | | |
| | | | | | | Responds to personal inquiry |
| Talks spontaneously | | | | | | |
| | | | | | | Talks spontaneously |
| Offers help* | | | | | | |
| | | | | | | Asks for help |
| Provides instruction | | | | | | |
| | | | | | | Responds to instruction |
| Asks questions | | | | | | |
| | | | | | | Answers questions |
| Answers questions | | | | | | |
| | | | | | | Asks questions |
| Clarifies instruction | | | | | | |
| | | | | | | Clarifies statement |
| Reviews student's work | | | | | | |

APPENDIX A (continued)

| ELDER BEHAVIOR | 1st min. | 2nd min. | 3rd min. | 4th min. | 5th min. | CHILD BEHAVIOR |
|---|---|---|---|---|---|---|
| Corrects student's work | | | | | | |
| | | | | | | |
| Encourages student | | | | | | |
| | | | | | | Responds to encouragement |
| Praises student | | | | | | |
| | | | | | | Responds to praise |
| Talks calmly to student | | | | | | |
| | | | | | | Talks calmly to elder |
| | | | | | | Expresses interest |
| | | | | | | Shows disinterest |
| | | | | | | Exhibits frustration |
| | | | | | | Expresses satisfaction |
| Corrects student's behavior | | | | | | |
| Helps refocus student | | | | | | |
| Expresses displeasure | | | | | | |
| | | | | | | Gestures |
| Demonstrates example | | | | | | |
| | | | | | | Engaged in task |
| Helps student | | | | | | |

*Offers help may mean listening to student reading, taking dictation, etc.
Note. The instrument as it is used has space at the bottom for "Notes on Non-Observed and Negative Behaviors" and "Other Comments."

## APPENDIX B

### Questions for the Teacher Interviews
### Regarding the Interaction Analysis Instrument
### and Classroom Observations

1. At Sto Rox, we noticed a high number of interactions where the elder offered help to the students. Are students more responsive to student-teacher help and student-student help as the result of the intergenerational mentoring received?

2. We noticed a high number of instances of the elder reviewing and correcting the student's work. As the result of the elder reviewing work, have you noticed:

_____ a difference in the quality of homework? in-classroom assignments? If so, what has changed?

_____ students taking more pride in their work?

_____ that homework is more likely to be completed?

_____ that students are more enthusiastic about their work?

3. There were many instances of the elder speaking calmly with students. As a result, do the children speak more quietly, for example, the day after tutoring?

4. We noted a high number of instances where the elder encouraged the children. As a result, are the children:

_____ more confident?

_____ more willing to participate?

_____ more persistent in completing a task, even in the face of failure during the first try?

_____ more assertive?

_____ more sociable?

_____ more cooperative?

5. As a result of the mentoring, have you noticed a change in the children's levels of self-control or individual's ability to manage his/her behavior when the elder is not present?

6. We noticed during tutoring that the children were engaged or on-task almost all of the time. As the result of the intergenerational tutoring, are the children more likely to stay on task when given an assignment in class?

7. We noticed a high number of instances of elders providing and clarifying instruction and asking the children content-related questions. Correspondingly, there were many instances of students responding to instruction and to questions. In the classroom, are the students who received tutoring exhibiting higher levels of comprehension of the homework and of other in-class assignments/work?

# SECTION FOUR:
# QUESTIONS AND CHALLENGES

# Corporate Opportunities for Intergenerational Linkages: A Human Resources Perspective

Rosanne Kocarnik Ponzetti
James J. Ponzetti, Jr.

**SUMMARY.** The potential impact of dependent care needs on corporate employers and employees is described. Recommendations are made regarding the development of effective intergenerational approaches to meet these needs and reduce their associated expenses. The roles of human resource personnel, intergenerational program developers and intergenerational program researchers in such initiatives are described. *[Article copies available for a fee from The Haworth Document Delivery Service: 1-800-342-9678. E-mail address: getinfo@haworthpressinc.com <Website: http://www.haworthpressinc.com>]*

**KEYWORDS.** Intergenerational, human resources, corporate

## INTRODUCTION

Demographic changes have prompted many corporations to evaluate and redesign their employee benefit programs to meet the needs of

Rosanne Kocarnik Ponzetti is affiliated with Legacy Health Systems, Human Resources Department, Emanuel Hospital, 2801 North Gantenbien, Portland, OR 97227. James J. Ponzetti, Jr. is affiliated with the Oregon Family Nurturing Center, Inc., 13852 Shireva Drive, Lake Oswego, OR 97034.

[Haworth co-indexing entry note]: "Corporate Opportunities for Intergenerational Linkages: A Human Resources Perspective." Kocarnik Ponzetti, Rosanne and James J. Ponzetti, Jr. Co-published simultaneously in *Child & Youth Services* (The Haworth Press, Inc.) Vol. 20, No. 1/2, 1999, pp. 149-159; and: *Intergenerational Programs: Understanding What We Have Created* (ed: Valerie S. Kuehne) The Haworth Press, Inc., 1999, pp. 149-159. Single or multiple copies of this article are available for a fee from The Haworth Document Delivery Service [1-800-342-9678, 9:00 a.m. - 5:00 p.m. (EST). E-mail address: getinfo@haworthpressinc.com].

a changing workforce. Significant demographic changes in family life, for example, single-parent families, increased labor force participation of women, and dual-earner families, have stimulated an interest in an array of policies, benefits, and programs to address the reality of balancing family and work responsibilities (McNeely & Fogarty, 1988; Raabe & Gessner, 1988; Tchida, 1991). In addition to acknowledging changing family structures and the increasing number of working women, companies are gradually recognizing the value of maximizing the diversity of today's workforce (Diamante, Reid, & Giglo, 1995). Attracting and retaining the best employees are critical challenges for employers.

To remain competitive, many businesses have adapted corporate policies, benefits, and programs to the specific requirements of potential employees as well as of existing employees. In response to the dependent-care issues of many workers, an increasing number of employers have made changes in their (a) personnel policies, (b) financial benefits, (c) caregiver information and assistance, and (d) support to community agencies (Barr, 1992; Kamerman & Kingston, 1982). On the whole, however, corporate culture is just beginning to examine employees' needs and responsibilities outside of the office (Bowen, 1988; Denton, Love, & Slate, 1990; Smith, 1991).

Many employees are faced with dependent-care needs for both children and dependent elders. Until recently, corporations that offered dependent-care benefits focused primarily on child-care needs. Increasingly, corporations are expanding benefits to include elder-care services (Denton et al., 1990; Keigher & Stone, 1994; Smith, 1991). Workers from the "middle generation," who may be faced with caring for both dependent children and older relatives, might benefit from dependent-care services that address the needs of multiple generations (Ventura-Merkel, Liederman & Ossofsky, 1989).

For the most part, intergenerational programs engage older and younger people in ongoing planned activities, often designed for mutual benefit. Similarly, an intergenerational approach to dependent-care benefits addresses employees' care needs with respect to both younger and older dependents. In this paper, we will discuss the potential impact that dependent-care needs have on employers, as well as corporate opportunities for utilizing intergenerational programs to address these concerns. Human-resource cost-analysis is one method of evaluating the expenses that employers may incur as a result of employee dependent-care concerns. The following discussion recommends effective strategies for using intergenerational programs to meet the dependent-care needs of workers and describes the roles of human resource professionals, intergenerational program developers, and intergenerational program researchers in such work.

## THE IMPACT OF DEPENDENT-CARE ISSUES UPON EMPLOYERS AND EMPLOYEES

Child-care needs of employees are diverse, multifaceted, and changing (Kossek, 1990). Some of the concerns that may be expressed by caregivers, their co-workers, and their employers about the problems associated with child-care include the (a) inability to be employed at all, (b) unavailability for specific shifts, (c) inability to return to work after a maternity leave, (d) inability to pursue work-related activities beyond the standard workday, (e) hindered advancement potential, (f) tardiness and absenteeism due to unexpected difficulties and emergencies during the course of the workday, (g) absenteeism due to ill dependents, (h) lower productivity due to low morale and/or lack of concentration on the part of caregivers, and (i) negative impact on co-workers who depend on employees who are caregivers (Martinez, 1993; McNeely & Fogarty, 1988; Mize & Freeman, 1989).

An increasing number of employees also may have caregiving responsibilities for elderly relatives (Keigher & Stone, 1994; Gibeau & Anastas, 1989; Smith, 1991). Elder-care may present difficulties with access to services, particularly medical services, because the majority of caregivers are employed and most agencies for elder-care operate during business hours (Gibeau, Anastas, & Larson, 1987). Employees with elder-care responsibilities may experience worry and time pressures that can affect job performance. They may consider quitting their job because of dependent-care concerns (Gibeau & Anastas, 1989). Arriving at work late or leaving work early and personal phone usage are some of the possible consequences of caring for an older relative (Lefkovich, 1992). Elder-care responsibilities can affect workplace productivity by increasing the rates of employee turnover as well as the frequencies of: (a) tardiness, (b) unscheduled days off, (c) the use of work time to make personal calls, (d) high rates of accidents and mistakes as a result of being distracted, (e) emotional distress for the caregiver, (f) the inability to engage in overtime, and, (g) low morale among co-workers, who must work harder to make up for decreases in the productivity of caregivers (Azarnoff & Scharlach, 1988; Dellman-Jenkins, Bennett, & Brahce, 1994).

Having recognized the challenges of providing both child- and elder-care, some corporations now offer work-family benefit programs that support the dependent-care needs of their employees (Davis & Krouze, 1994; Smith, 1991). These programs are based on the notion that just as employees vary in their need for life insurance and retirement planning, they also may have intergenerational dependent-care concerns that could be supported through employee-benefit programs. Some proponents of work-family initiatives have argued that corporate employers who recognize the wide range of worker age and the intergenerational nature of dependent-care needs can increase their competitive advantage by supporting the workforce. On the basis of anecdotal reports alone, many corporations expect to increase recruiting potential, morale, and productivity by offering benefits that address the dependent-care requirements of their workforce (Martinez, 1993). It is important that employees with dependent-care responsibilities become familiar with the potential for integrating child- and elder-care services through an intergenerational approach.

## *PROGRAM OPTIONS*

Until recently, most employer-sponsored, dependent-care benefit programs were directed primarily towards the care of children. Employers have a variety of available options for supporting child-care needs. Some of the most common direct-service benefits include: (a) referral services, (b) sponsorship of an on- or off-site facility, (c) some form of employer reimbursement or subsidy of child-care costs (such as a voucher system), (d) an off-site consortium, for example, a group of employers jointly finance one or more child-care centers, and (e) some form of vendor system, for example, an employer contracts for guaranteed slots in a child-care setting (Waldstein, 1989).

A small number of employers have provided on-site child-care, believing that such programs will increase worker morale and corporate productivity (Mize & Freeman, 1989). There is some support for this notion. Results of a recent study of the effects of on-site child-care indicated that supportive supervision and satisfaction with child-care arrangements were related to less work/family conflict. Also, less work/family conflict was related to lower levels of absenteeism (Goff, Mount, & Jamison, 1990). In a separate study, Sizemore and Jones (1990) found that following participation in elder-care programs, many employees reported experiencing reduced levels of stress, improved performance in the workplace, and increased confidence in being able to balance work and elder-care responsibilities. Findings such as these have important implications for the role of employers in addressing the dependent-care concerns of their employees.

Tchida (1991) predicted that the successful company of the future will offer a full set of employee assistance services such as flexible working arrangements, family leave, and dependent-care. However, expanded leave and caregiving benefits should be extended to include the caregiving relationships between adult children and their aging parents as well as those between parents and their young children. Although some professionals have described the current state of elder-care support services as confusing and disorganized (Keigher & Stone, 1994), others perceive a growing need for elder-care services and expect an increased emphasis on cooperative efforts and public/private partnerships (Thornburg, 1993). Integrating elder-care services with child-care programs might be an effective response to the variety of intergenerational relationships in employees' personal lives.

The specific nature of dependent-care assistance programs varies according to whether they are designed primarily for children, adults, or for a combination of the two. Care services may be offered directly or indirectly. Indirect services include (a) personnel policies, (b) education/information services, (c) financial assistance, (d) flexible work scheduling, (e) paid days-off for caring for sick family members, (f) dependent-care spending accounts, and dependent-care tax incentives, (g) leaves of absence for caregiving purposes, and (h) referral programs.

Direct services include (a) employer-provided support systems that augment the caregiver's services, such as on-site access to child-care or adult day-health programs, (b) home-care services, (c) contracts for care by external service-providers, (d) transportation services for dependents to/from care, and (e) case management and employee-assistance programs for employees who give care (Davis & Krouze, 1994; Denton et al., 1990; Lefkovich, 1992; Smith, 1994). Offering dependent-care services for both elders and children makes sense for the employer from both pragmatic and financial points of view.

## Intergenerational Care to Meet Dependent-Care Needs

Intergenerational programs have evolved over the past two decades (Newman, 1989). However, intergenerational program-providers have yet to market their programs and services to the corporate world. Integrating child-care and elder-care services into an "intergenerational care-service" program can be viewed as taking a lifespan approach to employees' caregiving responsibilities. This approach brings generations together while assisting employees to meet their dependent-care needs.

Adult day-care programs serve clients with degenerative diseases or chronic conditions, but who do not need daily nursing or medical care. The primary service objective is to provide a positive, supportive environment in which social and physical functioning can be maintained to whatever extent is possible. Child-care programs are designed to provide supervision and care in an environment that encourages security, growth, independence, and learning. It seems reasonable that intergenerational care-programs might achieve mutual goals by combining the resources and features of existing child- and elder-care services. An intergenerational approach would provide employees with centralized access to care services and would offer participants the benefits of multi-age programming.

### Program Models and Costs

Stride Rite and Lancaster Labs have developed intergenerational care programs that have been marketed to human-resource professionals as an option for meeting employees' dependent-care needs (Thornburg, 1993). However, such programs are rare, partly because of the high costs of implementing and operating them.

Establishing adult day-care programming can require a substantial investment, depending on the cost and availability of staff and facilities. Start-up costs are influenced by space and equipment requirements. Operating costs are influenced by the scope of the program and the size and qualifications of the staff (Tedesco & Oberlander, 1983).

Planning and implementing an intergenerational program involves a variety of expenses (Brummel, 1989; Helfgott, 1992). Care-providers who are interested in offering combined adult- and child-care services should have realistic estimates of program costs. Combining adult- and child-care programming may be more economical overall than providing separate dependent-care services, because of sharing the costs of (a) planning, (b) recruitment, (c) salaries, (d) orientation/training, (e) program activities, (f) meals/nutrition, (g) public relations, and (h) facilities maintenance.

To date there is little data available regarding the specific costs associated with intergenerational care programs. One exception is Chamberlain, Fetterman, and Maher (1992), who estimated the costs of providing care for elders and children in a rural intergenerational facility. However, it was our impression that their calculations underestimated the expenses associated with such care because, in their example, there was a heavy reliance on "in kind" contributions from the owner/operator.

When the high cost of direct-care services is considered, it seems likely that only a large company could afford to offer this form of care. Some businesses have considered collaborative, community services as an alternative solution. For example, the American Business Collaboration for Quality Dependent Care consists of 137 employers who have raised funds for expanding and improving the dependent-care services in their communities. Although it focuses primarily on child-care issues, the Collaboration has committed 6% of its budget to elder-care issues (Starcke, 1995).

Coordinating and marketing a multi-employer intergenerational-care program requires an extensive amount of planning and cooperation on the part of interested corporations. To attract the interest of corporate employers, proponents of the intergenerational-care model must be able to provide accurate assessments of both the costs and benefits of such programs.

### Assessing Employee Benefits

To market intergenerational-care programming successfully, program providers must use the same strategies to present a proposal as those used in the business world. Providers must understand how benefit plans are typically designed, and they must use the appropriate methods for estimating the costs incurred by businesses because of employee turnover, absenteeism, and poor motivation.

The design of employee-benefit plans is an ongoing process which reflects the changing conditions of the workforce. Employers must balance the demand for a specific benefit with the cost of provision, although some businesses have implemented intergenerational programs for other than strictly financial reasons. Occasionally, a corporation will offer dependent-care benefits without putting a dollar value on the benefit (Martinez, 1993). Generally, however, economic realities require that new benefits are justifiable financially.

It is usually the case that innovative dependent-care programs are initiated by a "champion" within the Human Resource Department of an organization (Martinez, 1990). Involvement and collaboration with Human Resource staff are important for gathering information about the costs and advantages associated with offering a new employee benefit.

An effective human-resource strategy is to pinpoint a particular business problem and to present a solution that will improve the "bottom line" (Mercer, 1989). For example, many corporations "cost out" specific employee behaviors such as turnover, absenteeism, personal problems, or attitudes. An accurate assessment of these costs allows a company to evaluate the extent of the problem and to develop strategies to reduce the financial impact on the organization (Cascio, 1991).

Intergenerational program researchers can assess the costs and benefits of care services by applying the same formulas that many organizations use to calculate the costs of specific employee behaviors (e.g., absenteeism, turnover, and tardiness). For example, Scharlach and Boyd (1989) noted that employees with dependent-care needs showed increased absenteeism and unscheduled time-off. Human resource professionals use specialized formulas to calculate the costs of absenteeism (Cascio, 1991). If the costs of providing dependent-care programs can be shown to be less than those associated with dependent-care absenteeism, an employer may decide to offer this benefit to employees.

An effective cost-benefits analysis must account for all of the factors that may be related to a specific employee behavior. Intergenerational program developers and researchers must work with human resource professionals in assessing the costs associated with the problematic behaviors that intergenerational-care programs are designed to address. One strategy is to compare the costs of providing intergenerational-care benefits with providing child- and elder-care services separately. Corporate employers should be shown that an integrated approach to dependent-care benefit plans can reduce costs as well as increase good public relations and employee satisfaction.

## CONCLUSION

In response to changing demographics, corporate policies toward employee benefits are also changing, and some companies now offer dependent-care services to their employees. Integrating child-care and elder-care services into "dependent-care services" seems a viable solution to the many problems faced by employees caring for young children and/or elderly relatives. However, most corporate employers require a fiscal return on their potential investment, in addition to the potential social benefits of intergenerational programs. Thus, intergenerational programmers and researchers must work together with corporate human resource professionals to make a case for incorporating their programs into employee benefit packages. To do so, all partners should become comfortable with the process used to design employee benefit plans and with the formulas used to cost employee behaviors. By providing corporate employers with calculations of the costs associated with employees' dependent-care responsibilities, employers can estimate the likely financial effect of new programs on reducing these expenses. In addition, employers can effectively discern the impact that an integrated, intergenerational approach to dependent care benefits will have on the corporate "bottom line."

## REFERENCES

Azarnoff, R. & Scharlack, A. (1988). Can employees carry the eldercare burden? *Personnel Journal, 67,* 60-65.

Barr, J. (1992, November). *Use of corporate elder care programs: a perspective from the employer.* Paper presented at the meeting of the National Council on Family Relations, Orlando, FL.

Brummel, S. (1989). Developing an intergenerational program. *Journal of Children in Contemporary Society, 20,* (3/4), 119-133.

Bowen, G. (1988). Corporate supports for the family lives of employees: A conceptual model for program planning and evaluation. *Family Relations, 37,* 183-188.

Cascio, W. (1991). *Costing human resources* (3rd ed.). Boston: PWS-Kent Publishing Co.

Chamberlain, V., Fetterman, E., & Maher, M. (1992). The economics of intergenerational community care. *Journal of Home Economics, 84,* (2), 17-19, 62.

Davis, E. & Krouze, M. (1994). A maturing benefit: Eldercare after a decade. *Employee Benefits Journal, 19,* (3), 16-20.

Dellmann-Jenkins, M., Bennett, J., & Brahce, C. (1994). Shaping the corporate response to workers with elder care commitments: Considerations for gerontologists. *Educational Gerontology, 20,* 395-405.

Denton, K., Love, L., & Slate, R. (1990). Eldercare in the '90s: Employee responsibility, employer challenge. *Families in Society, 71,* 349-359.

Diamante, T., Reid, C., & Giglo, L. (1995). Making the right training move. *HR Magazine, 40*(3), 60-65.

Gibeau, J., Anastas, J., & Larsen, P. (1987). Breadwinners, caregivers and employers: New alliances in an aging America. *Employee Benefit Journal, 12,* (3), 6-10.

Gibeau, J. & Anastas, J. (1989). Breadwinners and caregivers: Interviews with working women. *Journal of Gerontological Social Work, 14,* 19-40.

Goff, S., Mount, M., & Jamison, R. (1990). Employer supported child care, work/family conflict, and absenteeism: A field study. *Personnel Psychology, 43,* 794-809.

Helfgott, K. (1992). *Older adults caring for children: Intergenerational child care.* Washington, D.C.: Generations United.

Kamerman, S. & Kingston, P. (1982). Employer responses to the family responsibilities of employees. In S. Kamerman & C. Hayes (Eds.), *Families that work: Children in a changing world* (pp. 144-208). Washington, D.C.: National Academy Press.

Kossek, E. (1990). Diversity in child care assistance needs: Employee problems, preferences & work related outcomes. *Personnel Psychology, 43,* 769-791.

Keigher, S. & Stone, R. (1994). Family care in America: Evolution and evaluation. *Aging International, 21,* (1), 41-48.

Lefkovich, J. (1992). Business responds to elder-care needs. *HR Magazine, 37* (6), 103-108.

Martinez, M. (1990). Making room for work/family positions. *HR Magazine, 35,* 45-47.

Martinez, M. (1993). Family support makes business sense. *HR Magazine, 38*(1), 38-43.

McNeely, R., & Fogarty, B. (1988). Balancing parenthood and employment: Factors affecting company receptiveness to family-related innovations in the workplace. *Family Relations, 37,* 189-195.

Mercer, M. (1989). *Turning your human resource department into a profit center.* New York: American Management Association.

Mize, J., & Freeman, L. (1989). Employer-supported child care: Assessing the need and potential support. *Child & Youth Care Quarterly, 18*(4), 289-301.

Newman, S. (1989). A history of intergenerational programs. *Journal of Children in Contemporary Society, 20*(3/4), 1-15.

Raabe, P., & Gessner, J. (1988). Employer family-supportive policies: Diverse variations on the theme. *Family Relations, 37,* 196-202.

Scharlach, A., & Boyd, S. (1989). Caregiving and employment: Results of an employee survey. *The Gerontologist, 29,* 382-387.

Sizemore, M., & Jones, A. (1990). Eldercare and the workplace. *Educational Gerontology, 16,* 97-104.

Smith, D. (1991). *Kincare and the American corporation.* Homewood, IL: Business One Irwin.

Starcke, A. (1995, February). *HR News,* p. 2.

Tchida, M. (1991). Assessing employee dependent-care needs. *HR Magazine, 36*(9), 71-74.

Tedesco, J., & Oberlander, D. (1983). *Adult day care: A diversification option for hospitals*. Chicago: The Hospital Research and Educational Trust.

Thornburg, L. (1993). Day care for kids and elders is a natural. *HR Magazine, 38*(1), 48-49.

Ventura-Merkel, C., Liederman, D., & Ossofsky, J. (1989). Exemplary intergenerational programs. *Journal of Children in Contemporary Society, 2*(3/4), 173-180.

Waldstein, R., (1989). *Personnel Managers Handbook*. Englewood Cliffs, NJ: Prentice Hall Professional Newsletters.

# Designing for Change: Attitudes Toward the Elderly and Intergenerational Programming

Anne E. Vernon

**SUMMARY.** Common assumptions are examined about the prevalence of negative attitudes toward the elderly. This issue may have important implications for planning intergenerational programs aimed at attitude change. There is little historical evidence for the popular notion that intergenerational relations have been gradually eroding in Western society. Results of research suggest that negative attitudes about old age may vary according to situational, contextual, and social factors. In general, there is only a weak link between what people generally think about aging, and how they may behave toward elderly individuals. For maximum effectiveness, program planners should focus on changing demonstrably negative perceptions of old age within a specific context. It is important that activities and measures used in the design and evaluation of intergenerational programs are appropriate for the stated objectives. *[Article copies available for a fee from The Haworth Document Delivery Service: 1-800-342-9678. E-mail address: getinfo@haworthpressinc.com <Website: http://www.haworthpressinc.com>]*

**KEYWORDS.** Intergenerational, attitudes, research, programs

## *INTERGENERATIONAL PROGRAMMING AND ATTITUDINAL CHANGE*

Promoting positive interactions between younger and older individuals is an inherent goal of all intergenerational programming. That is,

---

Anne E. Vernon is affiliated with the Department of Behavioral Sciences, Mount Royal College, 4825 Richard Road S.W., Calgary, Alberta, Canada T3E 6K6.

[Haworth co-indexing entry note]: "Designing for Change: Attitudes Toward the Elderly and Intergenerational Programming." Vernon, Anne E. Co-published simultaneously in *Child & Youth Services* (The Haworth Press, Inc.) Vol. 20, No. 1/2, 1999, pp. 161-173; and: *Intergenerational Programs: Understanding What We Have Created* (ed: Valerie S. Kuehne) The Haworth Press, Inc., 1999, pp. 161-173. Single or multiple copies of this article are available for a fee from The Haworth Document Delivery Service [1-800-342-9678, 9:00 a.m. - 5:00 p.m. (EST). E-mail address: getinfo@haworthpressinc.com].

it is generally expected that participation in shared activities will be personally satisfying and socially enriching for people of all ages. Intergenerational programs seem to evoke good feelings within the community, perhaps because they are seen as forging connections between the generations. Many people believe that historically, ties between younger and older age-groups within Western societies used to be much stronger and more positive than they are now and that negative attitudes toward older adults prevail in modern society. Some might argue that communities should take a proactive approach to restoring intergenerational harmony. Many people see intergenerational programming as one way to achieve this goal.

Thus the primary objective of most intergenerational programming is to promote positive exchanges between younger and older participants. Many programs are aimed, at least indirectly, at dispelling disparaging stereotypes of aging or at fostering more favorable attitudes in children and youth toward the elderly. It is often expected that more positive perceptions of old age will, in turn, influence intergenerational relations within families or the community at large. For example, positive changes may be expected in the form of more frequent intergenerational contact, closer bonds between adult children and their parents, or in lower levels of intergenerational conflict in the workplace or the political arena. In other words, an *underlying* goal of some intergenerational programming may be to also change overt behavior.

This paper will address frequent assumptions about the nature, history, and prevalence of negative attitudes toward elderly persons, and about the relationship between age-group attitudes and behavior. For example, it is a common practice to use the terms "stereotype," "attitude," and "knowledge about aging" as essentially interchangeable. This practice implies a belief that to foster change in one aspect of age perceptions (e.g., knowledge about aging) is to promote change in another (e.g., contribute to more positive stereotypes of old age). However, there is considerable evidence that the association between people's attitudes, knowledge, and behavior may vary as a function of situational, contextual, and social variables.

These issues have important implications for planning, designing, and evaluating intergenerational programs that are intended to enhance public attitudes toward aging. The potential success of any program depends on the thoughtful selection and meaningful assessment of realistic goals and objectives. This topic seems especially pertinent in the current climate of reduced social spending and increased competition for available resources. There will likely be increasing pressure to show the need for and the likely benefits of publicly-funded intergenerational initiatives.

## WHAT'S IN AN ATTITUDE?

Although, by definition, an attitude is a broad construct that includes feelings, beliefs, and behaviors, most researchers use the term to describe the evaluative (feeling) component (Eagly & Chaiken, 1993). It is common to distinguish between attitudes (as inherently evaluative) and beliefs, many of which seem neutral. Thus attitudes can be thought of as essentially subjective appraisals that refer to one's likes or dislikes (Crockett & Hummert, 1987).

Common approaches to measuring evaluative perceptions of old age include the use of agree-disagree scales or semantic differential scales. Semantic differential scales require respondents to rate a generalized group such as "the elderly" or "older people" on a continuum whose end points are positive versus negative descriptors. The midpoint of the continuum denotes neutrality. Using this method, general attitudes (mostly feelings) toward older adults as a social group can be categorized as positive, negative, or even neutral.

In contrast to the essentially evaluative nature of attitudes, stereotypes about old age involve beliefs and expectations about the personal attributes, feelings, and behaviors of older adults as a group. Perhaps because most early studies in this area looked at stereotypes and attitudes in relation to prejudice toward the elderly, the two terms were often used interchangeably. It used to be generally assumed that holding a negative old-age stereotype implied having negative feelings toward elderly individuals. However, the bulk of recent studies have shown that stereotypes about all adult age-groups include both positive and negative images (Hummert, 1990, 1993, 1994; Hummert, Garstka, Shaner & Strahm, 1995; Schmidt & Boland, 1986).

These findings are consistent with an information-processing perspective, which holds that people use stereotypes frequently in their everyday lives because they are an "economical" way of organizing the massive amount of information in the external environment. According to this view, a stereotype is essentially descriptive and not necessarily negative in nature (Braithwaite, Lynd-Stevenson & Pi-gram, 1993).

However, it is still a common practice to focus on negative as opposed to positive images of aging. In the assessment of old-age stereotypes, respondents are required to rate the "typical older adult" on an adjective checklist or to sort descriptive terms into coherent, multiple images of older adults (Schmidt & Boland, 1986). Adjective checklists usually involve the attribution of personality traits, many of which are inherently evaluative (positive or negative) (Crockett & Hummert, 1987). Also, many researchers continue to assess age stereotypes in terms of their evaluative nature and view them as an indirect measure of people's prejudice toward the elderly.

For these reasons, stereotypical beliefs are generally viewed as distinct from factual beliefs about the elderly or old age. Knowledge measures typically require respondents to assess the "truth" value of objectively verifiable statements (e.g., Aged drivers have fewer accidents per driver than those under age 65; Palmore, 1988). Often, these measures are used to evaluate educational programs for people who work regularly with older adults, for example, in adult care settings).

Thus, there are important conceptual differences between an attitude, a stereotype, and a belief. Whereas the essence of an attitude is its evaluative component, a stereotype consists of images, beliefs, and expectations about a specific group that are not necessarily negative. Stereotypical beliefs differ from factual beliefs in that whereas the objective truth value is often difficult to establish for the former, it is at least a theoretical possibility for the latter. Because of these essential differences, planners of intergenerational programs should identify and articulate a conceptual focus well in advance. This is important to ensure that both the program's activities and evaluation measures are consistent with the explicit and implicit goals of the program.

For example, an intergenerational program aimed at improving younger people's attitudes toward aging might be designed to promote friendly interactions between younger and older individuals (e.g., matching older adults with pre-school children for play activities). In other words, if the goal is to change feelings, the program should focus on feelings. If the goal is to improve people's shared images of a social group's negative characteristics and attributes, the program should be designed to promote positive images. Thus a program directed toward changing negative age-group stereotypes might showcase the strengths, interests, and abilities of both youth and elderly individuals. Yet another approach might be to set up educational workshops (e.g., in employment settings) to provide information about the aging process itself or about the historical, social, and demographic characteristics of the current elderly population.

The following example from the research literature seems to illustrate this point. Roberto (1985) described a family-life program aimed at improving the relationships between adult children and their parents. A one-day intensive workshop was held to increase the adult children's knowledge about the aging process and community resources available for the elderly. The results of an evaluation showed that the workshop was highly successful in significantly increasing knowledge about old age and aging and in stimulating family discussions of community services for the elderly. The favorable outcome indicated that the workshop was well done in terms of educating participants and changing some behaviors. However, there were no significant differences between participants and a control group on scores from a measure of the parent-child relationship, the latter being the primary focus of the program. Given the educational focus of the workshop, this pattern of findings was unsurprising. That is, the essential focus of the workshop was on knowledge about aging in general; it did not focus directly or indirectly on any aspect of the parent-child relationship. A more effective approach might have been to foster face-to-face discussions between the adult children and their parents about the parent's personal experiences of aging. A relationship-oriented activity such as this seems to be conceptually consistent with the stated goals of the program.

### Assessing the Need for Attitudinal Change

There have been an increasing number and variety of intergenerational programs established over the past three decades. Most have received considerable public approval, and typically, public funding. However, in the current climate of diminished government spending, there may be increasing pressure on programmers to show the need for intergenerational projects and their potential benefits. Thus, it is important to consider where and how available resources might be used most effectively.

Many people would agree that programs promoting positive intergenerational contact are inherently beneficial for all participants.

Some might argue that intergenerational programming is essential for fostering healthy communities in a society marked by unprecedented levels of geographic mobility and age segregation. According to this view, there has been a gradual erosion of previously strong and "natural" connections between the old and the young in Western societies that is attributed to the unavoidable effects of increasing industrialization. It is presumed that intergenerational estrangement is reflected in widespread negative perceptions of old age that may add to the inherent difficulties of aging. Consistent with these beliefs, many intergenerational programs are directed toward re-forging links between the young and old, and to challenging negative perceptions of the elderly.

However, recent historical work on old age suggests that–contrary to popular notions of an idealized past–intergenerational relations in Western societies have been characterized by considerable stress since at least the Middle Ages. For example, Stearns (1989) discussed the various demographic, cultural, and economic factors in early Western society that contributed to conflict between the young and the old. He maintained that industrial forces gathering momentum during the early 19th century, with their emphasis on energy and adaptability, undeniably fostered a generalized preference for youth over old age. Simultaneously though, other aspects of an increasingly urban and industrial society alleviated the intergenerational tension within the family. Favorable changes included a decreased dependency on inherited wealth from parents and fewer instances of intergenerational habitation and shared work roles with older family members. Thus, growing industrialization, with its emphasis on youthful attributes, may have contributed to more negative evaluations of the elderly in the workplace. However, social and economic changes also associated with industrialization may have served to strengthen familial bonds. Stearns' conclusions suggest that levels of intergenerational conflict in Western society may have actually decreased overall with the coming of industrialization, and that negative views of aging may vary according to the social context.

Many reviewers have addressed the generic question of whether *contemporary* cultural perceptions are negatively biased toward the elderly (Brubaker & Powers, 1976; Crockett & Hummert, 1987; Kite & Johnson, 1988; Kogan, 1979; Lutsky, 1980; McTavish, 1971). Most have concurred that there is no definitive answer to this question, as results across studies have been often contradictory and inconsistent.

For example, Crockett and Hummert (1987) concluded that although generalized attitudes toward older adults may be somewhat more negative than views of their younger counterparts, there is no evidence of widespread negative evaluation. That is, ratings of the elderly, while often less favorable than those of younger people, still typically register on the positive end of attitudinal scales. This outcome is commonly interpreted as a negative bias toward the elderly, rather than being more accurately labeled as a positive bias toward the young. It is possible that neither interpretation is accurate, as researchers often use the terms, positive versus negative, to describe mean scores that may not be statistically different from the neutral point on a continuum scale.

Furthermore, the frequent emphasis on the overall evaluative tone of old-age perceptions may obscure the heterogeneous content of age-group stereotypes. Many studies have shown that people associate both positive and negative stereotypical traits with all adult age-groups (Hummert, 1990, 1993, 1994; Kite, Deaux, & Miele, 1991; Rosen & Jerdee, 1976; Rothbaum, 1983; Schmidt & Boland, 1986).

Because most research has focused on general attitudes and stereotypes of generalized age groups, for example, "old people" or the "typical older person," the extent of old-age bias toward specific individuals may have been overstated. Asking people to describe a generalized age-group places an artificial emphasis on chronological age as the sole focus of evaluation. In contrast, assessments of hypothetical individuals typically include personalized information that may influence and "flesh out" age perceptions (Kogan, 1979). Many studies have shown that judgments made about older individuals in specific situations may vary according to the particular attributes under consideration and their perceived relevance to the evaluative context (Erber, Szuchman, & Etheart, 1993; Gibson, Zerbe, & Franken, 1993). Some studies have found that people hold multiple stereotypes of the elderly (Hummert, 1990; Schmidt & Boland, 1986). The attitude expressed toward older individuals in a particular context may depend on the stereotype evoked by situational cues (Schmidt & Boland, 1986). Perceptions of specific individuals may also vary as a function of social roles, family roles, or motivational factors. For example, Vernon (1997) found that most university students believe that their parents, as compared to other adults, will undergo far fewer and far more moderate declines in everyday functioning with increasing age.

## The Attitude-Behavior Connection

It is a common tendency to assume that there is a necessary link between what members of one age-group know about, think about, and feel toward those in another. However, the findings from over forty years of research in this area have shown that change in one attitudinal dimension does not necessarily generalize to others. Most studies have found, at best, only modest association between false beliefs about old age and evaluative ratings of the elderly (Holtzman & Beck, 1979; Knox, Gekowski, & Johnson, 1986; O'Hanlon, Camp, & Osofsky, 1993; Schonfield, 1982). Little is known about how factual knowledge about aging may influence stereotypical images of the elderly.

Neither is it necessarily the case that people's attitudes are reflected in their overt behavior. The evidence is mixed for the common notion that individuals who express more favorable attitudes toward the elderly probably interact more frequently with older adults. Although some studies report that increasingly positive attitudes toward the elderly were related to increased contact (Naus, 1973; Rosencranz & McNevin, 1969) or to high quality contact (Knox et al., 1986), the correlations were generally low. Other researchers found no effect of contact (Weinberger & Millham, 1975).

The generally low correlation between attitude and overt behavior has been the focus of many critical reviews in the field of social psychology since the 1930s onward. Research in this area has shown that the attitude-behavior link varies according to the characteristics of the person who holds the attitude and those of the group about whom the attitude exists. Also, the strength of the relationship may change with the behavioral context, the perceived relevance of one's general attitude to specific situations, and the behavioral measure used (Eagly & Chaiken, 1993).

In person-perception studies, participants are asked to make attributional judgments about hypothetical individuals who possess various characteristics. This approach has been used to examine the influence of age-group perceptions on attributional judgments made about older people within everyday contexts. Age-cues are included along with other kinds of information given to the participants. Taken overall, theses studies have shown that the nature of judgments made about older adults may depend, in part, on the specific attributes being assessed, their relevance to the evaluative setting, and the kinds of other information available.

Many such studies have looked at attributional judgments of older people in a workplace context. Of course, the potential implications of negative perceptions of older adults in employment settings are substantial in terms of employee evaluations and decisions regarding promotion or advancement training. In one study (Gibson et al., 1993), actual employers rated hypothetical older workers, in comparison to their younger counterparts, as less effective, less quick to adopt new ideas, less contributing, and having less potential. However, older workers were also given more favorable ratings of stability, experience, and individual initiative than were younger ones. Moreover, there were many significant differences in the subjective importance attached to various attributes in the "ideal" employee depending upon whether the organizational setting was white-collar, blue-collar, or sales-and-service. Thus, how older workers per se are viewed by employers may vary greatly according to the specific characteristics valued in a given employment situation.

Other studies have shown that in some situational contexts the perception of valued traits in older adults may overshadow perceptions of declining competency. For example, Erber et al. (1993) reported that young adults preferred an older, as opposed to a younger (hypothetical) neighbor to do memory-related tasks for them, despite varying information provided concerning her recent memory failures. In a second study, they found that older individuals may be seen as having traits that are desirable and perhaps relevant to performing memory tasks. That is, older people, in comparison to their younger counterparts, were thought to be more responsible, trustworthy, and dependable.

As these studies seem to illustrate, some negative attributions associated with older adults may, in some contexts, be overridden by the perception of positive attributes. Further, specific characteristics may be more salient and seen as more desirable in some situations than in others. It seems likely also that some evaluative contexts, as compared to others, have stronger social norms, or even legal sanctions, against discriminatory behaviors, for example, those involving hiring practices or rental housing. Such norms or sanctions may suppress overt displays of negative attitudes toward older adults.

Thus, how people *behave* toward individual members of a social group in a particular situation may not reflect accurately how they *feel* about that social group in general. Many social psychologists have observed that the largest correlations between attitude and behavior are found where measured attitudes and behavior are similar in terms of specificity versus generality (Eagly & Chaiken, 1993). *General attitudes* are likely to be good predictors of measures summed across many attitude-relevant behaviors. *Specific attitudes*, such as attitudes toward a particular behavior on a particular occasion and in a particular context, will probably be good predictors of that specific behavior.

For example, managers' general attitudes toward older workers may be good indicators of aggregated measures of many management decisions related to the hiring, promoting, and retraining of older workers. However, because any single behavior is influenced by many situational factors, general attitudes are typically poor predictors of specific behaviors on a particular occasion in a particular context.

## *CONCLUSIONS*

There is little overall support for the notion that growing industrialization has eroded intergenerational relations in Western society. Similarly, there is mixed evidence for the common assumption that the elderly are always (or in all ways) viewed unfavorably. Negative perceptions about older adults, and if and how those perceptions are expressed in behavior, vary according to situational, contextual, and social factors. It is important to consider these potential sources of variability when interpreting the results of impact studies and when designing intergenerational programs. Also, changing people's subjective feelings or beliefs about the elderly are different goals from increasing factual knowledge about aging. The links are tenuous between what people generally feel, think, or believe about other age groups and how they behave toward individual members of those groups.

For programs aimed at meaningful attitudinal change, planners should target those specific contexts in which relations between age groups are likely to be most problematic. In addition, attention should be directed toward changing perceptions of old age that are demonstrably negative within a relevant context. For example, a program involving elderly persons as parent aides in a child abuse project may be effective for stimulating positive intergenerational contact and providing support to families in stress. However, it may be an inappropriate strategy for fostering meaningful change in age-group attitudes. Such a project seems inherently designed to reinforce *already positive* aspects of old-age stereotypes, for example, that the elderly possess valuable parenting experience and wisdom. It is unlikely that this type of program will alter other, negative aspects of old-age perceptions, which may be more salient in other situations. Alternatively, in a program where older adults serve as tutors for elementary school children, there is an implicit focus on the cognitive skills and abilities of the elderly. Such an approach may challenge negative perceptions of the elderly as more forgetful and less intellectually competent than younger adults.

When designing or evaluating an intergenerational program, the chosen activities and outcome measures should be appropriate to the program's stated objectives. Whereas an educational forum may be appropriate for training health care professionals who work with the elderly, interpersonal exercises might be more in line with a goal of improving parent-child relationships. It cannot be assumed the positive changes in one attitudinal dimension will generalize to others. Where behavioral change is the ultimate goal, the specificity of the targeted attitude should be consistent with that of the targeted behavior.

## REFERENCES

Braithwaite, V., Lynd-Stevenson, R., & Pigram, D. (1993). An empirical study of ageism: From polemics to scientific utility. *Australian Psychologist, 28*, (1), 9-15.

Brubaker, T.H., & Powers, E.A. (1976). The stereotype of "old": A review and alternative approach. *Journal of Gerontology, 31*, (4), 441-447.

Crockett, W.H., & Hummert, M.L. (1987). Perceptions of aging and the elderly. In K.W. Schaie (Ed.), *Annual Review of Gerontology and Geriatrics*, Vol. 7 (pp. 217-241). New York: Springer Publishing.

Eagly, A.H., & Chaiken, S. (1993). *The psychology of attitudes*. Fort Worth: Harcourt Brace Jovanovich College Publishers.

Erber, J.T., Szuchman, L.T., & Etheart, M.E. (1993). Age and forgetfulness: Young perceivers' impressions of young and older neighbors. *International Journal of Aging and Human Development, 37*, (2), 91-103.

Gibson, K.J., Zerbe, W.J., & Franken, R.E. (1993). The influence of rater and ratee age on judgments of work-related attributes. *The Journal of Psychology, 127*, (3), 271-280.

Holtzman, J.M., & Beck, J.D. (1979). Palmore's Facts on Aging Quiz: A reappraisal. *Gerontologist, 19*, (1), 116-120.

Hummert, M.L. (1990). Multiple stereotypes of elderly and young adults: A comparison of structure and evaluations. *Psychology and Aging, 5*, 182-193.

Hummert, M.L. (1993). Age and typicality judgments of stereotypes of the elderly: Perceptions of elderly vs. young adults. *International Journal of Aging and Human Development, 37*, (3), 217-226.

Hummert, M.L. (1994). Physiognomic cues to age and the activation of stereotypes of the elderly in interaction. *International Journal of Aging and Human Development, 39*, (1), 5-19.

Hummert, M.L., Garstka, T.A., Shaner, J.L., & Strahm, S. (1995). Judgments about stereotypes of the elderly: Attitudes, age associations, and typicality ratings of young, middle-aged, and elderly adults. *Research on Aging, 17*, (2), 168-189.

Kite, M.E., Deaux, K., & Miele, M. (1991). Stereotypes of young and old: Does age outweigh gender? *Psychology and Aging, 6*, (1), 19-27.

Kite, M.E., & Johnson, B.T. (1988). Attitudes toward older and younger adults: A meta analysis. *Psychology and Aging, 3*, (3), 233-244.

Knox, V.J., Gekowski, W.L., & Johnson, E.A. (1986). Contact with and perceptions of the elderly. *The Gerontologist, 26*, (3), 309-313.

Kogan, N. (1979). Beliefs, attitudes, and stereotypes about old people. *Research on Aging, 1*, (1), 11-36.

Lutsky, N.S. (1980). Attitudes toward old age and elderly persons. In C. Eisdorfer (Ed.), *Annual review of gerontology and geriatrics* (pp. 287-236). New York: Springer Publishing Co.

McTavish, D.G. (1971). Perceptions of old people: A review of research methodologies and findings. *The Gerontologist, 11*, 90-101.

Naus, P.J. (1973). Some correlations of attitudes towards old people. *International Journal of Aging and Human Development, 4*, (3), 229-243.

O'Hanlon, A.M., Camp, C.J., & Osofsky, H.J. (1993). Knowledge of and attitudes toward aging in young, middle-aged, and older college students: A comparison of two measures of knowledge of aging. *Educational Gerontology, 19*, 753-766.

Palmore, E.B. (1988). *The facts on aging quiz: A handbook of uses and results.* New York: Springer Publishing Company.

Roberto, K.A. (1985). Adult children and aging parents: A report of a program design and evaluation. *Activities, Adaptation & Aging, 6*, (4), 89-101.

Rosen, B., & Jerdee, T.H. (1976). The nature of job-related age stereotypes. *Journal of Applied Psychology, 61*, (2), 180-183.

Rosencrantz, H.A., & McNevin, T.E. (1969). A factor analysis of attitudes toward the aged. *Gerontologist, 9*, 55-59.

Rothbaum, F. (1983). Aging and age stereotypes. *Social Cognition, 2*, (2), 171-184.

Schonfield, D. (1982). Who is stereotyping whom and why? *The Gerontologist, 22*, (3), 267-272.

Schmidt, D.F., & Boland, S.M. (1986). Structure of perceptions of older adults: Evidence for multiple stereotypes. *Psychology and Aging, 1*, (3), 255-260.

Stearns, P.N. (1989). Historical trends in intergenerational contacts. In S. Newman, & S.W. Brummel (Eds.), *Intergenerational programs: Imperatives, strategies, impacts, trends* (pp. 21-32). New York: The Haworth Press, Inc.

Vernon, A.E. (1997). *Implicit theories of aging: Predictions of developmental change in parents versus generalized adults.* Unpublished doctoral dissertation, University of Victoria, Victoria, British Columbia, Canada.

Weinberger, L.E., & Millham, J. (1975). A multi-dimensional, multiple method analysis of attitudes toward the elderly. *Journal of Gerontology, 30*, (3), 343-348.

# Establishing School Volunteer Programs

Robert Strom
Shirley Strom

**SUMMARY.** Schools can no longer rely on students' mothers as a primary source of volunteers. Over the past decade, retired persons have contributed more assistance in the classroom than any other group. The partnership between schools and older members of the community can be viewed as a creative process that offers inherent benefits for both the children and the volunteers. The children may benefit from the individualized attention and from gaining knowledge about older people. For the adults, volunteering may make them feel more productive and may reduce feelings of loneliness or depression. Specific guidelines and a tool for providing volunteer feedback are offered to educators that are designed to maximize program success and sustained volunteer involvement. *[Article copies available for a fee from The Haworth Document Delivery Service: 1-800-342-9678. E-mail address: getinfo@haworthpressinc.com <Website: http://www.haworthpressinc.com>]*

**KEYWORDS.** Intergenerational, school, research, volunteer

During early and middle adulthood a person's job is often viewed as having a major influence on their sense of self-esteem. It is thought that as retirement approaches, the independence to do whatever one pleases replaces employment as the key to favorable self-impression. However, many elders have found that retirement is accompanied by a

---

Robert Strom and Shirley Strom are affiliated with the Division of Psychology in Education, Arizona State University, Box 870611, Tempe, AZ 85287-0611.

[Haworth co-indexing entry note]: "Establishing School Volunteer Programs." Strom, Robert and Shirley Strom. Co-published simultaneously in *Child & Youth Services* (The Haworth Press, Inc.) Vol. 20, No. 1/2, 1999, pp. 175-188; and: *Intergenerational Programs: Understanding What We Have Created* (ed: Valerie S. Kuehne) The Haworth Press, Inc., 1999, pp. 175-188. Single or multiple copies of this article are available for a fee from The Haworth Document Delivery Service [1-800-342-9678, 9:00 a.m. - 5:00 p.m. (EST). E-mail address: getinfo@haworthpressinc.com].

*175*

loss of purpose which must be restored to provide meaning for this stage of life. These elders regard community service as a worthwhile activity and recognize that fulfilling obligations to others is a basis for generating respect from them. This is why everyone is better off when older adults decide to share their talents with society. It all begins with volunteering.

## RECOGNIZING THE NEED TO VOLUNTEER

Sometimes people discover for themselves where they are needed. This was the case for Bill and Margaret Conrad of Phoenix, Arizona. One day Bill spotted the American flag flying upside down at an elementary school across the street from his home. Bill was a retired policeman so he knew that flying the flag upside down is considered a distress signal. He went to the principal's office to determine what was wrong. After a brief conversation, the principal asked Bill to help the sixth graders improve their flag-raising techniques. A few days later, Bill visited the principal again to inquire whether there was anything else he and his wife Margaret could do for the students. Soon Margaret was tutoring first graders in reading while Bill devoted time to fifth graders who had difficulty in mathematics.

Before long the school faculty invited Margaret to become the senior volunteers coordinator, an unpaid but important position. Together the Conrads went house to house in the neighborhood seeking possible helpers for the school. They visited churches and other organizations attended by seniors, inviting them to become involved with the children. This recruitment effort seemed to have paid off: At least one volunteer was visiting each of the school's 40 classrooms every day. Margaret described the motivation of the women and men whose work she coordinated as follows:

> There are great rewards for being a school volunteer. The more you are willing to give to this activity, the more you can receive. As you help children and encourage them with a pat on the shoulder, it isn't long until you get a lot of affection in return. It can provide a reason to get up in the morning, knowing that today I'm going to be with the children. And, of course, you feel useful, that is important at any age, but especially for older people.

Many people do not recognize their potential as a volunteer until someone else challenges them to become involved. Here again, Margaret provides an example:

> The kindergarten teachers requested that I find someone to assist on the playground in the morning as the buses arrived before the building was open. I stopped by the house across from school and asked the gentleman if he could help for 15 minutes in the morning. I knew his wife was ill but I figured she could be left by herself for a brief time. It would give him something worthwhile to do. He seemed uncertain and said that he would think about it. I identified some of the other neighbors who were volunteering at the school, ranging in age from 50 to 87. Following this conversation, he said he would come and give it a try. The next morning, after watching children on the playground, he came to my front door with a pleasant smile on his face and said that if anyone was needed for the afternoon kindergarten, he could do it. Mr. Zonn has been volunteering for six years and he puts in at least 10 hours a week.

These examples led us to conclude that having volunteers at school may help students and may provide satisfaction for those who spend time with them. Accordingly, it seems worthwhile to discover the best ways to make use of this support system.

## BECOMING A SCHOOL VOLUNTEER

Today's retirees are healthier and have more free time than any previous generation (Shapiro, 1997). We believe that they should be recognized by their communities as a valuable resource. This seems to be the belief also of an increasing number of teachers who want senior citizens as replacements for the many parents who are no longer able to provide assistance in the school. As nearly 80% of American mothers of school-age children are in the labor force, retirees have become the primary source of the nation's three million school volunteers (Herzog & Morgan, 1993).

It is common to assume that anyone who cares about the welfare of children would be a good volunteer. Certainly, the motivation to be helpful and a willingness to spend time with students would seem to be likely indicators of potential. However, some teachers and administrators have observed that specific attributes may make some older volunteers more effective than others. For example, many older adults demonstrate behaviors that are valued in the workplace, and that may indicate attributes such as dependability, punctuality, dedication, persistence, and adaptability. Many older adults also possess desirable qualities such as flexibility, spontaneity, patience, curiosity, and humor. Volunteering may help strengthen these qualities through interactions with students. The importance of modeling desirable characteristics is illustrated by the following examples of these qualities.

## Flexibility

Although many older adults worry about memory loss, they may tend to overlook the more significant loss of flexibility of thought. People who are inflexible can be identified at every stage in life, but this response pattern tends to increase with age (Blanchard-Fields & Hess, 1996; Sternberg, 1990). Inflexible persons are frequently described as being set in their ways. This means that they tend to like things to remain the same, to prefer predictable situations, and to not appreciate surprises. The main disadvantage of being inflexible is that it may preclude the growth that can come from seeing people, events, and circumstances in new ways.

Consider the example of Amy and Gwen, who seem to demonstrate inflexibility. Every week, they come to the senior center to hear recordings from the big-band era. The women have occupied the same front row seats since this program began three years ago. Recently, a new sound system was installed at the center. Although Amy and Gwen felt that the music from the new system was too loud, they said nothing. Finally, they complained to the director, who listened to their concerns and said, "Most people tell me the sound level is fine. One exception are the hard-of-hearing who would like the volume even higher. I suggest you move back a few rows and, if the music is still too loud, then go to the adjoining room and enjoy the band from there." Despite this, Amy and Gwen would not change their behavior to solve the problem. They refused to move from the front row seats that they had come to regard as their place. Each week they sat there, "imprisoned" by their need for sameness, locked into their routine, stuck in a rut of their own making due to a lack of flexibility.

Classroom volunteers who show flexibility are likely to have positive effects on students. Lois, for example, is prepared to accept the ever-changing feelings, moods and opinions of the sixth to eighth grade students with whom she works. Students seem to value Lois for making an effort to understand how they see things and for considering their ideas as important. She also tries helping them to look at situations from a variety of viewpoints, and encourages their careful consideration of alternatives for solving problems. Lois seems as willing to learn from the students as she is committed to supporting their learning. Students of all grades appreciate volunteers who consider new information, and who demonstrate flexibility in their thinking.

*Spontaneity*

It is important for classroom volunteers to exhibit spontaneity. This means showing the readiness to do some things without a lot of planning, being willing to depart from an agenda as it seems appropriate, and taking advantage of unforeseen opportunities when they arise. There is some evidence that people may become less spontaneous as they grow older (Blanchard-Fields & Hess, 1996; Sternberg, 1990). This appears to be the case with Grace, who lives in a retirement complex a few miles away from her son, Marshall, and his family. Marshall works in construction, which makes it difficult for him to forecast his free time. When he does get a break from the job, Marshall usually invites Grace for some family activity later that same day or the following day. These impromptu invitations bother Grace, who has become accustomed to living by a strict schedule. She prefers a lifestyle that allows her to know what will happen next and permits plenty of time to shift from one activity to another without her feeling stress. Thus, Grace usually tells Marshall that she cannot get ready with such short notice or that she is unable to participate because of prior plans to do something else. Unfortunately, Grace's unwillingness to act on "the spur-of-the-moment," to amend or delay any plans she has made, or to accommodate someone else's schedule, may carry a high cost. One consequence may be that Grace forfeits opportunities to enjoy the only times that the family can arrange to be with her. In a broader sense, giving up spontaneity may mean missing out on enjoyable interactions and experiencing the excitement associated with doing things that are unplanned.

Sometimes, parents and teachers deny children and themselves spontaneity by over-scheduling. At school, the defense may be, "We have limited time to cover so much material so we cannot wander from the topic or it will cause us to fall behind schedule." It is our belief that there are greater opportunities for learning when there is spontaneity. Students' motivation may increase when they learn to cope with uncertainty and learn to balance living for the present with living for the future. If children are given no chance to depart from what adults have planned for them, creative learning may seem "off-limits" and boredom with school may increase. For example, Evelyn is an older volunteer in a fourth-grade classroom who has come to appreciate why the teacher's plans are tentative. She has seen that plans must be revised often during a lesson according to how well the children respond to instruction. This means that both the teacher and Evelyn must improvise, react spontaneously to student difficulties, and forego anticipated activities in favor of other ones that may have a higher priority. On the one hand, it seems obvious to Evelyn that fourth graders are more present-oriented than adults, so they need practice in setting goals, amending aspirations, and realizing their need to delay gratification. On the other hand, Evelyn has found that interacting with students has increased her own sense of spontaneity. She believes students contribute to her self-improvement by their insistence on preparing for the future without sacrificing spontaneity.

## PREPARING VOLUNTEERS FOR THEIR ROLE

Successful partnerships are based on mutual consideration. When the needs of both partners are considered, relationships may be more productive and longer-lasting. This general principle can be applied to intergenerational programs linking schools with the community. Educators might benefit from knowing how to maximize volunteer effectiveness in the classroom. The degree of influence that volunteers may have on students and relative levels of volunteer satisfaction may depend partly on the support they are given by the faculty (Stevens, 1991). Recognizing the potential of older adults and utilizing their particular talents may increase levels of mutual respect in the teacher-volunteer relationship. The following recommendations may facilitate more productive partnerships between school staff and older adult volunteers.

*Teachers should identify specific tasks.* Although most teachers like the idea of having volunteers in their classroom, they may be uncertain at times about the things a volunteer should be expected to do. When expectations are vague and poorly defined, volunteers may experience anxiety and may be more likely to withdraw from participation. A better approach might be for the school principal to give a volunteer assignment request form to each participating faculty member. This form includes a checklist of tasks with which teachers may require assistance from volunteers. There is room on the form for teachers to describe additional kinds of assistance they may need. The assignment list we devised included (a) listening to students read, (b) giving corrective feedback for arithmetic problems, (c) reviewing spelling words, (d) going over lessons that a child missed through absence, and (e) monitoring vocabulary practice. Assignments that require group support included (a) playground supervision, (b) before- and after-school care, (c) drill-and-practice with flash cards, (d) leading discussions, and, (e) offering encouragement to troubled children.

In one survey of educators, 60% of teachers requested assistance with encouraging troubled children (Strom, 1996). When they were asked to explain their request, many stated a belief that there are more troubled children than is commonly supposed. Many perceived that patience in interacting with students is an important characteristic for volunteers in the classroom. The typical view expressed by young- and middle-aged teachers was that retired persons who volunteer in their classes generally possess patience to a greater degree than they do themselves. This finding seems to suggest the need for more older volunteers in the classroom than there are presently. Many elders have important emotional qualities that may contribute to children's development in and out of school (Goleman, 1995).

The clerical help often provided by elders also can allow teachers to perform other tasks. Volunteer clerical duties may include grading papers, preparing bulletin boards, reproducing written materials, locating library resources, and recording attendance. Older volunteers might also assume leadership for special activities such as (a) supervising arts and crafts projects, (b) monitoring computer tasks, (c) discussing hobbies, (d) reading or telling stories, and (e) giving language drills. Over the long run, these efforts may enhance student achievement.

*Volunteers should identify their interests.* Volunteers should be asked on an information form to provide some personal data that is needed in any workplace (e.g., volunteer's place of residence, phone number, health status, and who to contact in the event of an emergency). In addition, volunteers should be asked to state their preferences for when they want to volunteer and how they might like to spend their volunteer time in terms of the grade level, subject matter, and assignments. Knowledge about the specific hobbies, talents, and occupational experience of volunteers can be used by teachers and volunteer coordinators to make individualized matches between children and volunteers.

*Volunteer screening and orientation.* Security screening of volunteers is essential. School districts vary in the information that volunteers are expected to provide about themselves. In any case, the data form should include a place for disclosure of any arrest by the police. In the United States, the purpose of the National Child Protection Act (1996) is to protect students from encountering convicted felons who seek to work within the schools as volunteers, members of the staff or faculty. This legislation requires district participation in the national data bank that tracks abusers. Volunteers should be informed of this legislation and be told that similar investigations are done routinely in the certification of teachers. Efforts to safeguard children do not always work well. Nevertheless, there should be a high standard of screening for everyone who interacts with students.

*Volunteers should have a representative.* Most volunteers have occasional concerns, questions, and complaints about their working conditions. However, they may be uncertain about who should hear these matters and they may want to avoid "burdening" the teachers or the principal. Instead, they may prefer to express their views to a trusted person who has been designated as a volunteer coordinator at the school. The coordinator is responsible for recruitment, training, and placement of volunteers, as well as for representing them in discussions with the faculty and administration. Many retired people have work or volunteer experience that qualifies them to administer a school volunteer program. Indeed, parents are beginning to challenge schools that use paid staff to coordinate the work of volunteers. A more economical approach is to promote self-leadership among volunteers.

*Volunteers require inservice training.* To provide instruction for volunteers, teachers and staff should demonstrate how assigned tasks are to be performed. Subsequently, they should observe volunteers' performance and provide constructive feedback. Periodic training should emphasize issues related to child development and perceived difficulties in the classroom. This process may show volunteers how they can be more helpful and may contribute to a better understanding of standard operating procedures at the school. Specific topics for inservice training may vary, but any topic covered should include discussion of the perspectives and concerns of faculty, students, and volunteers.

*Volunteers should choose assignments.* Every volunteer should have a range of assignment options. This allows for an "easy exit" without a detailed explanation or embarrassment if a specific task is perceived by the volunteer as unacceptable. For example, a volunteer might imagine that working with first graders would be very satisfying, only to find with experience that this age group is too demanding of them or that they make too much noise. Another person might believe initially that working with the upper grades would offer the greatest intellectual challenge, but conclude later that members of this age group are moody and outspoken. At the outset, volunteers should be given several choices of age groups they might prefer to work with on a regular basis. It seems unreasonable to request binding decisions from people before they have had any direct experience. Getting involved with various tasks also helps volunteers feel comfortable knowing they are not obliged to continue working with the teachers to whom they were first assigned.

*Volunteers should decide their schedule.* Schedules for volunteers should be flexible enough to accommodate individual variability in obligations. Men and women may vary in the responsibilities they have outside of school. Some may have relatives or friends who count on them for personal care or other kinds of support. They may differ also in levels of health and stamina. Thus, some persons require a slower pace than others and may prefer relatively short work periods. Compared to these individuals, others are more energetic and may be available to help in the classroom for longer periods of time. Most retired people devote less than an hour a week to volunteering but make further commitments of their time when they feel competent (Herzog & Morgan, 1993). Being able to choose the time when they arrive at school is important to them and this choice should be respected. Every individual should be assured that the schedule they prefer will be acceptable and appreciated by the faculty, staff, and board of education.

*Volunteers should have a comfortable workload.* Sometimes, faculty members think that one way to show respect for volunteers is to increase their responsibility. For example, Nancy had done an excellent job shelving and checking out books. Because of this, the school librarian decided to put her in charge of the four other volunteers. However, when Nancy was informed of her new role as a supervisor, she stopped volunteering. This loss of a volunteer might have been prevented had the librarian discussed her plans with Nancy before implementing them. As it was, the change of assignment that the librarian saw as a promotion was seen by Nancy as a stressful and unsolicited task. Many volunteers have said they would never complain about an assignment, but would welcome a revision in what is expected of them if the possibility were raised by the teacher. Faculty members and the coordinator should periodically check with each volunteer regarding his or her level of comfort with the workload and nature of the assignment.

*Volunteers should be given feedback.* Volunteer performance should be assessed periodically. Volunteers often assert that volunteer activity enriches their lives. Because most are eager to perform well, they may feel disappointed when no feedback is given to them about their performance or about how they might be more effective. The potential benefits of giving volunteers feedback may include increasing their awareness of their influence in the classroom and using feedback to identify specific attitudes and behaviors for which there is a need for change (Strom & Strom, 1995).

As shown in Figure 1, we developed a "report card" for volunteers. Our instrument consists of 16 criteria used to record observations of volunteer behaviors as they are perceived by students, teachers, and the elders themselves. Students should be given assurance that their names will not be provided in feedback given to volunteers. To ensure this, volunteers should be given a summary profile form that combines the views of multiple observers. Many of the educators who have used this instrument have expressed the belief that giving individual feedback may bolster volunteers' self-esteem, support their motivation, and help shape their personal development.

*Volunteers should receive recognition.* Most teachers are accustomed to receiving compliments from parents for the assistance they give to students. These remarks may motivate teachers' continued hard work and personal development. Volunteers may benefit in a

FIGURE 1. School Volunteer Report Card

Name of Volunteer _____
Name of Evaluator _____

Directions: Check the blank beside the statements that describe this volunteer.
____ Encourages students to try again after they make a mistake
____ Helps students become self-confident in solving problems
____ Speaks clearly and uses words that can be easily understood
____ Shows a willingness to learn new things from the students
____ Gives students honest feedback about how well they are doing
____ Allows students enough time to think before giving answers
____ Wants students to ask questions about what they're studying
____ Likes to spend time with students who are at this grade level
____ Tries to get along with students who are difficult to be around
____ Protects students when they are mistreated by other people
____ Allows the students to judge some of their own schoolwork
____ Lets students know their ideas and opinions are important
____ Cares about students and is considered to be a good friend
____ Admits ignorance about the things that s/he does not know
____ Cooperates with the teacher and other members of the staff
____ Continues to try when problems and situations are difficult

You may have observed some other things this person does well or behaviors that you don't like and wish would improve. Write these feelings and ideas down on the other side of this paper.

Source: Office of Parent Development International, Arizona State University, Tempe, Arizona.

similar way when their contributions are recognized by the public. For example, several years ago one of the authors became chair of the board of directors for the Phoenix Retired Senior Volunteers Program. At the time, the customary method for recognition was to meet every 3 months in churches to give pins and certificates for a specified numbers of hours to the 1200 volunteers who have served in nonprofit settings such as hospitals, libraries, and schools. The recognition meetings were attended almost exclusively by the volunteers themselves, with only occasional visits from some official in city government. It was later decided to hold the recognition meetings in school settings. At the present time, the volunteer awards are given during ceremonies that also honor student and faculty accomplishments. By thanking volunteers in a public forum, schools provide a valuable lesson for students regarding the value of involvement with community service at every age (Clary, Snyder, & Ridge, 1992; Stevens, 1991).

*Benefits for students and volunteers.* Volunteers have much to offer the schools. For students, the benefits may include individual attention, getting to know people outside their own age-group, and finding out that many older people care about them. Students may also make greater academic gains. Researchers at Arizona State University compared the change across one year in scores on the California Achievement Test (CAT) for 147 elementary school students who were tutored by older adults with the change in scores for a similar number of untutored students from the same classrooms (Cooledge & Wurster, 1985). The results showed that students who had been tutored by elder volunteers made significantly greater gains on CAT scores than did their peers who did not receive any assistance.

Elders may also help make additional resources available for schools. Older adults' views of education may determine whether specific school-bond issues are passed.

In return for their assistance, older adults may benefit personally from working in schools. Volunteering offers them a chance to respond to the needs of others and may increase feelings of being useful and productive. Talking to children may present elders with new ways of looking at things, which may in turn broaden their personal perspective. Volunteer contact may also reduce feelings of loneliness and depression. These were some of the outcomes found in an assessment of an intervention program, in which culturally-diverse elders interacted with elementary and high school students (Strom & Strom, 1997).

In addition, the classroom environment provides considerable mental stimulation for older adults. Many people might suppose that nothing can be done about reversing intellectual decline. However, many studies have found that some declines in mental functioning can be slowed or even reversed by intervention (Druckman & Bjork, 1994; Lachman, 1997; Newman, 1991; Schaie, 1994). For example, Newman (1991) examined the memory performance of 50 retired men and women who had been invited to assist elementary and high school teachers in the classroom. None of these individuals, who ranged in age from 60-80 years, had ever served as school volunteers prior to their participation in the study. The research questions were (a) "Can weekly conversations between older adults and 6-18 year old students improve adult memory?" and (b) "Will interacting with students influence the general mood of older adults?" It was found that most of the volunteers perceived an improvement in their memory functioning as a result of their classroom experience. Newman reported also that subjective perceptions of memory improvement seemed positively associated with participant self-reports of higher self-esteem and a more optimistic outlook on life.

## CONCLUSION

Older adults want to have a sense of purpose and to feel that their life has meaning. These goals can be supported by their volunteering in schools. Older volunteers who are flexible, spontaneous, curious, and patient may be good replacements for parents whose employment prevents them from assisting in classes. However, the success of volunteers requires training and ongoing monitoring, facilitation and encouragement from faculty, administration, and staff. Specifically, volunteers should have (a) well-defined tasks, (b) a choice of assignments, (c) a self-determined schedule, (d) a comfortable workload, (e) systematic feedback on their efforts, (f) recognition for their accomplishments, and (g) a coordinator to represent them. Broader use of systematic feedback measures, like the instrument described here, and the dissemination of related results can only contribute to the quality of intergenerational programs and enrich the experiences of participating older volunteers and children.

## REFERENCES

Blanchard-Fields, F., & Hess, T. (1996). *Perspectives on cognitive change in adulthood and aging.* New York: McGraw-Hill.

Clary, E., Snyder, M., & Ridge, R. (1992). Volunteers' motivations. *Nonprofit management and leadership, 2,* 333-350.

Cooledge, N., & Wurster, S. (1985). Intergenerational tutoring and student achievement. *The Reading Teacher, 39* (3), 343-346.

Druckman, D., & Bjork, R. (1994). *Learning, remembering, believing: Enhancing human performance.* Washington, DC: National Academy Press.

Goleman, D. (1995). *Emotional intelligence.* New York: Bantam Books.

Herzog, A., & Morgan, J. (1993). Formal volunteer work of older Americans. In S. Bass, F. Caro, & Y. Chen (Eds.), *Achieving a productive society* (pp. 199-142). Westport, CT: Auburn House.

Lachman, M. (1997). *Your memory: What changes and what you can do about it.* Waltham, MA: National Policy and Resource Center on Women and Aging.

Newman, S. (1991). Everyday memory functions of older adults. *Intergenerational Clearinghouse, 10*(1), 1-2.

Schaie, K. (1994). The course of adult intellectual development. *American Psychologist, 49* (4), 304-313.

Shapiro, R. (1997). *The demographics of aging in America.* Washington, DC: Population Resource Center, 1-4.

Sternberg, R. (1990). *Wisdom, its nature, origins and development.* New York: Cambridge University Press.

Stevens, E. (1991). Toward satisfaction and retention of senior volunteers. *Journal of Gerontological Social Work, 16*, 33-41.

Strom, R. (1996). Establishing new traditions for a longevity society: Japan and the United States. *The Journal of Intercultural Studies, 23*(1), 1-13.

Strom, R., & Strom, S. (1995). Intergenerational learning: Grandparents in the schools. *Educational Gerontology, 21*, 321-335.

Strom, R., & Strom, S. (1997). Building a theory of grandparent development. *International Journal of Aging and Human Development, 45* (4), 1-31.

# Capacity-Building Partnerships Between Indigenous Youth and Elders

## Philip Cook

**SUMMARY.** Various strategies are discussed for creating intergenerational research opportunities that support the rights of indigenous children and youth. These strategies were developed during an international workshop that brought together indigenous elders and youth from 20 nations to discuss a global intergenerational action plan. Specific workshop goals were to (a) explore traditional values and teachings that nurture children, and (b) identify ways in which the United Nations Convention on the Rights of the Child might support indigenous peoples in developing research and training initiatives for strengthening the rights of indigenous children. The workshop applied traditional methods of mediation and dispute management to discussions of key child-rights issues relevant to indigenous children. The plan of action developed in the workshop included specific strategies for community and national level research based on information provided by Indigenous elders, children, and youth. Issues appropriate for study by intergenerational researchers include those related to discrimination, health, child protection, and increased participation of children and youth in cultural traditions. *[Article copies available for a fee from The Haworth Document Delivery Service: 1-800-342-9678. E-mail address: getinfo@haworthpressinc.com <Website: http://www.haworthpressinc.com>]*

**KEYWORDS.** Intergenerational, indigenous youth, elders

---

Philip Cook is affiliated with the School of Child and Youth Care, University of Victoria, P.O. Box 1700, Victoria, British Columbia, Canada V8W 2Y2.

[Haworth co-indexing entry note]: "Capacity-Building Partnerships Between Indigenous Youth and Elders." Cook, Philip. Co-published simultaneously in *Child & Youth Services* (The Haworth Press, Inc.) Vol. 20, No. 1/2, 1999, pp. 189-202; and: *Intergenerational Programs: Understanding What We Have Created* (ed: Valerie S. Kuehne) The Haworth Press, Inc., 1999, pp. 189-202. Single or multiple copies of this article are available for a fee from The Haworth Document Delivery Service [1-800-342-9678, 9:00 a.m. - 5:00 p.m. (EST). E-mail address: getinfo@haworthpressinc.com].

This paper describes a unique child-rights initiative that combines traditional knowledge gathered from indigenous elders (i.e., respected older persons) with the perspectives of indigenous children and youth considered "at risk." Recently, an international workshop was held to promote indigenous children's rights. The workshop was co-hosted by the School of Child and Youth Care and Aboriginal Liaison Office at the University of Victoria and the United Nations Children's Fund (UNICEF). The workshop brought together 85 people from 20 Indigenous nations, from the Inuit of Baffin Island to the Quechua of Ecuador, including 21 young people and a number of traditional Indigenous Elders.

The meeting was held at Dunsmuir Lodge on Láu-Wel-*New* Mountain, a Coast Salish Sacred site located north of Victoria, on Canada's west coast. The Salish cherish this mountain because, according to legend, the mountain saved their people during the great flood thousands of years ago and provided hope for future generations. It was considered a fitting place for a group of the world's Indigenous people to gather and to create a vision of saving their children and future generations from the "floods" of illness, disease, war, persecution, exploitation, and abuse that threaten their communities.

One of the young people at the workshop expressed the workshop theme in this way: "The vision created on this sacred mountain can become the dream carried forth by the young and the old to work together for children today. In this way, we create the guardians of the children for the future."

One Wayuu Elder who participated in the workshop quoted from Pocaterra (1994) when describing the importance of intergenerational relationships to Indigenous peoples:

> According to our vision of the world, it is impossible to speak of the family without reinstating our Elders as spiritual guides for our behaviour; the woman as advice giver, fighter, reproducer of life and backbone to the preservation of our people's identity; the youth as our future generations and the children as the community of our peoples, because they are our own lives. (p. 26)

Described below are the goals of the workshop, which seemed reflected in both its logo, the sacred Thunderbird surrounding and protecting young and old, and in its title, *Caring for Indigenous Children: Capacity Building to Support Indigenous Children's Rights*:

1. To explore the traditional Indigenous values and teachings used by Indigenous people to nurture children.
2. To identify ways in which the United Nations Convention on the Rights of the Child (CRC), within the International Decade of the World's Indigenous Peoples could support Indigenous peoples in developing research and training initiatives that are aimed at upholding the rights of Indigenous children.

Workshop participants were asked to develop practical research and training initiatives through the joint efforts of young and old Indigenous representatives. It was hoped that new ways would be discovered of looking at children's rights from a cross-cultural perspective. The approach taken in the workshop was based on the belief that children's rights are furthered best by child advocacy that is grounded in traditional cultural knowledge and in values that support children's well-being (de Cellar, 1996). Creating opportunities for young people to explore their cultural identity in collaboration with their Elders is an essential aspect of this process.

Self-definition is considered essential for Indigenous cultural distinctiveness. The Working Group on Indigenous Populations, operating within the U.N. Commission on Human Rights, has as mandates the promotion of the rights of Indigenous peoples and the formation of universal terminology for defining Indigenous peoples. In a 1996 working paper presented to the U.N. Economic and Social Council (United Nations Economic and Social Council, 1997), this group proposed that the concept of Indigenous peoples include the following:

- Priority in time, with respect to the occupation and the use of a specific territory.
- The voluntary perpetuation of cultural distinctiveness, that may include the aspects of language, social organizations, religion and spiritual values, modes of production, laws, and institutions.
- Self-identification, as well as recognition by other groups, or by State authorities, as a distinct collectivity.
- An experience of subjugation, marginalization, dispossession, exclusion or discrimination, whether or not these conditions persist.

Indigenous youth are often overrepresented in statistics of morbidity and mortality (Report of Royal Commission on Aboriginal

Peoples, 1996). The high incidence of these phenomena may be attributed to the breakdown of traditional family, community, and cultural supports. Reconnecting with cultural strengths may help to rebuild the links among culture, self-identity, and self-esteem. Typically, Indigenous Elders are the keepers of cultural values that underpin family well-being and community well-being.

Elders play an important role in many Indigenous societies. In Indigenous communities, age does not itself make one an Elder, and many Indigenous peoples have a name for Elders that distinguishes them as a group from the European-American category of senior citizens. Among the Inuit, for example, elderly people are referred to as *inutuqak*, but those considered Elders are referred to as *angijukqauqatigiit* (Report on the Royal Commission on Aboriginal Peoples, 1996). In a submission to the Canadian House of Commons study on Aboriginal Wellness, Elders are described as follows:

> For Indigenous people, authentic elders are living models of transcendence, that is they are the epitome of human experience in an awakened state of mind. . . . Authentic elders today are not necessarily chronologically old. Rather, they are individuals who are perceived to have many gifts with which they can perform multiple roles. The leadership hat is only one of the many that elders wear. They are also looked to as oral historians, teachers, cultural workers, ecologists, environmentalists and healers. (p. 21)

Intergenerational gatherings, such as the Caring for Indigenous Children Workshop, offer an opportunity to apply the values carried by the Elders to the issues challenging many Indigenous children and youth. One of the outcomes from the Victoria workshop was the creation of a Plan of Action for developing research and training strategies that promote the rights of Indigenous children. Specifically, the plan proposes that research be aimed at identifying community and national level indicators of Indigenous children's rights, as they were espoused in the Convention on the Rights of the Child during the International Decade of the World's Indigenous Peoples.

# THE U.N. CONVENTION ON THE RIGHTS OF THE CHILD AND INDIGENOUS CHILDREN

Since the adoption of the United Nations Convention on the Rights of the Child (CRC) in 1989, the global community has seen significant changes in the way that children are valued and their rights are respected. The CRC has been embraced to a greater extent than has any other international human-rights treaty in history. Currently, it is only two countries short (the United States and Somalia) of universal ratification.

Two parallel agreements, which were established at the World Summit for Children in 1990, have helped promote the CRC. These are the *World Declaration for the Survival, Development and Protection of Children*, and *First Call*. The former outlines practical goals and strategies for meeting children's health and education needs whereas the latter establishes guidelines for ensuring that children's developmental needs are met, irrespective of social or economic cycles (LeBlanc, 1995; Verhellen, 1994).The CRC is notable for its definition of childhood (i.e., ranging from 0-18 years of age) and for focusing attention on the world's most vulnerable children such as (a) those affected by armed conflict, (b) street children, (c) children with disabilities, and (d) children from minority or ethnic groups.

The rights addressed in the CRC, all of which are relevant to Indigenous children, include rights to health, education, protection, and participation. The Convention also refers specifically to the rights of Indigenous children, in Articles 17, 29, and 30. Article 30 states that:

> . . . a child . . . who is indigenous shall not be denied the right, in community with other members of his or her group, to enjoy his or her culture, to profess and practice his or her own religion, or to use his or her own language. (CRC Article 30)

Article 30 outlines the need to support the rights of Indigenous children in ways that uphold Indigenous cultures. This pertains especially to Indigenous children who are considered "at risk" due to racism and discrimination, which contributes to the breakdown of culture, community, and family. Article 8, which refers to the right to a name, nationality, and identity, seems pertinent to this issue as well. This is because of the importance placed on self-identity by Indigenous peoples and because of the loss of identity experienced by many

Indigenous children and youth. The spirit of both Articles 30 and 8 seems reflected in Article 12, which relates to the children's right for their views to be heard and considered. Article 12 emphasizes the importance of children's participation in the dialogue on culture and identity.

So that Indigenous children and Elders might identify common concerns and apply cultural balance and harmony to these concerns, two focus group sessions were held in Victoria, prior to the Workshop. These sessions were facilitated by a child-rights expert and an Indigenous person with traditional-cultural training. Participants included 10-15 Indigenous children and Elders from Canada and Latin America. Some of the child-rights issues discussed in the focus groups were (a) protection from bonded child labor, (b) culturally sensitive health initiatives to combat diseases, (c) malnutrition and long-term disability, and (d) action to reduce poverty, homelessness, discriminatory practices against marginalized youth (e.g., street youth).

New partnerships among Indigenous Elders, youth, and community-based child-rights advocates can "breathe life" into the Convention by applying traditional Indigenous values of healing and balance to current issues that may place youth at risk. In this way, children's-rights strategies are developed intergenerationally and from the "ground up" rather than being imposed by state governments or international organizations.

The CRC can also be used as a framework for Indigenous peoples, governments, and non-governmental organizations (NGO's) for devising, implementing, and evaluating community-level children's programs in a culturally appropriate manner. Now that it is approaching universal ratification, the CRC may be a powerful advocacy tool for putting Indigenous children's issues on the global community's agenda.

Although the U.N. Committee on the Rights of the Child is the official body that monitors it, the CRC works in collaboration with UNICEF and other U.N. bodies and non-governmental organizations. UNICEF is active in supporting children's rights through a variety of programs in developing countries (Cohen, 1990). Although senior UNICEF policy advisors have participated annually in the inter-agency meetings held during the International Decade of the World's Indigenous Peoples, UNICEF has yet to develop any specific policy or programmatic response to "Decade" activities. The Caring for Indigenous Children workshop appears to have been a first response, an

extension of current programming in child protection, health, education, and participation.

## THE INTERNATIONAL DECADE
## OF THE WORLD'S INDIGENOUS PEOPLES

In its resolution 48/163 of December 21, 1993, the U.N. General
Assembly proclaimed the International Decade of the World's Indigenous Peoples as being from 1995 to 2004. The goal of Decade activities is to strengthen international cooperation in addressing problems
faced by Indigenous peoples, in areas such as human rights, the environment, education, and health.

The Decade was envisioned as a time in which community-level,
action-oriented programs would be developed in partnership with Indigenous peoples. The General Assembly instructed the U.N. financial
and development institutions, operational programs, and specialized
agencies to achieve these goals by: (a) giving priority and resources to
improving the conditions of Indigenous peoples, (b) launching special
projects in collaboration with Indigenous peoples for the purpose of
strengthening community-level initiatives, and (c) designating focal
points of Decade activities in coordination with the Centre for Human
Rights.

An important part of this work is developing programs that address
the needs of Indigenous children. Indigenous children comprise a
disproportionate number of children in difficult circumstances around
the world. They face some of the greatest threats to survival, protection, and healthy human development, including those of: (a) bonded
child labour; (b) a high incidence of AIDS and other diseases, (c) substance abuse, (d) poverty, (e) malnutrition, (f) homelessness, (g) long-
term disability, (h) the negative impact of environmental degradation,
(i) the breakdown of intergenerational relationships and loss of Indigenous languages and culture, and (j) discriminatory practices.

Elders can provide important support to Indigenous children by
implementing child- and youth-focused programs (Clarkson, Morrisette, & Regallet, 1992). Also, elders can provide Indigenous children
with a greater sense of connection with the strengths of their family,
community and culture, thus helping to build self-esteem (Pepper &
Henry, 1995).

For advocacy to be effective at both the national and community levels, strategies are needed that are based on an understanding of the relationship between traditional teachings about children's survival, growth, and development, and the values in the CRC. The almost universal ratification of the CRC, as it coincides with the U.N. Decade for the World's Indigenous Peoples, suggests that it is an ideal time to begin this task. One of the objectives of the Victoria workshop was to increase the attention given during the International Decade to the rights of Indigenous children.

Workshop participants examined both the congruity and the dissonance between the holistic vision for children inherent in traditional Indigenous values and the vision espoused by the CRC. From this process came a plan for social democracy in support of the world's Indigenous children. Ideally, the conceptual links between these two visions for Indigenous children would be applied to culturally-grounded, community-based research, training programs, and policy development. The plan of action would be used as a conceptual scaffold for training government, NGO, UNICEF and other U.N. Agency staff who work with Indigenous peoples.

## WORKSHOP PARTICIPANTS AND OVERVIEW

Participants at the workshop included: (a) traditional Indigenous representatives (e.g., Elders, healers), (b) Indigenous youth, (c) representatives from Indigenous NGOs, (d) UNICEF program officers, (e) representatives from other UN agencies, and (f) child-focused specialists with a background in research, policy, or training relating to programming for Indigenous children and youth. In total, 85 delegates attended the workshop. The ages of the child participants ranged from 10-18 years and the oldest Elder was 75 years of age.

Twenty Indigenous nations were represented at the workshop, including the Coast Salish (Canada), Kwagiulth (Canada), Inuit (Canada), Maori (New Zealand/Aotearoa), Kelabit (Sarawak), Mextica (Mexico), Maya (Guatemala), Rupununi (Guayana), and Wayuu (Venezuela).

Across the six days of the workshop, there were four "theme-days," which focused on Health, Education, Protection, and Participation. The theme days were preceded by a day of introduction and orientation, and were followed by a day of activities based on the traditional teachings, discussions, and issues of the theme days. The "talking circle," a widely-used method of Indigenous group discussion and dispute resolution, was used in many of the large- and small-group discussions.

The activities of each theme day were scheduled as follows:

*Ceremony:* In Indigenous ceremony, strengths and values are expressed in song, dance, and prayer. Coast Salish peoples began each day of the workshop with a traditional welcome to Indigenous people from around the world. Delegates from other nations returned this welcome. Through the opening and closing ceremonies, the Coast Salish and other Indigenous Elder delegates surrounded and protected the youth, who met to celebrate and honour old connections and to protect those who will be the bearers of culture–the children.

*Traditional teachings:* The workshop was meant to (a) harvest the strengths of the past and to apply them to the future, (b) learn about traditional, holistic models of personal balance and see how these traditional practices could be applied to a modern context, and (c) address issues of family and community breakdown. During the Traditional Teachings, the Indigenous peoples shared, through words, song, and dance, the traditional methods, ancient teachings, and key spiritual values surrounding the theme of the day. The Traditional Teachings was a "solution first" approach, which prepared participants to listen to the issues under discussion, with the strong voices of the Indigenous peoples echoing in their minds.

*Global overview:* During this segment, individuals from UNICEF and other U.N. agencies and NGOs provided workshop participants with a global overview of the issues affecting Indigenous children, with specific references to the theme of the day and the CRC.

*Model showcase:* Descriptions were presented of successful, ongoing community-development models that support Indigenous children and youth. These examples were used to illustrate some of the ways in which Indigenous children's rights may be sustained by traditional cultures.

*Group discussion:* Elders, youth, technical participants and training participants met in small groups or remained in the larger talking circle to discuss specific issues and to brainstorm about how the Traditional Teachings and Models could be applied to the issues in the Global Overview.

*Children's presentations:* At the end of each day, the child and youth participants, who had been meeting in their own small group, met with the larger group to present the results of their group activities. It seemed appropriate to end each day by listening to the children to remind delegates of the central purpose of the workshop.

## THE PLAN OF ACTION AS A TOOL FOR RESEARCH

Figure 1 depicts the plan of action that was developed during the workshop. The plan was based primarily on the perceived links among Indigenous cultures, children's rights, and priorities for human development. It was intended to be used as a rough guide for multi-level discussion of the rights of Indigenous children (Halldorson, Bramly, Cook, & White, 1997), and for designing research focused on children's rights.

The action plan highlights three essential components of community-based and global initiatives in support of children's rights:

- Traditions and cultural values that support the child's right to a life with dignity. This is a central focus of initiatives aimed at strengthening the rights of Indigenous children and youth.
- Children's active participation in cultural traditions and teachings, thus promoting personal balance and well-being.
- The application of these components to child-rights issues of Indigenous children.

The fundamental value at the heart of both the Indigenous values supporting children and the CRC is the child's right to be treated with dignity. The value of human dignity was espoused by all cultures and delegates at the workshop. The preamble of the CRC lists the following values, all of which support a child's right to life with dignity.

- Children are entitled to special care and assistance.
- The family is the ideal environment for the growth and well-being of children.
- Traditional and cultural values are considered to be essential for the protection and healthy development of the child.
- It is the responsibility of all governments to work together in support of these goals.

FIGURE 1. Strategies Based on the UN Convention on the Rights of the Child to Support Indigenous Children's Rights

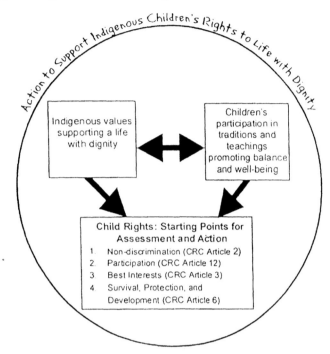

The overarching value of children's dignity was seen by Indigenous Elders, children, and child-rights experts as being nested in family, community, and culture. The CRC recognizes the family as the ideal support mechanism for children's development. Several articles in the CRC (articles 2, 3, 5, 9) pertain to values that support the protection of children and parents (e.g., that the perspective of the parents should be taken into account when considering the best interests of the child, and that the roles and duties of the parents, extended family, and community are to be respected). These values are in harmony with the values of Indigenous cultures, as described by Elders in the talking-circle discussions. Also, article 30 of the CRC articulates the important role of Indigenous culture in supporting Indigenous children's language rights and religious rights.

Many of the workshop discussions touched on Indigenous children's identity and self-esteem as they may be linked to their land, their language, and their cultural values. The key to reinforcing a child's cultural values is their participation in cultural traditions and teachings that promote personal balance and well-being. Cultural participation is the best vehicle for promoting a child's healthy development and membership in his or her culture. Culture is flexible: Children retain certain cultural values and beliefs and add to these as they participate, learn and grow in their families and in their communities.

The CRC (articles 12, 13, 14, 15, 16) states that the objective of promoting participation is to help children grow into contributing community members. This is done by fostering their active participation in family and community matters. The family guides and informs the child in this process according to the child's evolving capacities (developmental level), the family's child-rearing practices, and the child's participation in civil society.

Research strategies developed in the workshop included examining the form and extent to which Indigenous children and youth participate in cultural activities. For example, street children are often denied access to traditional practices that may serve as protective mechanisms. However, some traditional practices may be harmful to children, such as the marriage of girls at a young age. These intergenerational issues need further study in light of the CRC articles.

Some delegates challenged the notion that children are expected to listen and to not speak in the presence of adults or Elders. It was suggested that research might explore how children's "voice" might be integrated into intergenerational community discussion and decision-making.

Some workshop participants pointed out that some Indigenous peoples have unique ways of discussing and debating issues pertaining to children, such as the talking circle. These culturally-based, information-gathering, and dissemination procedures might be applied to community focus groups or participatory action research. Elders can play a key role in initiating community discussion that is culturally appropriate. Youth facilitators with a background in children's rights can help create a safe environment for youth to participate in these discussions.

The CRC provides four guiding principles that can be used to assess and take action on children's rights, and to guide research. These four principles are based on children's rights to (a) non-discrimination (CRC article 2), (b) participation (CRC article 12), (c) best interests (CRC article 3), and (d) survival, protection, and development (CRC article 6).

Participants at the workshop continually reaffirmed the notion that Indigenous child rights are linked to the land, the sacred, past history, and to the traditional teachings of the Elders. Discrimination was seen as a constant threat to these links insofar as it precludes Indigenous children from learning their history and from practicing their religion. Discriminatory practices may also keep Indigenous peoples from their land and may impede their access to basic services such as health care and education. Discriminatory practices may increase the vulnerability of Indigenous children to the devastating impact of armed conflict, diseases such as HIV/AIDS, and the multiple risks of life on the street.

Many of the children and youth at the workshop expressed the view that they are not passive victims, but rather, are articulate, action-oriented advocates for their own and others' best interests. They described participation as a form of relationship, a constant give-and-take of responsibilities between older and younger generations.

Many participants proposed that Indigenous peoples' own values be taken into account whenever the *Best Interests Test* is applied to their children, particularly in child-custody legal procedures. That is, it was felt that the Best Interests Test should be modified to reflect local Indigenous cultural values and beliefs, before it is applied to Indigenous children.

Indigenous participants, in general, called for higher-quality and more culturally-based education, health care, and child-protection services. For traditional teachings and healing mechanisms to be used effectively in achieving these goals, more intergenerational partnerships must be established among Indigenous organizations and communities, government agencies, and children's advocacy organizations on all levels (Halldorson, Bramly, Cook, & White, 1997).

Overall, these CRC guiding principles can be used to identify community or national research-indicators of Indigenous children's rights. The articles provide benchmarks against which the current situation of Indigenous children may be measured. The general perspective taken in the workshop was that the research process must reflect the values of Indigenous cultures and the priorities of local community members of all ages.

The plan of action arising from the workshop provides a framework for promoting the rights of Indigenous children during the Decade of

Indigenous Peoples through both intergenerational research and social action. Children and Elders can and should be active partners in this process of helping to deconstruct the language of human rights into meaningful, culturally-relevant practices.

# REFERENCES

Clarkson, L., Morrisette, V., & Regallet, G. (1992). *Our responsibility to the seventh generation: Indigenous Peoples and sustainable development.* Winnipeg: International Institute for Sustainable Development.

Cohen, C. P. (1990). The role of non-governmental organizations in the drafting of the Convention. *Human Rights Quarterly, 12,* 137-147.

de Cellar, P. (1996). *Our creative diversity: Report on the World Commission on Culture and Development.* Paris: UNESCO Publishing.

Halldorson, L., Bramly L., Cook, P., & White, W. (1997). *Claiming our place in the circle: A report on the Caring for Indigenous Children Capacity Building Workshop and a Plan of Action.* Victoria: Unpublished Report.

Himes, J. (1995). *Implementing the Convention on the rights of the child: Resource mobilization in low-income countries.* The Hague: Martinus Nijhoff Publishers.

Karp, J. (1997). *Human dignity and the Convention on the Rights of the Child.* Unpublished paper presented at the Caring for Indigenous children: Capacity building to support Indigenous children's rights workshop. Victoria, Canada: University of Victoria.

LeBlanc, L. (1995). *The Convention on the Rights of the Child.* Lincoln: University of Nebraska Press.

Pepper, F., & Henry, S. (1995). An Indian perspective on self esteem. In S. Selkirk & J. Archibald (Eds.), *Selected papers from the Mokakit conference,* pp. 97-124. Vancouver: Mokakit Education and Research Association.

Pocaterra, N. (1994). Speech to the United Nations opening ceremony of the International Year of the World's Indigenous People. In United Nations (1994), *Seeds of a new partnership: Indigenous Peoples and the United Nations.* New York: United Nations Department of Public Information.

Report of the Royal Commission on Aboriginal Peoples (1996). *Perspectives and Realities* (Volume 4). Ottawa: Canada Communication Group.

House of Commons Standing Committee on Health (1995). *Towards holistic wellness in the Aboriginal peoples.* Ottawa: Government of Canada.

Suttles, W. (1987). *Coast Salish essays.* Seattle: University of Washington Press.

United Nations Economic and Social Council (1996). Working paper by the Chairperson-Rapporteur, Mrs. Erica-Irene Daes, on the concept of Indigenous people. Geneva: Commission on Human Rights.

Verhellen, E. (1994). *Convention on the Rights of the Child.* Apeldoorn, Holland: Garant Press.

# EPILOGUE

# Intergenerational Contact
# as Intergroup Communication

Jessica Abrams
Howard Giles

**SUMMARY.** This Epilogue highlights important progress in the area of intergenerational contact research and identifies some important operational and empirical lacunae. The diverse array of intergenerational programs is discussed as are the potential consequences of program contact for older adults, children and youth. We highlight for researchers and program planners the likelihood that pre-existing stereotypes can affect program experiences (and the communicative patterns within them) as well as the need to articulate program goals more clearly. The paper's main thrust is in drawing attention to several theoretical models that can usefully guide future research. A theoretical framework based on intergroup communication is outlined that explores the motivations and communicative behaviors likely during intergenerational exchange. Researchers should investigate communicative strategies that promote

Jessica Abrams and Howard Giles are affiliated with the Department of Communication, University of California, Santa Barbara, CA 93106-4020.

[Haworth co-indexing entry note]: "Intergenerational Contact as Intergroup Communication." Abrams, Jessica and Howard Giles. Co-published simultaneously in *Child & Youth Services* (The Haworth Press, Inc.) Vol. 20, No. 1/2, 1999, pp. 203-217; and: *Intergenerational Programs: Understanding What We Have Created* (ed: Valerie S. Kuehne) The Haworth Press, Inc., 1999, pp. 203-217. Single or multiple copies of this article are available for a fee from The Haworth Document Delivery Service [1-800-342-9678, 9:00 a.m. - 5:00 p.m. (EST). E-mail address: getinfo@haworthpressinc.com].

successful intergenerational contact. *[Article copies available for a fee from The Haworth Document Delivery Service: 1-800-342-9678. E-mail address: getinfo@haworthpressinc.com <Website: http://www.haworthpressinc.com>]*

**KEYWORDS.** Intergenerational, research, contact, communication

A large literature in Western social gerontology attests to negative stereotypes and attitudes associated with older adults (e.g., Kite & Johnson, 1988). Largely because of this, an array of programs has been established to facilitate positive interactions between younger and older individuals. The so-called "contact programs" have been designed primarily under the assumption that predominantly favorable perceptions of elderly people garnered through them will assist in reducing ageist attitudes of youth. Over the last 25 years, there have been numerous investigations into whether such intergenerational contact has been successful along these lines.

The papers in this volume indicate clearly that research efforts by intergenerational scholars have come a long way and we have now more sophisticated insights into what happens when youth and elderly people interact. A number of the papers extend significantly the traditional brief of contact programs mentioned above. While varying in their conceptualizations of the contact, use of different dependent variables, and contrasting goals, they provide an excellent window into the diverse intergenerational contact programs now in place. From this collection, we learn that for youth, intergenerational contact is significantly related to: (a) increased school attendance, (b) more positive attitudes regarding the elderly, the future, and community service, (c) a reduced inclination to use drugs, and (d) an increased sense of well-being.

Not all the contributions deal directly with intergenerational programs; several of them challenge extant approaches. For example, VanderVen reminds us that as young scholars we were taught to develop and argue from theory. Yet, she argues that theory is glaringly absent from contemporary work in the intergenerational field. Theory, along with research and practice, links the "knowledge triangle." Kocarnik Ponzetti and Ponzetti bring to mind the difficulties that people may face when trying to care for their dependents. They argue that because people are living longer, families may need care for both generations of dependents, young and old. These authors recommend that employers integrate elder care services with child care programs as an effective means of satisfying employees' needs while maintaining employee productivity. Travis and Stremmel support this by noting that unification of child and adult care may be a way for developing mutual respect, sharing knowledge, and developing meaningful relationships between the generations. Be this as it may, they demonstrate that the likelihood of administrators providing intergenerational activities is significantly related to the latter's *attitudes* toward intergenerational exchange.

The foregoing papers illustrate that while the overarching theme is intergenerational program research, each contribution brings with it different and valuable perspectives and foci. Space precludes any comprehensive analysis of all the important issues and problems emerging from them and we take the liberty of selecting from amongst those that afford a concise and coherent discussion.

## *INTERGENERATIONAL PROGRAMS: THEIR NATURE AND GOAL ORIENTATION*

One obvious departure that many of the papers here make from prior research is that intergenerational contact can take place in more "naturalistic" settings than previously conceived. Specifically, the authors answer the call to take intergenerational contact outside of institutions (i.e., hospitals and nursing homes) and this increases generality of findings (Fox & Giles, 1993). Throughout the volume, we see intergenerational contact taking place in a wide variety of settings: Inside the school classroom as well as tutoring outside it (Newman, Morris, & Streetman), in child day care (Angersbach & Jones-Forster) and a mental health center (Griff), on school trips, attending sports or cultural events, and participating in community service activities (Taylor, LoSciuto, Fox, Hilbert, & Sonkowsky), providing escorts and delivering meals (Brabazon), and finally, in collaborative decision-making activities between youth and older adults (Cook). By continuing to examine intergenerational contact in such a wide variety of settings we can move toward a more general picture of "what works" and "what doesn't": A state of the art which will assist in our ability to educate program planners and policy makers. As Vernon reminds us, it is critical that planners especially are aware of the complex contextual factors involved in designing their programs as some are more conducive to improving attitudes and stereotypes than others. While we may not be at such an emancipatory stage as yet, partly because of the different goals and foci of planners and researchers, we are at least on the road. What is required as a next important step forward (beyond the structural classification of Fox and Giles [1993]) is a multidimensional taxonomy of contact programs which will allow us to more systematically locate most of the programs within it. Thereby, we can assess programs' parameters analytically, compare and contrast them cogently with other programs having similar and dissimilar goals, and determine which underlying structural, psychological, communicative, and other ingredients are associated with variably desired outcomes. Ultimately, such a taxonomy will provide us with a template enabling the most productive intergenerational programs to be designed.

The design of many intergenerational contact programs occurs without much academic discussion, yet such dialogue is extremely important. Indeed, programs should be designed with a specific purpose(s) in mind that is linked to research and/or evaluation, and this does not always appear to be the case. Whether contact is being designed to counter attitudes certain youth have of the elderly or whether older adults are involved due to their convenience as a newly discovered social resource is sometimes difficult to discern. The fact that youth can have negative perceptions of elderly folk should not be ignored in program design (Williams, Ota, Giles, Pierson, Gallois, Ng, Lim, Tyan, Somera, Maher & Harwood, 1997). For example, as Vernon notes, if the elderly are perceived to be forgetful, then such (oftentimes erroneous) preconceptions can be challenged. That said, it should not be assumed that contact will alter attitudes (Fox & Giles, 1993). Some older people also may sometimes unwittingly behave and self-stereotype in ways that perpetuate them. Accordingly, youths may internalize further these stereotypes and enter old age themselves with unfavorable expectations about aging (Bieman-Copland, Ryan, & Cassano, 1998). Hence, although elderly volunteer-mentors may be a tremendous resource, program designers may wish to consider and challenge such negative perceptions that can of course also be *reciprocally* negative (see Giles & Williams, 1994).

Although the goals of some of these papers may not always be made explicit enough for theoretical tastes, they do, again, succeed at broadening the documented scope of intergenerational contact and related research. They illustrate well the many different functions and roles that older adults can play in our communities. One particularly evident role was mentor, which may serve both younger *and* older folks well. Taylor et al. report that mentoring gave older people "a reason to get up in the morning." Prior work suggests that younger people perceive the elderly as being worthy of supplying useful advice and assistance. Specifically, Harwood (1998) examined age-based, stereotyped expectations, arguing that youth often bring so-called "intergenerational communication schemas" (ICSs) with them as they engage older people in interaction. These ICSs comprise such features as the anticipated talk patterns of both participants, expected emotions in the encounter, and predicted topics of conversation.

The "Learning" ICS was one category emerging from this work where young adults mentioned the wisdom of older people, learning something from the conversation and being inspired. It was reported that younger people were often interested in learning about historical events or interested in older persons disseminating prudent advice regarding personal issues. Older people mentoring younger people who already embrace such an ICS would seem a good program match. If having the elderly mentoring youth is as beneficial as many of the current papers suggest (Angersbach & Jones; Brabazon; Newman, Morris, & Streetman), then Strom and Strom's call for elderly volunteers to serve in this capacity in schools is warranted. In this way, older adults can contribute to society while simultaneously challenging any negative ICSs youth may possess.

Although considerable research has investigated intergenerational mentoring between youth and older adults who are strangers (Fox & Giles, 1993), we know less about such contact within our own families (Peterson, 1989). If the elderly serve as good community-based mentors, then one might be disposed toward believing that grandparents should be "built-in" family mentors. However, Griff shows us that in the context of play therapy this will only be successful if the grandparent has a healthy relationship with the parent. In this vein, Fitzpatrick (1990) noted a typology of four grandparent-parent types (viz., pluralistic, protective, laissez-fair, and consensual) and that these can usefully predict communication patterns within families. It may be that families are only receptive to the elderly as mentors in their own families when grandparent-parent communication is pluralistic, that is, valuing open communication and the discussion of differing opinions. Indeed, there are instances where the elderly are not appreciated in their own families. In Brabazon's paper, volunteer mentors reported that they decided to become mentors to share the knowledge, skills, and wisdom learned over a lifetime; they also reported, however, that their own children and grandchildren did not value their life experiences. Kalbfleisch and Anderson (1997) report that while grandparents often provide emotional and physical support to their grandchildren, sometimes grandparents are not the recipients of emotional support from their grandchildren in turn. Future research should be aimed at investigating further the dynamics of intergenerational relationships within families, specifically when and why certain elderly family members are not appreciated in the familial context (Fox, 1993).

People adapt to the aging process through their interactions with others, and a person's internalized conceptions of the aging process are socialized into their make-up early in life, including anticipation of being grandparents themselves one day. As we have argued elsewhere, many young people do not have a clear idea of their own position along the lifespan (Giles & Harwood, 1997) and when they do, it is often with negative anticipation. Moreover, we (James Honneycutt, personal communication, June 14, 1998) would speculate that most youth feel that when they become older, become parents, and eventually perhaps grandparents, that somehow they will fulfill these roles and identities more satisfactorily than the present generation; in other words, "I will not be anything near like *them!*" Our lack of systematic attention to viewing youth education in lifespan terms due in part to the exigencies of contemporary, immediate needs, probably means that we are not inviting sufficient models for young people to access both now and later as they cope with moving across the different subcultures that constitute maturing adult life (Giles, Fox, Harwood, & Williams, 1994).

Over the years, there has been a call for longitudinal work in the intergenerational domain. While the current collection does not respond to that plea, some important conclusions do emerge. Taylor et al. demonstrate the benefit of contact occurring over a number of years, if the opportunity is provided. They found that "at risk" mentees who spend at least 8 hours a week with their mentor fared far better than those who spent much less time; they noted that "developing a sustained, trusting relationship takes time." A good mentorship relationship can operate only when quality contact is established over the long haul and, as our interaction analysis papers suggest (Angersbach & Jones; Newman et al.) when group size permits younger and older participants to interact freely.

## IMPORTANT CONCEPTUAL AND EMPIRICAL LACUNAE

Intergenerational contact has been operationalized in many ways; indeed, different operationalizations of contact emerge for virtually every paper in this collection. We have observed that the field in general tends to combine all interactions which take place between someone over 55 years of age with someone younger than 18 years and labels them "intergenerational contact," typically in the context of a community based, organized program. It is not the label that makes this problematic but, rather, the need to operationalize it more succinctly. Specifically, a number of important factors such as chronological and psychological age, objective and subjective health of the older adults, and the type and duration of contact can influence the program experience for either or both participant groups. In essence, this is why goal setting and taxonomic planning are advisable.

Authors here have also used different operationalizations for the "older adult" participants in intergenerational programs; with regard to their age alone, they range from 55 to 91 years. Because people are healthier and living longer, this wide age range may be problematic both theoretically and practically as VanderVen describes. There are huge inter-individual differences in health, mobility, financial security, and activity between persons aged 55 and 91. Indeed, someone in their 60s or 70s, for example, may not even define themselves according to age despite certain others' categorical attributions of them in these terms. When participants vary unbeknownst to each other in the relative importance and social meanings of their age, miscommunication can result (Ota, Harwood, Williams & Takai, 1998). If robust conclusions are to be drawn about intergenerational contacts, operationalizations of their variable nature and what it means to be older and younger should be expressed more clearly and better understood, both in practice and research.

Interestingly, while the foregoing papers overwhelmingly support the idea that intergenerational contact is beneficial to both age groups, we know very little about *why* the contact is rewarding. For example, while researchers are informed that both younger and older people typically enter contact with stereotypes about each other (input), and that contact can sometimes alter or change attitudes and stereotypes (output), we know little about why and how this occurs (thruput). What is needed is a focus on processes of communicative exchange. For example, what information is exchanged in intergenerational interactions, how and why, and who has what kinds of control? Both Newman et al. and Angersbach and Jones's interaction analysis papers offer potential means by which communicative data can be gleaned; Ward and Smith and Yeager's call for ethnographic research is also warranted in supplying us with means of ascertaining what transpires during intergenerational contact.

Other important questions emerge such as: "What happens when contact is *taken away?*" After a certain period of time, relationships are formed and the participants come to depend on one another to meet certain needs. While having these needs met may be rewarding and positive, it can be so only as long as the relationship continues. As applied intergenerational researchers, we have a social responsibility to help ensure that contact between younger and older people is positive or helpful long-term. In order to address this, future research should consider what happens longitudinally *after* intergenerational contact is terminated. If outcomes dissipate or are reversed, then contact may need to be amended with these future outcomes in mind. For example, what happens to the elder's sense of self-worth when the very rewarding intergenerational program is terminated without any other possibilities for continuing contact with other young mentees?

## THEORY REVISITED

Although each of the papers in this volume conceptualizes intergenerational contact differently, taken together they clearly suggest that such contact benefits both younger and older participants. Even so, research in this field has failed to address sufficiently certain areas that are required if robust conclusions can be generated about intergenerational programs' effects on participants. As already highlighted by VanderVen, work is often atheoretical; this is why she recommends an intergenerational theory while Coupland (1997) has called for a more multidisciplinary approach with emphasis on sociolinguistic and communication theory.

Over the years, we have been working with a theoretical model that could be useful in this respect called the Communication Predicament of Aging (CPA) (Harwood, Giles, Fox, Ryan, & Williams, 1993; Ryan, Giles, Bartolucci, & Henwood, 1986). This addresses the predicament that arises as people make well-intended changes to their communication to meet the needs of older people. Specifically, the CPA model proposes that in situations where negative stereotypes toward the elderly are present, younger people may constrain the communication situation in such a way that unfavorable and dissatisfying communication occurs for both participants (Williams & Giles, 1996). That is, younger speakers may recognize and attend to old-age cues (e.g., posture, walking aids) and in turn these cues may elicit common stereotypes about the elderly (e.g., incompetence). Therefore, the speaker is likely to assume the older person has memory, hearing, or cognitive problems which require accommodating through their communication with them, for example, by speaking slowly, over-simply, and loudly (Ryan, Hummert, & Boich, 1995). Such communication reinforces negative age stereotypes and usually results in dissatisfying communication. The consequences of long-term exposure to such negative and dissatisfying communication for the older person include lowered self-esteem and psychological well-being. For the youth, this can result in the reinforcement of negative stereotypes along with a heightened fear of their own aging.

Noticeably absent from the current collection of papers was explicit empirical recognition that youth can and do stereotype older people (Coupland, Coupland, & Giles, 1991; Thimm, Rademacher, & Kruse, 1998). This absence is particularly relevant to the CPA Model. Because stereotyped expectations are hypothesized to lead to particular styles of talk by the younger person to the older, addressing youth's attitudinal armory and communicative predispositions is fundamentally important. As Travis and Stremmel underscore, stereotypes are all too alive and well! That said, as we are implying here (see also Hummert, 1994) and is also demonstrated by both Griff's and Cook's contributions, not all stereotypes are negative. Yet unfortunately, in addition to the Learning ICS described earlier, Harwood (1998) details five other ICS varieties, not all of which are complimentary to older people. For instance, the Pity ICS describes how younger people feel sorry for, sad about, or even pity older people, and the Gerontophobic ICS illustrates young people's discomfort or anxiety when communicating with an older adult. Such issues and their roles in contact need real attention in program design and research, otherwise the field will be missing critical factors related to program success and failure. It is important to note that any intergenerational program should challenge unfavorable stereotypes youth and older adults may have of one another.

The Communication Enhancement of Aging (CEA) model was developed in an attempt to reduce the gap between stereotyped expectations and individual competence that may result from potential intergenerational miscommunications. Specifically, it focuses on the need for "personalized" encounters between younger and older people. The CEA process begins with speakers having a better understanding of so-called "normal" aging processes (see Williams & Coupland [1998] for an articulation of distinct types of these) and being prepared to communicate on a more consultative and participatory basis than is typically the case. In this way, and after an educational intergenerational program, speakers are expected to have positive expectations and stereotypes of older people in general. This change in stereotypes will enable speakers to recognize more about an older person as an *individual* and not as an undifferentiated member of a socially stigmatized category. This assessment can enable youths to make more appropriate adjustments in communication style which could also increase the satisfaction of both partners, empowering the older person, reinforcing their competence, and enhancing their well-being and self-esteem.

Taken together, the CPA-CEA theoretical package can provide intergenerational scholars with a worthwhile framework for understanding how and why intergenerational miscommunication can occur during youth-elderly exchanges and suggest ways in which these communications can be improved. Both these models, with due attention to any social ramifications of the gender make-up of intergenerational mentor-mentee contact, can assist program planners and researchers to understand the presence and eradication of stereotypes.

## TOWARD AN INTEGRATIVE, THEORETICAL GAUNTLET

One theory alluded to here and worthy of special note is social identity theory (e.g., Tajfel & Turner, 1986), particularly as it has been applied to the intergenerational sphere by Harwood, Giles, and Ryan

(1995). This theory is based on the concepts of personal and social identities. The former can be construed as a sense of self as an individual entity based on interpersonal comparisons with people in one's own social group. *Social* identity, however, derives from the social comparisons we make between different groups in society and especially comparing the position of our own ingroup with that of relevant outgroups. Hence, and depending on the situation, we may make relative judgments about the position of our age group (e.g., youth) with that of other (e.g., older) age groups. Given media portrayals, cosmetic advertisements, and the existence of age stereotypes, it is not uncommon for younger and older individuals to possess more positive and unfavorable social identities, respectively (Giles, 1991). When age categories are situationally salient, as they unavoidably are in most intergenerational contact programs, self- and other-stereotyping can take place. Hence, communicating with another as a more or less typical member of an age group rather than as a specific individual where age is not very salient will render the exchange being based on stereotypes rather than on discrete and fine-tuned individual qualities.

In this way, Fox and Giles (1993) formulated an intergenerational contact model based on Hewstone and Brown's (1986) "intergroup contact theory." Given that intergenerational exchange has been conceptualized as intercultural contact (Giles & Coupland, 1992), Fox and Giles incorporated Bochner's (1982) typology of cross-cultural contact variables into their framework, including: Location of interaction (on whose territory), time-span (long vs. short-term), type of involvement (helper or help recipient), frequency of contact (high, medium, or low), degree of intimacy between participants (i.e., social distance), relative status and power (unequal or equal), and numerical valence (majority vs. minority). Earlier we advocated that a future goal of research and program design ought to develop a typology of contact situations. Together with the distinction as to whether personal or social identities are at the fore, that is, whether the intergenerational exchange is more "interpersonal" or "intergroup," this theory might be a useful starting point toward such a goal. Also useful is that Fox and Giles's model is transactional; it recognizes the attitudes, feelings, and goals of both youth and older people in encounters.

Taking up further the notion that intergenerational exchanges can be usefully framed in intercultural terms, researchers should find Gallois and Callan (1997) particularly helpful (see Giles [in press] for a critical review). They offer guidelines and communicative strategies for promoting effective communication between different ethnic groups which relies heavily on notions of different cultural norms and habits. While little research has attended to the unique social and communicative norms that different age groups bring to an encounter, Gallois and Callan's proposals could minimize difficulties in intergenerational program contact. While the CPA and CEA (as above) lay out some of the problems of intergenerational communication and offer potential (and somewhat abstract) solutions, they do not provide communicative strategies about how to approach specific intergenerational contact nor guidelines for their application in a range of different contexts. If neither generation is informed of the variable (and historically, ever-changing) rules and norms of "how" to behave in a communicatively harmonious way, then researchers and program designers may not be very successful in changing negative stereotypes each generation has of one another, issues we contend are critical to successful contact, no matter what the specific purpose of it.

With this in mind, future theory development may be usefully oriented to combine many of the recommended communicative strategies offered by Gallois and Callan together with the above mentioned models; we anticipate that such a grand rapprochement might yield significant practical gains. A range of methodologies and even epistemologies can be useful to this end (Giles & Coupland, 1992), from ethnographic and social constructionist approaches to the controlled and tightly evaluated experimental paradigm. All generations can benefit from understanding the social and communicative perils that we encounter along the path to maturity. Increasing our sophistication about these processes and phenomena will assist in promoting healthy interpersonal and community environments, educational and occupational aspirations for youth, and lifespan satisfaction and multigenerational understandings for all. This notwithstanding, the research advances reported in this important collection are substantial; they also have underscored the tremendous and still somewhat untapped resources available to our society through creative intergenerational contact. Hopefully, the theoretical paths in intergroup communication we have proposed will add to the research agenda emerging from this volume and provide intergenerational researchers with additional, valuable new areas for consideration.

# REFERENCES

Bieman-Copland, S., Ryan, E. B., & Cassano, J. (1998). Responding to the challenges of late life: Strategies for maintaining and enhancing competence. In D. Pushkar, W. Bukowski, A. Schwartzman, D. Stack, & D. White (Eds.), *Improving competence across the lifespan* (pp. 141-157). New York: Plenum Press.

Bochner, S. (1982). Introduction. In S. Bochner (Ed.), *Cultures in contact: the psychology of desegregation* (pp 1-38). New York: Pergamon Press.

Coupland, N. (1997). Language, aging and ageism: A project for applied linguistics? *International Journal of Applied Linguistics, 7*, 26-48.

Coupland, N., Coupland, J., & Giles, H. (1991). *Language, society and the elderly: Discourse, identity and aging.* Oxford: Basil Blackwell.

Edwards, H., & Giles, H. (1998). Prologue on two dimensions: The risk of management of intergenerational miscommunication. *Journal of Applied Communication, 26*, 1-12.

Fitzpatrick, M. A. (1990). Aging, health and family communication: A theoretical perspective. In H. Giles, N. Coupland, & J. M. Wiemann (Eds.), *Communication, health and the elderly* (pp. 213-228). Fulbright papers, Vol. 8. Manchester, England: Manchester University Press.

Fox, S. (1993). The development of communication in families over the lifespan. Communication Dept., Western Michigan University, Kalamazoo. Manuscript submitted for publication.

Fox, S., & Giles, H. (1993). Accommodating intergenerational contact: A critique and theoretical model. *Journal of Aging Studies, 7*, 423-451.

Gallois, C., & Callan, V. (1997). *Communication and culture: A guide for practice.* New York, NY: John Wiley & Sons.

Giles, H. (1991). "Gosh, you don't look it! A sociolinguistics of ageing. *The Psychologist, 4*, 99-106.

Giles, H. (in press). Review of C. Gallois, & V. Callan (1997). *Communication and culture: A guide for practice.* New York, NY: John Wiley & Sons. *Journal of Occupational and Organizational Psychology.*

Giles, H., & Coupland, N. (1992). *Language: Contexts and consequences.* Pacific Grove, CA: Brooks/Cole.

Giles, H., Fox, S., Harwood, J., & Williams, A. (1994). Talking of age and aging talk: Communication through the lifespan. In M. L. Hummert, J. M. Wiemann, & J. F. Nussbaum (Eds.), *Interpersonal communication in older adulthood: Interdisciplinary research* (pp. 130-161). Thousand Oaks, CA: Sage.

Giles, H., & Harwood, J. (1997). Managing intergroup communication: Lifespan issues and consequences. In S. Eliasson & E. H. Jahr (Eds.), *Language and its ecology: Essays in memory of Einar Haugen* (pp. 105-130). Berlin: Mouton de Gruyter.

Giles, H., & Williams, A. (1994). Patronizing the young: Forms and evaluations. *International Journal of Aging and Human Development, 39*, 33-53.

Giles, H., Williams, A., & Coupland, N. (1990). Communication, health and the elderly: Frameworks, agenda and a model. In H. Giles, N. Coupland, & J. M. Wiemann (Eds.), *Communication, health and the elderly* (pp. 1-28). Fulbright papers, Vol. 8. Manchester, England: Manchester University Press.

Harwood, J. (1998). Young adults' cognitive representations of intergenerational conversations. *Journal of Applied Communication Research, 26,* 13-31.

Harwood, J., Giles, H., Fox, S., Ryan, E. B., & Williams, A. (1993). Patronizing speech and reactive responses. *Journal of Applied Communication Research, 21,* 211-226.

Harwood, J., Giles, H., & Ryan, E. B. (1995). Aging, communication, and intergroup theory: Social identity and intergenerational communication. In J. F. Nussbaum & J. Coupland (Eds.), *Handbook of communication and aging research* (pp. 133-159). Mahwah, NJ: Erlbaum.

Hewstone, M., & Brown, R. H. (1986). Contact is not enough: An intergroup perspective on the contact hypothesis. In M. Hewstone & R. Brown (Eds.), *Contact and conflict in intergroup encounters: Social psychology and society* (pp. 1-44). Oxford: Basil Blackwell.

Hummert, M. L. (1994). Stereotypes of the elderly and patronizing speech. In M. L. Hummert, J. M. Wiemann, & J. F. Nussbaum (Eds.), *Interpersonal communication in older adulthood: Interdisciplinary research* (pp. 162-184). Thousand Oaks, CA: Sage.

Kalbfleisch, P. J., & Anderson, A. (1997). Mentoring across generations: Culture, family, and mentoring relationships. In H. S. Noor Al-Deen (Eds.), *Cross-cultural communication and aging in the united states* (pp. 97-120). Mahwah, New Jersey: Erlbaum.

Kite, M. E., & Johnson, B. T. (1988). Attitudes toward older and younger adults: A meta-analysis. *Psychology and Aging, 3,* 233-244.

Ota, H., Harwood, J., Williams, A., & Takai, J. (1998, March). *A cross-cultural analysis of age identity: Japan and the United States.* Paper presented at the Conference on Interdisciplinary Theory and Research on Intercultural Relations, California State University, Fullerton. (Education Center for International Students, Nagoya University, Japan.)

Peterson, E. T. (1989). Grandparenting. In S. J. Bahr & E. T. Peterson (Eds.), *Aging and the family* (pp. 159-174). Lexington, MA: Lexington.

Ryan, E. B., Giles, H., Bartolucci, G., & Henwood, K. (1986). Psycholinguistic and social psychological components of communication by and with the elderly. Special Issue: Language, communication and the elderly. *Language and Communication, 6,* 1-24.

Ryan, E. B., Hummert, M. L., & Boich, L. H. (1995). Communication predicament of aging: Patronizing behavior toward older adults. *Journal of Language & Social Psychology, 14,* 144-166.

Ryan, E. B., Meredith, S. D., MacLean, M. J., & Orange, J. B. (1995). Changing the way we talk with elders: Promoting health using the Communication Enhancement Model. *International Journal of Aging and Human Development, 14,* 87-105.

Tajfel, H., & Turner, J. C. (1986). An integrative theory of intergroup relations. In S. Worchel & W. G. Austin (Eds.), *Psychology of intergroup relations* (pp. 7-24). Chicago: Nelson-Hall.

Thimm, C., Rademacher, U., & Kruse, L. (1998). Age stereotypes and patronizing messages: Features of age-adapted speech in technical instructions to the elderly. *Journal of Applied Communication Research, 26,* 66-82.

Williams, A., & Coupland, N. (1998). Epilogue: The socio-political framing of communication and aging. *Journal of Applied Communication, 26*, 139-154.

Williams, A., & Giles, H. (1996). Intergenerational conversations: Young adults retrospective accounts. *Human Communication Research, 23*, 220-250.

Williams, A., Ota, H., Giles, H., Pierson, H. D., Gallois, C., Ng, S. H., Lim, T-S., Ryan, E.B., Somera, L., Maher, J., & Harwood, J. (1997). Young peoples' beliefs about intergenerational communication: An initial cross-cultural comparison. *Communication Research, 24*, 370-393.

# Index

Numbers in *italics* indicate figures.